Star Chamber Matters
An Early Modern Court and Its Records

Star Chamber Matters
An Early Modern Court and Its Records

Edited by
K. J. Kesselring and Natalie Mears

UNIVERSITY OF LONDON PRESS
INSTITUTE OF HISTORICAL RESEARCH

First published in 2021 by
UNIVERSITY OF LONDON PRESS
SCHOOL OF ADVANCED STUDY
INSTITUTE OF HISTORICAL RESEARCH
Senate House, Malet Street, London WC1E 7HU

Available to download free at http://www.humanities-digital-library.org or to purchase at https://www.sas.ac.uk/publications

ISBN
978-1-912702-89-3 (hardback edition)
978-1-912702-90-9 (.pdf edition)
978-1-912702-91-6 (.epub edition)
978-1-912702-92-3 (.mobi edition)

DOI: 10.14296/2109.9781912702909

Cover image: The British Library Board, Maps. C.29.e.1,A.

INSTITUTE OF HISTORICAL RESEARCH | SCHOOL OF ADVANCED STUDY UNIVERSITY OF LONDON

Contents

Notes on contributors

Clare Egan is a lecturer in medieval and early modern literature at Lancaster University. Her research interests include early drama and performance, especially the study of spectatorship, and provincial libels tried at the court of Star Chamber under James I. Other areas of research interest include spatial humanities and ecocriticism. She has recently had articles published in the journals *Medieval English Theatre* and *Early Theatre*.

Daniel Gosling is the Early Modern Legal Records Specialist at The National Archives of the UK. His PhD thesis (University of Leeds, 2016) examined the use and interpretation of the Statute of Praemunire in the late medieval and early modern periods. His current research includes the legal records relating to the Bear Garden in Elizabethan and Jacobean Southwark, the inns of court, regicides and writ development in the late medieval period.

Simon Healy was a researcher at the History of Parliament Trust for many years, writing almost a million words on members of the House of Commons and House of Lords from 1604–29. In 2015, he completed a doctorate on crown finances and the political culture of early Stuart England at Birkbeck College, London, where he worked (for the most part) under the supervision of the late professor Barry Coward. His contribution to this volume derives from an investigation of the money supply in early modern England.

Sadie Jarrett is currently the Economic History Society Postan Fellow at the Institute of Historical Research and is affiliated with Cardiff University. She is an honorary research associate at Bangor University's Institute for the Study of Welsh Estates, where she completed her PhD. Her doctoral thesis comprised an extended case study of the Salesburys of Rhug and Bachymbyd, an early modern Welsh gentry family from northeast Wales. Her research interests include expressions of gentility in the early modern world, the role of women in gentry families and regional participation in the power structures of the early modern state.

Emily Kadens is a professor of law at the Northwestern University Pritzker School of Law in Chicago, USA. Her research focuses primarily on the medieval and early modern history of commercial law and practice. She is currently working on a book on the history of commercial cheating in early modern England.

K. J. Kesselring is a professor of history at Dalhousie University, Halifax, Canada. She has published three books that drew, to varying degrees, on Star Chamber records, including most recently *Making Murder Public: Homicide in Early Modern England* (2019). In addition to writing a set of articles on subjects such as felony forfeiture and coverture, she has also edited or co-edited several volumes of essays and documents, including *Star Chamber Reports: BL Harley MS 2143* (List and Index Society, Special Series 57, 2018).

Louis A. Knafla is professor emeritus at the University of Calgary and a legal historian of early modern England and western Canada. His most recent publication is 'Legal-historical writing for the Canadian prairies: past, present, future', in *Canada's Legal Pasts: Looking Forward, Looking Back* (Calgary, 2020), pp. 271–96. Volume seven of his series *Kent at Law 1602* on *Courts of Equity – The Equity Side of Exchequer*, is in press.

Natalie Mears is an associate professor (reader) in Tudor and early Stuart history at Durham University. She has published widely on Elizabethan politics and religion, including *Queenship and Public Discourse in the Elizabethan Realms* (2005), and was co-investigator on the AHRC-funded project, 'British state prayers', acting as lead editor for the first of four volumes, *National Worship* (2013). She was host and co-organizer of the conference 'Star Chamber and its records' held in Durham in July 2019.

Hillary Taylor is a temporary lecturer in early modern British social and economic history at the University of Cambridge and a fellow of Jesus College. She is finishing a book on social relations and the class politics of language and is beginning a new project on workplace violence, both focused on early modern England. She received her PhD from Yale University in 2016.

Ian Williams is an associate professor in the Faculty of Laws, University College London. His research focuses on early modern English law, ranging from the history of legal ideas to book history and more political topics.

Deborah Youngs is a professor of history at Swansea University with research interests in the social, legal and cultural histories of late medieval England and Wales. She is currently engaged on a series of projects relating to women's litigation and with a specific focus on Star Chamber. She is also co-editing (with Teresa Phipps) a collection of essays entitled *Litigating Women: Gender and Justice in Courts of Law, c.1300–c.1750*, to be published by Routledge.

List of figures and tables

Figures

Tables

Acknowledgements

This volume emerges from a conference on the court of Star Chamber and its records held at Durham University in July 2019. Based on papers given at or arising from the event, the chapters gathered here represent only a portion of the work-in-progress then discussed. As such, we wish to thank all the participants at the event for their contributions, which have fed into this volume in a variety of ways. We want to single out in particular Helen Good, who made available the results of some of her prodigious work on the Elizabethan Star Chamber, a project to make its records more accessible to researchers not just in the academy but also well beyond. We wish to thank, too, the funders who made the event possible and so enjoyable. The co-organizers were able to draw upon the generosity of Durham University's Institute of Medieval and Early Modern Studies and the Social Sciences and Humanities Research Council of Canada. We also thank Steve Hindle, W. M. Keck Foundation Director of Research at the Huntington Library, who not only presented material from his own ongoing research but also secured funding for our reception and conference dinner from the Huntington, with an eye to increasing awareness of the Library's own rich store of materials related to Star Chamber. To IMEMS, SSHRC and the Huntington, our thanks.

We also wish to thank Melissa Glass for her work on copyediting, as well as Julie Spraggon at the Institute of Historical Research, Kerry Whitston at the University of London Press and Robert Davies for their assistance in seeing this collection through to publication. We are especially pleased to be able to publish with the IHR/ULP partnership for Open Access scholarship and are grateful for their support.

K. J. Kesselring
Dalhousie University

Natalie Mears
Durham University

14 January 2021

1. Introduction: Star Chamber matters*

K. J. Kesselring with Natalie Mears

The court of Star Chamber remains notorious even now: commentators sometimes invoke its name to suggest that a judicial body or legal action is not quite lawful, something secretive and illegitimate. The court provoked concern in its own time, too, though its vilification deepened after its death. With roots in the mid fourteenth century, Star Chamber became institutionalized as a judicial body somewhat distinguishable from the king's executive Privy Council by 1540. Akin to contemporaneous experiments with conciliar justice in other European jurisdictions, though, the court's ties to the royal council remained close. Star Chamber drew its authorization directly from the monarch and operated outside the procedures of the common-law courts, without juries and with judges drawn primarily from the royal council, supplemented in time by justices of the high court bench. Sitting as a court, the lords heard a wide range of amorphously defined wrongs and crafted punishments at their discretion, just short of death. They adjudicated disputes that arose from many aspects of early modern political, religious and cultural development. Trying both civil and criminal cases over its history, at the instance of both private plaintiffs and royal officials, the court heard quarrels framed as cases of riot, fraud, libel, perjury and more. Star Chamber offered some people relatively fast, flexible solutions to problems that other courts could not address, even while it provided others with evidence of the dangers of royal power when unchecked by law. Indeed, in 1641, a little over a hundred years after its emergence as a distinct judicial tribunal, Star Chamber was abolished by members of a parliament about to embark on civil war and revolution for what they deemed egregious abuses of royal power and law.

Today, Star Chamber's records offer riches to scholars interested in broad swathes of early modern history. And yet, despite the court's continued notoriety, its own history might still be more fully explored to better

* Our thanks to Louis Knafla for reviewing a draft of this chapter and the Social Sciences and Humanities Research Council of Canada for funding the research from which parts of it derive.

understand these records as well as the political and legal conflicts of its time. As the chapters gathered here demonstrate, we can learn much about the history of an age through both the practices of its courts and the disputes of the people who came before them. With Star Chamber, moreover, we have not just any court, but one that came of age and was later killed off on either side of one of the great formative periods in English legal history, in the middle of an era of religious, political and social transformation. We also have a court that left an unusual wealth of documentation, though in records that come with a few challenges of their own.

The court's contemporary defenders and critics debated whether Star Chamber constituted a 'court of record', and its occasional use of oral proceedings without a written bill proved one of its more contentious aspects.[1] Even so, it produced written records in abundance. True, it lacked the Latin-language parchment rolls of decisions that lawyers would come to insist upon over the early 1600s as a formal 'record', but it generated a wealth of documentation otherwise – in contrast to the common-law assize courts, with their formulaic indictments in crabbed Latin on little stubs of parchment and oral proceedings now lost to history. With cases in Star Chamber typically begun by voluble English bills of complaint, framed as petitions to the sovereign with elaborate narratives of alleged wrongs, they often then generated written rejoinders, demurrers, interrogatories and depositions. Indeed, contemporaries sometimes complained about the volume of the pleadings and proofs, with officers occasionally making futile efforts to limit the length of bills and to add efficiencies to the court's operation. In William Prynne's infamous 1634 trial for libel and sedition, when asked to review all the exhibits one judge observed that 'this would require the leisure of a vacation to be read over. I hope your Lordships do not require that'. No, he was assured, he did not need to read it all.[2] A mocking critique of the court published at its closure had a 'Christopher Cob-web', keeper of the court's records, comment on the large, lucrative (or costly) bundles of papers and parchments that had been 'copied, engrossed,

[1] On the disputes over Star Chamber's status as a 'court of record', see W. S. Holdsworth, *The History of English Law* (17 vols., London, 1956–66), v. 157–61 and S. E. Thorne, 'Courts of record and Sir Edward Coke', *University of Toronto Law Journal*, ii (1937), 24–49. See, too, the text of the Act for the Abolition of the Court of Star Chamber, 17 Car. I, c. 10 (1641), which repeatedly contrasted Star Chamber with the 'courts of record' in which most proceedings should occur. K. Peters, '"Friction in the archives": access and the politics of record-keeping in revolutionary England', in *Archives and Information in the Early Modern World*, ed. L. Corens, K. Peters and A. Walsham, *Proceedings of the British Academy*, ccxii (2018), 151–76 is useful here, too.

[2] Harvard Library, MS. Eng 1350, unfoliated.

written, rescribed, prescribed and transcribed forty times over'. Copyists who charged by the sheet produced bills the size of cloaks, he lamented.[3]

Modern scholars have their own reasons to find Star Chamber's records a mixed blessing. For one, the court's records of judgements have disappeared. At the court's dissolution in 1641, the heaps of older pleadings and proofs that were stored in the Star Chamber itself survived, but at some point thereafter the court's working files kept in the clerks' office in Gray's Inn disappeared, including most of the proceedings from the reign of King Charles and all the order and decree books. What do we do in their absence? How do we read and make use of the competing narratives crafted by plaintiffs and defendants? How can we make better use of the manuscript law reports and contemporary notes on cases to compensate at least somewhat for the missing order and decree books? Furthermore, the sheer bulk of proofs and pleadings impedes access and efforts to catalogue. The nearly 40,000 files surviving from Queen Elizabeth's long reign are particularly poorly served by finding aids. On the other hand, these bills and depositions offer both exceptional accounts of extraordinary occurrences and unparalleled insights into the everyday. Scholars have already used Star Chamber records to great effect in examinations of rebellions and riots, community disputes, gender relations, lay piety, puritanism, suicide, libel, witchcraft, censorship, popular perceptions of the past – *et cetera* – but anyone who has dipped into the archive knows that much more might yet be done with greater attention to the court's records and processes, and with more collaboration between archivists and the range of scholars who use the archives in their care.

The chapters collected in this volume emerge from a conference held at Durham University in July 2019 on the court of Star Chamber and its records. The event brought together archivists, geographers, historians and specialists in both law and literature who had an interest either in the court itself or in the subjects that can be so fruitfully explored through its unusually rich records. The interdisciplinary mix of scholars gathered at the Durham conference responded to a call for papers that asked them to consider creatively, constructively and imaginatively the Star Chamber archive. How might we use its records to better understand the court and its role in early modern political culture, or to study the range of behaviours

[3] Anon., *The Star-chamber epitomized, or, A dialogue between Inquisition, a news smeller, and Christopher Cob-web, a keeper of the records for the Star-Chamber, as they met at the office in Grayes-Inne. Wherein they discourse how the clerkes used to exact fees* (London, 1641), pp. 2, 4. One wonders if the author had known of Lord Chancellor Egerton's fining of a plaintiff's counsel who had produced a bill of 125 sheets in length, accompanied by talk of having the man wear it 'as a herald's coat' through the courts of Westminster: J. Hawarde, *Les Reportes del Cases in Camera Stellata, 1593–1609*, ed. W. P. Baildon (London, 1894), p. 263.

and disputes brought into Star Chamber? How might we make these records more 'accessible', in all senses of the word? We wanted to see how such a mix of scholars might shed new light on the court and its archive – and, vice versa, how a shared focus on one court and its records might foster meaningful interdisciplinary conversations. We hope that this volume of chapters based on papers given at or prompted by the conference will draw more people into these exchanges.

***

The court of Star Chamber itself is overdue for a full-scale evaluation, for which this collection should help to break the ground and lay foundations. Revisionist historians of the mid to late twentieth century chipped away at older Whiggish accounts of the court, building upon important early work by Cora Louise Scofield and Elfreda Skelton.[4] Geoffrey Elton influentially countered portrayals of the court's tyranny by asserting that plaintiffs appreciated its flexibility and relative speed.[5] Thomas Garden Barnes highlighted its role in modernizing the law and dealing creatively with the problems of a new socio-economic age.[6] In addition to his valuable survey of the court's archives up to the reign of Elizabeth, John Guy linked Star Chamber's development to the reformist agenda of Henry VIII's first chief minister, Lord Chancellor Thomas Wolsey.[7] More recently, some scholars have depicted the court as a venue for the popular legalism central

[4] C. L. Scofield, *A Study of the Court of Star Chamber* (Chicago, 1900); E. Skelton, 'The court of Star Chamber in the reign of queen Elizabeth' (unpublished University of London MA thesis, 1930).

[5] G. R. Elton, *Star Chamber Stories* (London, 1958).

[6] T. G. Barnes's work on the court includes: 'Star Chamber mythology', *American Journal of Legal History*, v (1961), 1–11; 'Due process and slow process in the late Elizabethan-early Stuart Star Chamber', parts I and II, *American Journal of Legal History*, vi (1962), 221–49, 315–46; 'The archives and archival problems of the Elizabethan and early Stuart Star Chamber', in *Prisca Munimenta: Studies in Archival and Administrative History*, ed. F. Ranger (London, 1973), pp. 130–49; 'Star Chamber and the sophistication of the criminal law', *Criminal Law Review* (1977), 316–26; 'Star Chamber litigants and their counsel, 1596–1641', in *Legal Records and the Historian*, ed. J. H. Baker (London, 1978), pp. 7–28; 'A Cheshire seductress, precedent and a "sore blow" to Star Chamber', in *On the Laws and Customs of England*, ed. M. S. Arnold et al. (Chapel Hill, 1981), pp. 359–82. See, too, his *List and Index to the Proceedings in Star Chamber for the Reign of James I (1603–1625) in the Public Record Office, London, Class STAC 8* (3 vols., London, 1975).

[7] J. A. Guy, 'Wolsey's Star Chamber: a study in archival reconstruction', *Journal of the Society of Archivists*, v (1975), 169–80; *The Cardinal's Court: The Impact of Thomas Wolsey in Star Chamber* (Hassocks, 1977); *The Court of Star Chamber and its Records to the Reign of Elizabeth I* (London, 1985).

to state formation and the 'negotiation of authority'.[8] However well-used or modernizing the court was, though, other scholars have continued to insist upon its repressive functions, pointing to its taming of obstreperous lawyers, for example.[9] Despite these disagreements and despite its profound significance in early modern English history, as Louis Knafla has noted, Star Chamber has not yet been the focus of a large-scale effort at reconstruction and analysis.[10] Barnes did extraordinary work on opening its Jacobean records to continued use, but since his death in 2010, the promise of his early examinations of the court's own history has gone unfulfilled. Moreover, post-revisionist reanalyses of early Stuart political culture suggest that the view of the court developed by Elton and Barnes now warrants refocusing. The chapters gathered in this volume go some way towards reviving and revisiting the history of the court itself.

One piece of ground-clearing to be done at the outset is to set aside the tendency either to vilify or vindicate the court, deeming it 'bad' or 'good' by some subsequent set of standards. The latter position has produced a problematic insistence upon the court's 'popularity', made by historians invested in refuting the caricatured Whiggish denunciations of the court as a despotic body. In his 1958 *Star Chamber Stories*, Elton wrote that the court did not deserve its evil reputation because it 'commanded great popularity', at least under the Tudors. In his 1988 text on *The Stuart Constitution*, J. P. Kenyon carried this assertion forward with the claim that 'it is clear that right up to 1640 the court retained its popularity with litigants'. Others still reiterate this notion.[11] But what do we mean by describing the court as 'popular', and why insist that it was? Such characterizations of the court obstruct the view and rest on weak footings. They have helped push explanations for the court's demise to ever later dates and have made them ever more contingent. They too quickly become positive, partisan defences of the court, shaping our interpretation of the court's place in political culture and our understanding of its uses for litigants. This section revisits the nature and timing of complaints made against Star Chamber, the numbers of cases brought before it and the profile of its litigants.

[8] See, e.g., S. Hindle, *The State and Social Change in Early Modern England, c.1550–1640* (New York, 2000), pp. 66–93.

[9] R. P. Alford, 'The Star Chamber and the regulation of the legal profession, 1570–1640', *American Journal of Legal History*, li (2011), 639–726.

[10] L. A. Knafla, *Kent at Law, 1602: III. Star Chamber* (List and Index Society, Special Series 51, 2012).

[11] Elton, *Star Chamber Stories*, pp. 11–12; J. P. Kenyon, *The Stuart Constitution, 1603–1688* (Cambridge, 1988), p. 117. For more characterizations of the court as 'popular', see, e.g., M. Stuckey, *The High Court of Star Chamber* (Holmes Beach, Fla., 1988), pp. 4, 67 and B. Shapiro, *Law Reform in Early Modern England* (Cambridge, 2020), pp. 46, 97.

It ends with a brief discussion of the intellectual context and consequences of assertions of the court's 'popularity' and suggests that historical assessments of the court and its cases might now best discard them and their allied tendencies to take sides in the disputes of centuries past.

For one, the court's modern advocates tell us that complaints about Star Chamber did not begin until the Stuart era, or even that they only began in Charles's reign,[12] but objections arose earlier. Unsurprisingly, some people criticized the court for judgements in their own cases – and were punished for doing so, at least as early as 1554. The jurors sanctioned in Star Chamber for acquitting Nicholas Throckmorton in his treason trial, who then complained that truer men had never left the court, subsequently faced time in the Tower, for example.[13] In 1594, John Golburne and Thomas Swyfte dispersed a 'slanderous libel or writing against a judgement formerly passed' in the court; for this criticism, Swyfte stood to lose his ears and to spend seven years in the hole at the Fleet prison. Golburne eventually received a pardon of his £500 fine, but only after spending at least four years locked away.[14] It did not do to voice one's concerns about the court too loudly. Some such complaints spoke of more than personal grievance, too. One Carew, tried in 1603 for his opposition to the Elizabethan Prayer Book, cited Magna Carta's famous chapter twenty-nine in his own critique, arguing that he should face legal sanction not in Star Chamber but only 'by judgement of his peers or by the law of the land'.[15] While we do not have his words directly, and his criticism emerged from self-interest, it seems that as

[12] See, e.g., D. L. Vande Zande, 'Coercive power and the demise of the Star Chamber', *American Journal of Legal History*, l (2008–10), 326–49. Vande Zande opens by asserting that 'the perception of infamy engendered by the Star Chamber stems principally from its conduct in the decade immediately prior to the first of the English civil wars' and sets as his problem the explanation of how the court failed so quickly and precipitously (p. 327). He continued to write that 'the Star Chamber maintained an honoured history throughout the Tudor and early Stuart monarchies. In fact, there is little evidence of opposition to the Star Chamber until immediately prior to its abolition' (p. 330). Stuckey maintained that 'only the political trials of Charles's reign brought it into the sights of the king's enemies' (*Star Chamber*, p. 4). J. R. Tanner, *Constitutional Documents of the Reign of James I* (Cambridge, 1952), p. 140, says that the decline in the popularity of the court had 'scarcely begun' in the reign of James I. The problem is to account for how a court 'hitherto useful and even popular perished in a storm of execration in 1641'.

[13] *Star Chamber Reports: Harley MS 2143*, ed. K. J. Kesselring (London, 2018), no. 11. See also nos. 50, 51, 78, 207, 404, 839, 841, 979 and 989.

[14] *Harley MS 2143*, no. 917 and The National Archives of the UK, C 66/1508, mm. 5–6.

[15] W. Hudson, 'A Treatise on the court of Star Chamber', in *Collectanea Juridica*, ed. F. Hargrave (2 vols., London, 1792), ii. 1–240, at p. 4. For this case, see also Hawarde, *Les Reportes del Cases in Camera Stellata*, p. 164.

early as 1603, a defendant argued in Star Chamber itself that its procedures violated the liberties of the subject.

Even those writers who extolled the court offered evidence that others had found reasons to criticize the body. William Lambarde praised the court in his *Archeion*, completed in 1591, but also included in his text a 'confutation of some objections against the Star Chamber'. He noted that some people argued that the court should deal only with complaints as specified in relevant parliamentary acts that had authorized it to hear specific concerns. He noted, too, that some people objected even then to the purely oral proceedings *ore tenus*, insisting that a written bill of information ought to be necessary to start a trial. Lambarde thought the 'assaults of all those objections which some are wont to make against certain proceedings of this court' unjustified, but clearly, he did not speak for all.[16]

Another of the court's defenders, William Hudson, produced a treatise in 1621 that both responded to criticisms and expressed a few qualms of his own. Hudson opened by addressing two contentions. The first held 'that this court is but an usurpation of monarchy upon the common law of England, and in prejudice of the liberties granted to the subject by the Great Charter, especially where persons are produced, without legal prosecution to punishment, at the bar without oath or testimony'. The second alleged 'that it is no settled ordinary court of judicature, but only an assembly for consultation at the king's command'. Hudson sought to refute both accusations – 'although a high court, yet it is an ordinary court of justice in this kingdom', he insisted – but seemed more sympathetic to other concerns. On complaints about the inability to examine witnesses' credibility, for example, he acknowledged it to be 'a great imputation to our English courts, that witnesses are privately produced, and how base or simple soever they be … yet they make as good a sound, being read out of paper, as the best'. He countered claims that it was not a proper court of record, while admitting that negligence recently crept in had impaired the care and custody of its documentation. He also recognized some validity in complaints about oral proceedings *ore tenus*, which was 'much blamed, as seeming to oppose the Great Charter'. He defended the practice, but allowed that 'therein sometimes there is a dangerous excess' and an 'exuberancy of prerogative'.[17]

[16] W. Lambarde, *Archeion*, ed. C. H. McIlwain and P. L. Ward (Cambridge, Mass., 1957), pp. 93–6. The complaints appear in the manuscript version from 1591, too: British Library, Add. MS. 48055, fos. 36d–38d, 50d, 77d, 83d–87.

[17] Hudson, 'Treatise', pp. 3–4, 36, 127, 200, 224. Hudson produced his treatise primarily for the instruction of the new lord keeper, John Williams, bishop of Lincoln, who assumed office in July 1621. Multiple copies of the manuscript survive; it was first printed in 1792,

Signs of reservations about the court also appeared in some of the manuscript reports on cases it heard. In notes on cases he observed between 1593 and 1609, John Hawarde intimated a degree of concern about Star Chamber's proceeding on proclamations rather than statutes in his discussion of the 1597 suit that Attorney General Edward Coke brought against the maltsters of Kent. Hawarde noted Francis Bacon's speech, which suggested that the queen's councillors intended to proceed against engrossers and forestallers 'by the Queen's prerogative only, and by proclamation, councils, orders, and letters'. As such, he observed, their 'proclamations and orders shall be a firm and forcible law, and of the like force as the common law or an Act of Parliament'. The privy councillors intended 'to attribute to their councils and orders the vigour, force and power of a firm law, and of high[er] virtue and force, jurisdiction, and preeminence than any positive law, whether it be the common law or statute law'. Hawarde thought that the councillors sought to be the most 'commanding lords in all the world', in part because they also proceeded against builders of cottages on proclamation and not on statute, and because the councillors prosecuted some justices of the peace for negligence in failing to execute conciliar orders.[18] When did Hawarde record this passage? Contemporaneously, in 1597, or at some later point before his death in 1631? In his study of the proclamations of the Tudor queens, Frederic Youngs asserted that Hawarde was simply 'wrong' in his evaluation of the 1597 proceedings, and accused him of reading back concerns of the Stuart era.[19] It is possible, of course, though it seems improbable that Hawarde penned *post hoc* concerns any later than 1611, the year in which he succeeded to his father's estates and which W. P. Baildon, the editor of Hawarde's manuscript, thought to be the latest possible date for him to have edited his papers.[20] At the very least, Hawarde's concerns predated the disputes of Charles's reign.

Looking even further back, signs of opposition exist in the defeat of a bill to extend Star Chamber's powers in 1584.[21] Evidence of concern appeared,

---

with some errors in transcription. On Hudson and his treatise, see T. G. Barnes, 'Mr. Hudson's Star Chamber', in *Tudor Rule and Revolution*, ed. D. J. Guth and J. W. McKenna (Cambridge, 1982), pp. 285–308, and his introduction to a Lawbook Exchange reprint of Hargrave's edition of Hudson's work, under the title *A Treatise of the Court of Star Chamber* (Clark, N. J., 2008).

18 Hawarde, *Camera Stellata*, p. 79.

19 F. A. Youngs, *The Proclamations of the Tudor Queens* (Cambridge 1976), p. 57.

20 Hawarde, *Camera Stellata*, p. viii. Hawarde notes that he compiled the manuscript from notes taken in court, p. 357.

21 Brit. Libr., Harley MS. 6847, fo. 133ff, reprinted in Skelton, 'Star Chamber', pp. cxxxv–cxxxviii, and *Proceedings in the Parliaments of Elizabeth I*, ed. T. E. Hartley (3 vols., Leicester, 1981–95), ii. 107.

too, in the 1551 order that English bill courts such as Star Chamber no longer hear litigation that could be heard in the common-law courts. The order seems to have prompted Star Chamber's re-direction from civil to criminal disputes, and was reportedly provoked by 'the disorders that have been used in this court … to the derogation of the common law'.[22] At the very least, this 1551 order suggests the error in claims such as Kenyon's, that the court did not arouse the 'jealousy of the common law courts' before 1640.[23] Other Elizabethan disputes over jurisdiction lay behind the efforts of people such as William Mill, the court's long-time clerk, to prove the court's antiquity – including one dispute that prompted a resolution by all the common-law judges in 1565, in Onslow's Case, that Star Chamber could not hear cases on perjury committed in the church courts and ought to be limited to the offences laid out in the supposed originating statute of 1487.[24] Evidently, substantive concerns about Star Chamber were expressed well before 1640, well before Charles's reign, and even before the Stuart era began. Modern defenders of the court have argued that these complaints were unfair; maybe so, but the complaints and concerns existed.

Modern proponents of the court's popularity do not just rely on dismissing evidence of complaints; they see the strongest support for their claim in the simple fact that people continued to use Star Chamber, and turned to it in increasing numbers over Elizabeth's reign. True, but we should put these numbers in context to understand the significance of getting caught up in proceedings in this court as opposed to others. John Guy's counts of bills filed in Star Chamber indicate averages of about 150 suits per annum between Wolsey's reforms and the end of Henry VIII's reign; 145 per annum under Edward VI; and 147 per annum under Mary I.[25] Under Queen Elizabeth, numbers did go up: Elfreda Skelton counted seventy-two bills in Elizabeth's first regnal year and some 732 in the final year of her reign. As a rough indicator of cases filed in between, the calendars of surviving files include an average of 381 dated bills per annum in Elizabeth's reign, with the surge beyond earlier averages beginning in the 1570s and numbers

[22] Guy, *Star Chamber … to the Reign of Elizabeth*, p. 57.

[23] Kenyon, *Stuart Constitution*, p. 117.

[24] Skelton, 'Star Chamber', p. 45; Brit. Libr., Hargrave MS. 216, fo. 100, re: the 1565 dispute with King's Bench over perjury; for Onslow's Case (1565), see 2 Dyer 242b (73 *English Reports* 537) and J. H. Baker, *Reports from the Lost Notebooks of Sir James Dyer* (2 vols., London, 1994; Selden Society, v. 109–110), i. xci. See, too, Brit. Libr., Add. MS. 4521, fo. 64, 'a discourse concerning the antiquity of the court occasioned by certain articles made by the attorneys against the court and clarks of the same, anno. 1590' and Lansdowne MS. 639, fo. 147b, another Elizabethan reference to debate about the age of the court.

[25] Guy, *Star Chamber … to the Reign of Elizabeth*, p. 9.

continuing to mount in the later decades.[26] Thereafter, we see a bit of a reduction: according to Thomas Barnes and Henry Phillips, under King James, the court received an average of 358 bills of complaint per annum; some 435 per annum in the early 1630s; and then a drop to about 250 or so per annum towards the end.[27]

How does the volume of bills filed compare to the level of business in other courts? Even at its peak, it was the smallest drop in the sea. Chris Brooks suggested that in 1560, the courts of King's Bench and Common Pleas had some 5278 cases in advanced stages. In 1606, the number reached 23,147. By 1640, it was 28,734.[28] Robert Palmer has more recently queried these estimates based on his own prodigious work with the court rolls, arguing that Brooks overestimated the cases in King's Bench and significantly underestimated the number of cases begun in Common Pleas. For the common-law side of the Exchequer, moreover, Palmer demonstrates that the numbers were 'well in excess of 2000' cases per year in the early 1600s. Whereas Brooks had calculated that some 54,075 cases were begun in all the central courts in 1606, Palmer suggests a rough estimate of 'something in excess of 112,000 cases'.[29] For present purposes, we might simply observe that both estimates vastly outnumber the few hundred bills brought to Star Chamber each year.

Furthermore, the averages calculated by Guy, Skelton and others refer to bills filed, not cases heard. The court typically sat only two days a week, in term time; only so much could ever be done within such constraints. The

[26] As a rough indicator of cases filed in between, a count of catalogued entries for the *unconsolidated* case files from 1560–9 shows an average of 279 entries per year, ranging from a low of 166 to a high of 368. If we use the factor suggested by L. Knafla (0.47 to 1), that gives an average of 131 cases. Given the problems with divided case files, bills with multiple copies and suspected gaps in the catalogue, we should not give this number much weight, but it is within the range of annual averages from earlier reigns. The average in the text comes from the 'Hidden Archives STAC 5 and 7' Excel file produced by Amanda Bevan et al. at The National Archives, incorporating work done by Helen Good that is now available via 'The Elizabethan Star Chamber project' website <https://waalt.uh.edu/index.php/Elizabethan_Star_Chamber_Project> [accessed 7 Nov. 2020].

[27] Skelton, 'Star Chamber', p. 165; Guy, *Star Chamber … to the Reign of Elizabeth*, p. 9; Barnes, 'Litigants', p. 17; see charts in Knafla, *Star Chamber*, p. xxii and Barnes, 'Due Process', p. 330.

[28] C. W. Brooks, *Pettyfoggers and Vipers of the Commonwealth: the 'Lower Branch' of the Legal Profession in Early Modern England* (Cambridge, 2004), pp. 49–51, 56–7, 78.

[29] Brooks had estimated some 100–150 cases per annum on the common-law side of Exchequer, but Palmer points to a few series and categories he overlooked, including the *qui tam* litigation to enforce statutes. See Palmer, 'The level of litigation in 1607', part of his study of 'Litigiousness in early modern England and Wales' <http://aalt.law.uh.edu/Litigiousness/Litigation.html> [accessed 7 Nov. 2020].

working papers of privy councillor Sir Julius Caesar for 1608/9 show an average of four to five cases on the docket each day. At that rate, assuming the usual thirty-four sitting days a year, the court could only have heard, at most, some 150 cases, and probably fewer as some cases extended over several days.[30] Based on the writ and process books for the 1630s, Henry Philips suggested that 'the number of cases heard during the course of a single year averaged rather less than fifty'.[31] Plaintiffs dropped many suits. They compounded some out of court on their own. Committees of the court also dismissed many as being unsuited to Star Chamber.[32] Such committees also arbitrated or compounded others outside a formal hearing in the full court, a practice that Hudson worried could lead to abuses and injustices, with one person 'made judge of the whole cause, which is most prejudicial'. At the very least, he wrote, it constituted 'an insufferable indignity' that threatened the court's reputation.[33] In short, plaintiffs initiated far fewer cases in Star Chamber than in other courts and many of their complaints did not make it to a full hearing.

When looking at the bills filed, moreover, it becomes clear that Star Chamber had a more restricted litigant profile than some other courts. By 'popularity' we cannot mean 'pertaining to the common people'.[34] Barnes deemed 54% of the plaintiffs who filed bills in James's reign to have been of gentle status or higher.[35] A small, in-progress sample of Elizabethan bills shows a similar percentage, with 60% of the plaintiffs identifying as gentlemen, knights or noblemen.[36] This stands in contrast to the proportion of plaintiffs in King's Bench and Common Pleas of similar high status: Brooks noted 25% and 28% respectively in 1606.[37] True, categorizing petitioners to the court, and their complaints, is complicated by the jointly

[30] Alnwick MS. (on microfilm at the Brit. Libr.), vol. 9, passim. The 34 sitting days comes from Barnes, 'Due Process', p. 335.

[31] H. E. I. Phillips, 'The last years of the court of Star Chamber, 1630–41', *Transactions of the Royal Historical Society*, 4th ser., xxi (1930), 103–31, at p. 111.

[32] See, e.g., Brit. Libr., Add. MS. 37045. And the unsuitability of a case for the court was, of course, a common rejoinder from defendants.

[33] Hudson, 'Treatise', p. 20 (see also pp. 28–9).

[34] One might remember, too, that 'popularity' had negative connotations for some contemporaries: *Politics, Religion, and Popularity in Early Stuart Britain,* ed. T. Cogswell, R. Cust and P. Lake; C. Cuttica, 'Popularity in early modern England (ca. 1580–1642): looking again at *thing* and *concept*', *Journal of British Studies,* lviii (2019), 1–27.

[35] Barnes, 'Litigants', p. 10. See also A. Fox, *Oral and Literate Culture in England, 1500–1700* (Oxford, 2000), p. 308. Guy also observed that bills under Wolsey came predominantly from the 'upper echelons' of society; *Court*, p. 62.

[36] Based on a tally of 82 bills: nobility, 3; knights and esquires, 16; gentlemen, 30; also, clergy, 4; yeomen, 9; husbandmen, 3; merchants, 7; tradesmen, 8; plus two others.

[37] Brooks, *Pettyfoggers*, p. 282.

filed bills with multiple plaintiffs and issues.[38] Some bills named dozens of commoners as plaintiffs, or as defendants, in suits over disputed common rights. Commoners might more readily proceed against their 'betters' in Star Chamber than elsewhere, but the court's profile of plaintiffs tilted heavily towards the elite.

One might also note Tim Stretton's observation that of all the central courts, Star Chamber had 'the smallest female presence', with women named as plaintiffs or defendants in just over 10% of actions between individuals in an Elizabethan sample and in some 8.5% cent of Jacobean cases.[39] New datafiles produced from calendars of the Elizabethan records let us see that just 4% of the files with bills name a woman as either a sole or joint complainant – a proportion that had declined from the 14% of women-led complaints Deborah Youngs found for cases begun under Henry VIII.[40] In contrast, roughly 20% of plaintiffs in Chancery and Requests were women.[41] None of the central courts earned a high percentage of their business from women plaintiffs, but by no standard was Star Chamber 'popular' among women, who turned to other courts in greater numbers and proportions.

Another point should be made about plaintiffs and the counts of bills filed: the bills do not include all cases launched by the attorneys general.[42] Counts of bills filed in Star Chamber are dwarfed by litigation in other central courts and they in turn significantly outnumber the cases actually heard in open court, but they also miss some cases that *did* proceed to

[38] For a good discussion of the difficulties in categorizing plaintiffs and complaints in the English bill courts that offered discretionary conciliar justice, see L. Flannigan, 'Litigants in the English "Court of Poor Men's Causes", or court of Requests, 1515–25', *Law and History Review*, xxxviii (2020), 303–37.

[39] T. Stretton, *Women Waging Law in Elizabethan England* (Cambridge, 1998), p. 40, noting that women were named as plaintiffs or defendants in 36 of a sample of 346 Elizabethan suits, and in 657 of 7715 Jacobean suits, based on the manuscript calendar and Barnes indexes respectively.

[40] 'Hidden Archives' file for STAC 5 and 7 (694/17710); the percentage of all (unconsolidated) calendar entries with a female plaintiff was 3.7 in the 1560s and 4.3 in the 1590s, so there does not seem to have been any particular decline over the latter part of the period, suggesting that the decline set in earlier, perhaps around the time the court switched from its civil to criminal focus, *c.*1551–60; D. Youngs, '"A besy woman … and full of lawe': female litigants in early Tudor Star Chamber', *Journal of British Studies*, lviii (2019), 735–50, at p. 740.

[41] Stretton, *Women Waging Law*, p. 40. The STAC numbers may be comparable to KB and CP, though possibly lower: Brooks found that of cases in advanced stages in these courts widows were plaintiffs in 6% in 1560, 2–3% in 1606, but Stretton's samples of cases initiated in 1560, drawn from KB 27's warrants of attorneys, show that women comprised 13% of all litigants, both plaintiffs and defendants.

[42] On this point, see Baker, *Dyer*, i. lxxxviii–lxxxix.

trial: those launched *ore tenus*, or orally without written proceedings. Assertions of the court's 'popularity' also sometimes accompany claims that the attorneys general did not use the court as an instrument of royal prerogative and state policy quite so much as the court's later vilification would suggest.[43] Perhaps so. But it is easy to underestimate how much of a role the prosecutions by attorneys general played in the court's time and in the public's perceptions of the court if we simply count the bills they filed and then compare them to the total number of bills. Barnes observed that of his set of some 8228 actions in the court between 1603 and 1624, only 600 of the cases began upon an attorney general's information; furthermore, he suggested that only fifty-two of them were really *pro rege* proceedings 'in furtherance of the greater interests of Crown and Commonwealth'.[44] But any estimate of the involvement of attorneys general based on the bills surviving in the Star Chamber archive will miss the causes launched *ore tenus* and thus underestimate that officer's use of the court. When we look at one sizeable collection of trial reports, most cases between private parties have matching bills of complaint in the surviving Star Chamber files, but some 67% (49/73) of the cases launched by attorneys general do not.[45] Cases launched by an attorney general almost invariably made it to a hearing, too. Yes, private plaintiffs launched the majority of cases filed and heard, but someone attending sittings of the court would have seen cases begun by the crown's attorney taking up a greater proportion of the court's time than we might think by looking at the full set of bills filed.[46]

In short, some people offered substantive complaints about Star Chamber much earlier than modern advocates of the court suggest; its litigant profile tended to be rather more elite, and more male, than those of other courts; the numbers of cases brought before the court and the numbers actually heard were dwarfed by the numbers in other central courts; and cases launched by the attorneys general played a bigger part of the court's public performance than has previously been suggested by some scholars. Recognizing these facts might give us a better understanding of the individual cases that we study. Yes, people continued to use the court until its end. And yes, Star Chamber performed functions that some people

[43] See, e.g., Stuckey, *Star Chamber*, p. 48.

[44] Barnes, 'Litigants', p. 9.

[45] Working from reports transcribed in *Harley MS 2143*: of 73 cases that were clearly launched by the attorneys general, only 24 have yet been found in the STAC files. The others may have had bills that were subsequently lost, but most were presumably launched *ore tenus*, without a written bill.

[46] As an example, of the 89 cases listed in Sir Julius Caesar's working notes in 1608/9, 8 were AG cases. Alnwick MS., vol. 9.

at the time considered valuable. Indeed, the court's remit, like that of other English bill courts, was actively created in partnership with plaintiffs who brought a wide range of amorphously defined grievances to the lords of the council in their petitions.[47] But why insist upon the court's 'popularity'?

The insistence may well have roots in something akin to the well-known propensity of biographers to fall in love with their subjects. But it gained traction within the context of revisionist assaults on Whig history and efforts to refocus from long-term to short-term and contingent causes for wholly unrevolutionary civil wars. A number of these revisionists cited Elfreda Skelton's 1930 MA thesis for evidence of the court's popularity, but she made the claim almost secondarily, with reservations, and in passing – noting near the end of her work that the court 'seems to have been popular with the people', based on the increasing volume of bills and the praise offered by one plaintiff who hoped to secure a favourable judgement.[48] Assertions of popularity became orthodoxy only when historians started to turn away from any talk of long-term causes for the civil wars. They became a proxy or prop for positive evaluations of the court's place in a largely stable polity. Star Chamber is overdue for a post-revisionist reanalysis that looks at its uses and significance in its own time and place, and that does not simply return to older depictions of the court as unpopular.

We might also remember that the negative characterizations of the court that some early and mid twentieth-century historians argued against were never attempts at disinterested historical analysis, but rather partisan eighteenth-century accounts that sought to make polemical, political points in the context of debates over high-profile libel cases, like that of John Wilkes.[49] We can presumably do better than simply inverting the heavy-handed moralizing of these politically invested works when affecting to write as historians. Barnes had noted his own unease with the 'chief argument in justification of the court' made by some works, observing that 'popularity

[47] See, e.g., the discussion of bills alleging duelling in K. J. Kesselring, *Making Murder Public: Homicide in Early Modern England, 1480–1680* (Oxford, 2019), pp. 105–13.

[48] Skelton, 'Star Chamber', p. 204. On p. 207, Skelton notes that 'no murmur of discontent was heard in Elizabeth's reign', but elsewhere in the thesis, Skelton does note some such complaints (e.g., p. 45).

[49] See, e.g., Anon., *The Court of Star Chamber or Seat of Oppression* (London, 1768), quoted as a stand-in for the views that D. L. Vande Zande argues against, 'Coercive Power', p. 326, also cited in Barnes, 'Star Chamber mythology', 2 n. 4. For evidence of this Whiggish view Barnes also cites Anon., *An Inquiry into the History and Abolition of the Court of Star Chamber upon the Principles of Law and the Constitution, particularly as it relates to Prosecutions for Libels* (n.d., mid 18th century) and F. K. Holt, *The Law of Libel* (London, 1816).

is not a test recognized by the canons of historical jurisprudence'.[50] He suggested that we might best evaluate Star Chamber by asking whether it did 'substantial justice by the lights of justice in its day', even while apologizing 'if at times [he] sounded like counsel retained by Star Chamber against the Whig historians'. Perhaps we might avoid the temptation to try to justify or condemn the court at all. Rather than reprising the categories of debate in 1641 (or the 1760s) in the guise of scholarly analysis, we might instead focus on explaining the court's functions and meanings for those who used it or were drawn into its operations. As Ethan Shagan has observed in another context, we might best step aside from the normative moral judgements offered by the people under study: 'allowing historical categories of debate to masquerade as scholarly categories of analysis … normalizes and naturalizes one position' over others.[51]

Allowing that the court was contentious decades before its demise (and for reasons that may or may not have had anything to do with that demise), that it heard far fewer cases than other courts, and that the attorneys general did make distinctive use of the venue can allow scholars who work with its records a richer appreciation of the stakes at play in a person's decision to launch a case in this court as opposed to others. We can better situate the individual cases we want to study when we recognize that claims for Star Chamber being an 'ordinary' rather than extraordinary court, disputes about its origins and arguments over the status of its records were part of broader disagreements. More broadly, if we set aside assertions of the court's popularity and temptations to become its defenders (or attackers), we will better understand its functions and meanings in its own day. We might also appreciate more fully the conditions in which the records we rely upon were produced and used.

***

The chapters that follow offer a variety of insights into Star Chamber and the disputes that came before it. The first and final chapters offer detailed guides to the surviving records of and about the court. Daniel Gosling surveys Star Chamber collections in The National Archives of the UK and elsewhere, updating previous overviews and describing ongoing efforts to improve cataloguing and access. Ian Williams not only revisits debates about why Star Chamber came under attack in the opening salvos of the Long

[50] Barnes, 'Star Chamber mythology', p. 11.

[51] E. Shagan, *The Rule of Moderation: Violence, Religion, and the Politics of Restraint in Early Modern England* (Cambridge, 2011), p. 19.

Parliament, but also provides valuable lists of extant manuscript reports and notes on cases in the court, resources that will repay further attention. As Gosling observes, these notes can fill some of the gaps left by the loss of the order and decree books; as Williams explains, some such reports circulated widely, extending the audience for Star Chamber hearings well beyond the crowds that jostled for space in the court itself.

Several chapters touch on the political uses of the court, broadly understood. Hillary Taylor examines the politics of deposing to demonstrate the significant constraints on poor people's agency in the court, for example. Louis Knafla explores a case that saw Sir Edward Coke, as attorney general, bring the central court's weight to bear on a local eruption of violent disorder to help godly ministers effect the moral reformation of their community. Sadie Jarrett's chapter reminds us of Star Chamber's role in integrating Wales into the polity governed from Westminster. Simon Healy dissects one attempt in the reign of King James to use Star Chamber as a revenue collection agency for a cash-strapped crown. Williams demonstrates the political tensions that arose from the increasing role of bishops among the court's judges in the fraught Caroline years.

Some chapters speak to Star Chamber's distinctive remit and contributions to legal developments beyond its walls. The chapters by Healy and Emily Kadens address remarkable allegations of fraud, one of the crimes of covin and deceit that became a special focus for the court, while offering insight into the particular endeavours in which the frauds were said to have occurred: the international bullion trade and marine insurance, respectively. Claire Egan's contribution examines libel cases, another area in which the court developed a particular interest and expertise, and explores the dynamics of publication, performance and 'rehearsal' of libels as they moved from local audiences into Star Chamber.

Chapters by Jarrett, Knafla, Kesselring and Deborah Youngs touch on women as plaintiffs or defendants in the court. Star Chamber was not just yet another venue for disputes involving women; it was one in which norms about marriage formation and (married) women's legal responsibility were re-negotiated and asserted. In addressing how women used this court and were treated by its judges, these chapters contribute to ongoing discussions of women's access to justice in early modern Britain. They also speak to issues of sexual violence, with chapters addressing cases of marital abduction or sexual assault that came before the court and showing again the wealth of insights into early modern life that can be gleaned from these records.

The chapters provide a variety of answers to two questions that recurred at the conference from which the volume arose. One asked how far we might 'believe' the stories presented in the court documents, and how we might use them even while recognizing them as narratives constructed for a particular purpose. Taylor's contribution highlights an additional reason for caution in attending to the effects of relations of deference or dependency between deponents and the people for whom they testified. Here the authors show themselves attentive to issues of the sort raised by scholars such as Natalie Zemon Davis, Frances Dolan and others on the uses of petitions and depositions as evidence.[52] Youngs, Egan and others show how much can be gained by attentive reading of the language plaintiffs or their counsel used in crafting bills. They all demonstrate the usefulness of reading those narratives in the context of other, ancillary documents and with a well-informed understanding of the court for which they were produced.

Another recurring question was 'why Star Chamber'? Why take a case to *this* court, as opposed to another? The chapters show a variety of motives at play, whether it was a Welsh gentlewoman hoping for treatment more to her liking from a Westminster court than a local one, as in Jarrett's chapter; a Dorset yeoman looking for the particular defence of his good name that Star Chamber could provide, as in Egan's; or the merchants using a Star Chamber bill as a collateral suit to secure domestic jurisdiction for an offence at sea, as discussed by Kadens. Some plaintiffs turned to the court because the wrongs they wanted righted did not clearly fit common-law categories; others preferred the types of remedies potentially to be had there to those available elsewhere. Some simply sought to vex their foes or to shore up suits pending in other courts. Some wanted the publicity and heft of a prosecution in this extraordinary court to vindicate themselves. Whatever their varied motivations, their suits helped make the court what it was. The chapters that follow can thus contribute to our understanding of jurisdictional conflict, legal pluralism and the contested co-creation of 'justice' within early modern England and Wales. Collectively, too, they help us 'look *at* our archives, not just through them', attentive to the broader social relations that shaped the production of the documents we read as both sources and texts.[53]

[52] See, e.g., N. Z. Davis, *Fiction in the Archives: Pardon Tales and Their Tellers in Sixteenth-Century France* (Stanford, 1987) and F. E. Dolan, *True Relations: Reading, Literature, and Evidence in Seventeenth-Century England* (Philadelphia, 2013). For a particularly helpful examination of the processes behind the production of depositions in Star Chamber and similar courts, see H. Falvey, 'Relating early modern depositions', in *Remembering Protest in Britain Since 1500,* ed. C. J. Griffin and B. McDonagh (Cham, 2018), pp. 89–100 and H. Taylor, 'The price of the poor's words: social relations and the economics of deposing for one's "betters" in early modern England', *Economic History Review*, cxxii (2019), 828–47.

[53] For an introduction to the literature on the 'archival turn', see K. Burns, 'Notaries, truth, and consequences', *American Historical Review,* cx (2005), 350–79, quote at p. 355, and papers in *The Social History of the Archives: Record-Keeping in Early Modern Europe*, *Past and*

Sadly, because of the pressures of our current epidemiological context, we lost a few of our anticipated chapters as the contributors found themselves unable to complete archival work or to spare the time from all the other demands that arose. Riot remains almost untouched here now, unfortunately, despite being one of the subjects for which the court and its records are perhaps best known. We also lost a chapter that promised to explore connections between cases in the Elizabethan Star Chamber and the drama of the era. We can end, though, with a brief allusion to the opening of Shakespeare's *Merry Wives of Windsor*, where one character threatens to turn a petty local dispute into 'a Star-chamber matter'. With their shared attentiveness to the nature and limits of an archive, the chapters that are gathered here allow better insight into a wide range of matters brought before the court and into the ways in which Star Chamber itself mattered in early modern history. Judging even from the conference alone, many more Star Chamber matters are yet to come to light.

Present, ccxxx (2016), supplement 11.

2. The records of the court of Star Chamber at The National Archives and elsewhere*

Daniel Gosling

The records of the court of Star Chamber are incomplete. The separation of material in the early seventeenth century means that today, the records preserved at The National Archives represent approximately half of the original Star Chamber archive. This chapter describes the current arrangement and content of these records, with reference to material held elsewhere, and explains how they survived when others were lost. It is not the first to do so, though it is a topic that often needs renewing. When Cora Scofield published her thesis on the surviving records of Star Chamber in 1900, the only records at the Public Record Office (as it was then known) outside of the dedicated series of Star Chamber proceedings were 'a few estreats of fines'.[1] In the twentieth century, Thomas G. Barnes and John Guy provided more detailed surveys of the Star Chamber collections, which identified related records to help piece together what was lost.[2] Since the publication of these works much has changed. The Public Record Office was moved from its former home on Chancery Lane, London, to Kew and merged with the Historical Manuscripts Commission to form The National Archives of the UK.[3] Three new Star Chamber series were added to the main collection, created from unsorted miscellanea.[4] The paper catalogue moved online, incorporating descriptions of records held at more than 2500 archives across the United Kingdom. Most recently, The National Archives

* Unless otherwise specified, all document references refer to The National Archives of the UK.

[1] C. L. Scofield, *A Study of the Court of Star Chamber, Largely Based on Manuscripts in the British Museum and the Public Record Office* (Chicago, 1900), p. v.

[2] T. G. Barnes, 'The archives and archival problems of the Elizabethan and early Stuart Star Chamber', *Journal of the Society of Archivists*, ii (1963), 345–360; J. A. Guy, *The Court of Star Chamber and its Records to the Reign of Elizabeth I* (London, 1985).

[3] The Public Record Office still exists as a legal entity, bound by the Public Records Act 1958 (6 & 7 Eliz. II, c. 51), which remains in force.

[4] STAC 11–13.

D. Gosling, 'The records of the court of Star Chamber at The National Archives and elsewhere' in *Star Chamber Matters: An Early Modern Court and Its Records*, ed. K. Kesselring and N. Mears (London, 2021), pp. 19–39.

has embarked upon a project – the Star Chamber Archive – comprising catalogue improvements, the sorting of miscellanea and increased data connectivity, to draw together virtually Star Chamber material spread across record series and repositories.

The exact origins of a definable court of Star Chamber are uncertain. The 1641 act that abolished the court claimed it was created by Henry VII's 1487 statute against liveries and retaining, which empowered the lord chancellor, lord treasurer and keeper of the privy seal to act judicially with the council.[5] The 1487 parliament roll seems initially to support this. The act is annotated, '*Pro Camera Stellata.* An acte geving the court of Starchamber aucthority to punnyshe dyvers mydemeanors'.[6] However, this annotation was a later, sixteenth-century, addition.[7] The starred chamber (*Camera Stellata*) in the Palace of Westminster, from which the court took its name, had acted as a meeting place for the council to conduct business since its construction in 1347; an inner chamber was used for state business, while the outer chamber was used to hear petitions for justice.[8] In the later medieval period, enquiries were made before the king and his council in the Star Chamber, defendants were ordered to appear before them to answer charges, and matters of legal ambiguity were taken there for judgement. The formal court probably developed from this judicial business.[9]

The main series of Star Chamber proceedings at The National Archives suggest at least a regularization of judicial business in the starred chamber around the accession of Henry VII; the earliest series of proceedings for the court – STAC 1 – contains records dating predominantly from this reign. The accumulation of proceedings in the sixteenth century necessitated the construction of nine large presses of wainscot in 1608 in the court room itself to house these records.[10] However, even this could not accommodate

[5] For Star Chamber's abolition see 16 Chas I, c. 10, citing 3 Hen. VII c. 1.

[6] C 65/125, m. 10 (Item 17).

[7] *Select Cases in the Council of Henry VII*, ed. C. G. Bayne and W. H. Dunham Jr (Selden Society 75, 1958), pp. lxiv–lxxii.

[8] See, e.g., the 1383 document concerning the king's wars which was made in Star Chamber (E 30/304). The ceiling of the chamber was spangled with stars on an azure background, contemporary depictions of which can be seen in illuminated initials in E 33/1/1, E 33/1/2 and E 33/2.

[9] E.g. *Year Book* [*YB*] Mich. 5 Edw. IV, pl. Long Quinto [3], fos. 58a–61b (1465); *YB* Pasch. 13 Edw. IV, pl. 5, fos. 9a–10b (1473); *YB* Mich. 2 Hen VII, pl. 9, fo. 3a (1486), taken from *Medieval English Legal History: An Index and Paraphrase of Printed Year Book Reports, 1268–1535*, ed. D. J. Seipp <https://www.bu.edu/law/faculty-scholarship/legal-history-the-year-books/> [accessed 9 Dec. 2020]. See also C 49/22/18, describing the examination of witnesses in Star Chamber before Henry VI and his council.

[10] E 407/55, fos. 165–168.

the whole of the Star Chamber archive, and so a separate office was created in the Holborn court of Gray's Inn.[11] This satellite repository served as an office for the clerk of the court. Those records which the clerk needed to refer to most often, the decrees and orders for the duration of the court's existence – which recorded, among other things, the final judgement of a case – as well as Caroline court proceedings, were deposited there for easy reference. A prudent decision at the time, but one that would ultimately lead to the loss of these records.

The fate of these records and the location of those now in the care of The National Archives are detailed in a report made in 1705 by John Lowe and Peter Le Neve, deputy chamberlains of the Exchequer. The 'bills, answers, replications, etc, of the dissolved Court of Star Chamber' – those records of proceedings formerly kept in the court itself – were reported as being in the Chapter House at Westminster, along with several other public records. After the court of Star Chamber's abolition, these records had been put into the care of the usher of the Exchequer, until the foundation of the Annuity Offices in the 1690s prompted their move to the Chapter House.[12] Lowe and Le Neve also noted that, 'none of the decrees of the said court are to be found ... they were [last] in a house in St Bartholomew's Close, London'.[13] That the records made it to St Bart's gives us cause for hope that they survived, as the area was extraordinarily resilient to the many fires afflicting London in the latter part of the seventeenth century.[14] However, they have not yet resurfaced.

It is remarkable that the remainder of the Star Chamber collection survives. In 1701, prior to their report on the contents of the Chapter House, Lowe and Le Neve wrote to Christopher Wren to complain that the glazing there needed urgent repair, because the 'raine beats in & endamageth' the records.[15] An up-to-date report on the records of the Chapter House was made in 1719 by Dudley Downes and John Lawton, then deputy chamberlains. This report remarked that the Star Chamber records had 'lain many years in a very great heap, undigested, without any

[11] Barnes, 'Archival problems', p. 358.

[12] The report is reproduced as 'An Account of the several Records, in the Court of the Receipt of the Exchequer, in the Custody of the Lord Treasurer, or the Right Honourable the Lords Commissioners of the Treasury, for the Time being, the Chamberlains of the Exchequer, and their Deputies' in *Journal of the House of Lords: Volume 21, 1718–1721* (London, 1767–1830), pp. 136–9.

[13] *Journal of the House of Lords, 1718–1721*, p. 137. Still missing in 1732 when John Lawton, keeper of the records in the Exchequer, reported, 'the decrees of this court are not at present anywhere to be found' (SP 46/140).

[14] Gray's Inn, with its many wooden structures, fared less well.

[15] E 36/253, fo. 294.

covering from dust, or security from rats and mice'.[16] Thankfully, since then the records have been better kept, and The National Archives now holds a substantial collection of Star Chamber material, drawn predominantly from this Chapter House collection.

There are four main types of record relating to Star Chamber. The first, original records of proceedings, makes up the bulk of the collection at The National Archives. Proceedings began with a bill of complaint.[17] The bill was in English and outlined the matter at issue, including certain fictions alleging riot or other force that brought the matter within the court's jurisdiction. These bills were often addressed to the monarch or lord chancellor and concluded with a request that the defendant appear to answer their complaint.

If the plea was accepted, a writ of subpoena was issued to summon the defendant.[18] Before 1500, a precis of the order, or the prescribed date for appearance, was entered at the foot of the bill itself. If the defendant appeared, they provided a written answer, stating that the plaintiff's complaint was false. If the defendant presented a demurrer – a denial of the court's suitability to hear the matter – proceedings were stayed until it could be confirmed, usually by a common-law judge, that the matter should rightly be heard in Star Chamber.[19] Defendants who submitted a failed demurrer were liable to pay costs and ordered to answer the plaintiff's original bill.[20] If the defendant did not appear, a writ of attachment was sent to the sheriff of the county where the defendant was 'most resident' to apprehend them. If the defendant could still not be found, the clerk of the court of Star Chamber could award a commission of rebellion to seven or eight named persons, authorizing them to apprehend and imprison the defendant.[21] After the answer, the plaintiff made their replication, restating their complaint; this could be countered by a rejoinder from the defendant, again requesting dismissal. Even then the pleadings were not necessarily complete, as plaintiffs and defendants could respond with surreplications and surrejoinders.[22]

[16] *Journal of the House of Lords, 1718–1721*, pp. 141–2.

[17] Prosecutions brought by the attorney general were brought instead by information.

[18] Any person could serve the subpoena to the defendant, provided they informed the defendant of 'certain knowledge thereof before the return of the process' (E 163/24/9, p. 1r).

[19] T. G. Barnes, 'Due process and slow process in the late Elizabethan – early Stuart Star Chamber', *The American Journal of Legal History*, vi (1962), 221–249, at p. 228. See British Library, Add. MS. 37045 for a register of such opinions made in Star Chamber.

[20] Barnes, 'Due process and slow process', p. 228, citing Huntington Library, Ellesmere MS. 2680.

[21] E 163/24/9, p. 1r.

[22] Cases which are known to have reached this stage (by virtue of a surviving surrejoinder)

After the pleadings came the proofs, whereby the court tried to ascertain the truth of the matter. First, a set of interrogatories was drawn up by the plaintiff's counsel and put to the defendant (by impartial examiners), dealing with each grievance in the bill of complaint. Following this, each side was allowed to draft interrogatories to put to witnesses.[23] These pleadings and proofs make up the bulk of the records held at The National Archives in STAC 1–9. The third stage of proceedings was the trial hearing. If the defendant was found innocent of the charges laid against them, the judges dismissed the case (with fines put to the plaintiff). If they were found guilty, punishment could vary from a fine, to imprisonment, banishment or even corporal punishment.[24] Throughout this process, and at the end of the case, the court created entry books for orders and decrees. The decree recorded the final judgement of a case; the orders recorded any court decisions made throughout proceedings.[25] It is these entry books, along with the majority of the Caroline proceedings, which have not been seen since before 1705.

Original records of proceedings are arranged by reign in the series STAC 1–9. It is estimated that these records account for approximately half of the former Star Chamber archive, the remainder comprising the lost decree and order books.[26] Some misfiling has occurred, and records relating to earlier and later reigns can be found among the proceedings for specific monarchs.[27] The survival of each stage of proceedings varies. In some cases, particularly those that were settled out of court, only a single stage survives; others have preserved almost every part of the case.[28] Pleadings, written on parchment, have a better rate of survival than the proofs, written on

include STAC 2/1/25 (*Alen* v *Alen*), STAC 2/22/136 (*Ferror* v *Hastinges*) and STAC 2/22/273 (*Spenser* v *Hopkins*).

[23] Interrogatories described on the catalogue rarely specify whether they were put to the defendants or witnesses.

[24] Barnes, 'Due process and slow process', p. 229.

[25] Barnes, 'Archival problems', p. 350.

[26] Guy, *Court of Star Chamber*, p. 19.

[27] E.g. the proceedings for Henry VII contain records from both before (STAC 1/1/18, *Tayllour* v *Atwyll*, temp. Edw. IV) and after (STAC 1/2/55, *Middelton* v *Willisthorp*, temp. Hen. VIII) his reign. So too does the Marian series of Star Chamber proceedings contain Elizabethan cases (e.g. STAC 4/11/19, *Goodwin* v *Bysshop*, after 26 Eliz. I; STAC 4/11/56 *Shelley* v *Jefferson*, 1574).

[28] E.g. STAC 2/26/212 (*Dyes* v *Elkyn*) and STAC 4/7/41 (*Hartgill* v *Lord Stourton*) contain only a bill or draft bill; STAC 1/2/129 (*Mille* v *Guldeford*) and STAC 8/314/20 (*Hunt* v *Jenkins*) contain only an answer. Conversely, STAC 2/2/49 (*Aston* v *Baskerfeld*), STAC 5/U1/9 (*Unwyn* v *Sneyd*), and STAC 10/1/52 (*Tenaunt* v *Sparowe*) all contain at least a bill, answer, replication and rejoinder; STAC 2/1/25 (*Alen* v *Alen*) is particularly complete, containing a bill, answers, replication, rejoinder, interrogatories, depositions, certificate and surrejoinder.

paper. In the nineteenth century, the majority of this collection was re-sorted, drawing together several elements of the pleadings and proofs into an alphabetical arrangement of files. However, STAC 5 and parts of STAC 8 retain their original eighteenth-century arrangement where different stages of pleadings were filed according to the first letter of the plaintiff's surname. The proofs were gathered together, with separate sequences for examinations taken by the officers of the court and for depositions. Where documents have been preserved as a case file, it should be read in reverse. Thus, the bill will usually appear at the back of the file, with other pleadings and proofs arranged in reverse chronological order.[29]

STAC 1 is formed of the surviving records of equity proceedings heard before Henry VII's council, comprising 135 items across two bound volumes. As there was not yet a clear distinction between Star Chamber and council proceedings, the records can only be ascribed to proceedings before the council during that reign, 'which are analogous to Star Chamber proceedings, [and] may probably be accepted as such'.[30] For this reason, material otherwise identical to that in STAC 1 can be found in other series relating to the judicial business of the council.[31] The series also contains records of proceedings heard and determined by other conciliar courts, such as the court of Requests.[32]

During Henry VIII's reign, particularly under the chancellorship of Thomas Wolsey (1515–29), the business of Star Chamber increased. STAC 2 – which collects Star Chamber proceedings for the reign of Henry VIII – contains over 6500 items across thirty-five pieces. A piece – often the archival level at which a reference becomes orderable – in STAC 2 can refer to either a bound volume or box of loose files. Despite bills alleging riot (to justify bringing the case before Star Chamber), the majority of actions related to disputed titles to property. STAC 2 contains some records from the reigns of Henry VI through to James I, caused in part by the generic address in a bill of complaint to the (unspecified) king. In several cases, further details in the body of the bill are required to date a document. One such record sees James Amore addressing 'the king our sovereign lord' in the bill; it is only from his citing his presence on the 'fields of Barnet and

[29] When a bill comprised multiple pages, they would also often be arranged in reverse order, such as in STAC 2/1/68 (*Alyson* v *Knyghtley*).

[30] Scofield, *Study of the Court of Star Chamber*, p. v.

[31] E.g. E 28/96.

[32] E.g. STAC 1/1/20, a dispute concerning the manor of Dowdeswell, Gloucestershire, or STAC 1/2/82, concerning assaults in Bishop's Norton, Lincolnshire.

Tewkesbury' in the body of the bill that it can be dated to Edward IV's second reign.[33]

Worthy, but incomplete, attempts to arrange STAC 2 in the nineteenth century mean that the first sixteen pieces (STAC 2/1–16) are bound volumes, broadly alphabetized by plaintiff. This sorting is not consistent across the whole series and other 'A' plaintiffs can be found among the remaining nineteen bundles (STAC 2/17–35), arranged as loose parchment bundles in boxes.[34] Files relating to the same plaintiff, too, can be spread across several pieces.[35] Royal officers are alphabetized by their office rather than surname; actions brought by the king's almoner, most often concerning the goods of suicides, are therefore sorted as 'Almoner'.[36] As with STAC 1, documents relating to Star Chamber proceedings from Henry VIII's reign can be found in other equity series.[37] Since 2019, some catalogue descriptions for items in STAC 2 have been improved to include more accurate dates and a note recording document type (bills, answers, etc).[38]

STAC 3, Star Chamber proceedings for Edward VI, contains just over 1000 items across nine pieces. Despite his minority, most of the bills are still addressed to the king, though some are addressed to Protector Somerset.[39] Business still mainly concerned civil proceedings, and files include actions of breach of contract, debt, fraud and tithe disputes. The impact of the Reformation can be seen from disputes over ecclesiastical jurisdictions and questions of title concerning ex-monastic land (commonly heard before the court of Augmentations). STAC 4, Marian Star Chamber proceedings, contains a little over 750 items across eleven boxed pieces. Proceedings from Mary's reign, particularly after her marriage to Philip, are easier to identify and date because of the double address to the king and queen. Additionally, after 1556 the chancellor Nicholas Heath provided that all bills of complaint be endorsed with the exact date of filing.[40]

33 STAC 2/1/74 (*Amore* v *Chapman*).

34 E.g. STAC 2/17/231 (*Astley* v *Cotes*).

35 See, for instance, John Aldersey, who appears in several Cheshire cases across STAC 2/19/166, STAC 2/20/182, 306, and STAC 2/28/39.

36 STAC 2/1/41–60.

37 E.g. REQ 2/9/150 (*Buyke* v *Geffreisun*), an answer to a bill in STAC 2/18/186 (*Buyke* v *Gascoigne*); E 163/11/48/3, describing the wrongdoing of William Pygod, linked to STAC 2/3, fos. 201–205 (*Barton* v *Pygott*).

38 E.g. STAC 2/1–2.

39 For bills addressed to Somerset, see STAC 3/3/64 (*Barantyne* v *Dormer*), STAC 3/4/80 (*Harrys* v *Longe*), and STAC 3/6/50 (*Markham* v *Manby*).

40 The catalogue entries for STAC 4 only give the date range for Mary's reign. Researchers can therefore find more precise dates for Marian bills of complaint by looking at the original documents.

During Elizabeth's reign, Star Chamber's jurisdiction transformed from largely civil – as it had been under Henry VIII – to almost exclusively criminal.[41] STAC 5, which forms the bulk of the Elizabethan Star Chamber proceedings, is by far the largest STAC series, comprising over 35,000 items across 982 pieces. It is also the only STAC series that retains much of its original eighteenth-century sorting. This is represented on the catalogue by a slightly different referencing system to other series. Bundles are arranged by the first letter of the lead plaintiff, and the piece number contains both this letter and a number. For example, STAC 5/G17/18 refers to the eighteenth item in the seventeenth bundle of 'G' plaintiffs.[42] Royal officers, and certain other plaintiffs, continue to be sorted by their office. Cases relating to suicides or deodands (the object or instrument that was the cause of death, to be forfeited to the crown), within the jurisdiction of and brought by the queen's almoner, are therefore sorted among the 'A' bundles.[43] STAC 6 formerly contained supplementary Elizabethan proceedings, though was formally removed as a series in 1964 as its records had been absorbed into STAC 5 (a process begun in 1896).[44]

Part of The National Archives' Star Chamber Archive project will incorporate new case references to Star Chamber proceedings. These do not appear on the records themselves but were created to make it easier to reassemble virtually separate parts of a suit. STAC 5, which provides the largest dataset of Star Chamber material in a single series, is the first collection to receive these case references, which will allow users to connect files relating to the same case spread across multiple pieces (and, when the project is complete, series and repositories).[45] These case references and improved catalogue descriptions incorporate and supersede both the original four-volume catalogue created in the 1740s and indices created in the 1960s.[46]

[41] Guy, *Court of Star Chamber*, pp. 57–60.

[42] STAC 5/G17/18 (*Goslinge* v *Osborne*).

[43] Over 350 such items are contained in STAC 5. E.g. STAC 5/A1/7 (*Queen's Almoner* v *Robinson*); STAC 5/A54/34 (*Queen's Almoner* v *Goddard*); STAC 5/A59/40 (*Queen's Almoner* v *Cooper*).

[44] For the removal of STAC 6, see PRO 13/33. For the obsolete series list, see OBS 1/1367.

[45] The 'A' plaintiffs for STAC 5 have already received these unique case references. So STAC 5/A1/3, STAC 5/A23/14 and STAC 5/A31/24 can now be identified as forming part of the same case, from the unique case reference SCEL – 14898.

[46] For more details about these case references see the online series description for STAC 5, which describes the catalogue changes <https://discovery.nationalarchives.gov.uk/details/r/C13674> [accessed 9 Dec. 2020].

STAC 7, comprising thirty-one pieces of around 1300 items, also contains Elizabethan proceedings. These differ from STAC 5 in that they went through the nineteenth-century re-sorting process that the majority of the Star Chamber collection underwent.[47] Though they are not in their original letter bundles, they have been arranged in alphabetical sequence. The example of suicide and deodand cases brought by the queen's almoner again illustrates this point.[48] STAC 7 is arranged into three sequences, each commencing with the beginning of the alphabet. These are STAC 7/1–9, 10–16 and 17–31.[49] For STAC 7/17 onwards, the subject is mostly listed as 'incomplete', denoting a file without a bill of complaint (though much information can still be gleaned from these records). At least two cases in STAC 7 indicate that the case was brought before parliament at some point, and several further cases note crown intervention.[50]

STAC 8, collecting Star Chamber pleadings and proofs for James I's reign, is second in size only to STAC 5 and contains more than 8500 items across 314 pieces. This series has benefited considerably from the work of Thomas G. Barnes, most notably his three-volume list and index of these proceedings.[51] During the compiling of this index, Barnes was given permission to reunite separate parts of many law suits, formerly arranged in separate files.[52] Some documents in STAC 8 retain their original arrangement, whereby bills, answers and demurrers and replications and rejoinders were each filed in separate series according to the first letter of the lead plaintiff's surname.[53]

[47] This can be seen from the Public Record Office ink stamping on these records, a product of this re-sort.

[48] STAC 7/1/10–14, 16, 19; STAC 7/17/9–14.

[49] So STAC 7/1, 10 and 17 all contain proceedings for lead plaintiffs with surnames beginning with 'A', and so forth.

[50] For cases brought before parliament, see STAC 7/2/26 (*Elwes* v *Kempe*) and STAC 7/2/39 (*Goodwyn* v *Ap Jankyn*). For crown intervention, see STAC 7/10/28 (*Brigges* v *Gybson*), STAC 7/11/15 (*Conway* v *Lawgher*), STAC 7/12/4 (*Evans* v *Fortescue*), STAC 7/13/27 (*Littleton* v *Lee*), and STAC 7/15/26 (*Saxbye* v *Bowland*).

[51] *List and Index to the Proceedings in Star Chamber for the Reign of James I (1603–1625)*, ed. T. G. Barnes (3 vols., Chicago, 1975).

[52] Notes of these moves are published by Barnes in the first volume of his *List and Index to the Proceedings in Star Chamber for the Reign of James I.*

[53] These files are: STAC 8/61/1–66 (bills, 'B' plaintiffs); STAC 8/120/1–18 (bills, 'D' plaintiffs); STAC 8/138/1–13 (bills, 'E' plaintiffs); STAC 8/152/1–15 (bills, 'G' plaintiffs); STAC 8/178/1–34 (bills, 'H' plaintiffs); STAC 8/185/1–10 (bills, 'I/J' plaintiffs); STAC 8/190/31–40 (bills, 'K' plaintiffs); STAC 8/203/1–32 (bills, 'L' plaintiffs); STAC 8/207/1–27 (bills, 'M' plaintiffs); STAC 8/225/1–9 (bills, 'O' plaintiffs); STAC 8/232/7–22 (answers, 'P' plaintiffs); STAC 8/258/1–31 (bills, 'S' plaintiffs); STAC 8/280/1–19 (bills, 'T' plaintiffs); STAC 8/304/1–45 (bills, 'W' plaintiffs); STAC 8/309/7–28 (answers and demurrers, 'W'

In 2019, catalogue descriptions for STAC 8 were updated utilizing existing indices. The most noteworthy additions were subject categories for each case, taken from Barnes's index. These subject categories reflect the change in jurisdiction of the court during the sixteenth century. The new subject search terms comprise: abduction, assault, attempt, compounding a felony, conspiracy/confederation, conspiracy to indict, contempt, counterfeiting, defamation, destruction of property, duelling, embezzlement, embracery, engrossing, extortion, forgery, fraud, hunting, lawyers' offences, maintenance (including jury offences), officers' malfeasance, offences against religion, perjury, proclamation contemned, religious differences, rescue, riot/rout/unlawful assembly, sedition, subornation, subversion, theatre, trade deceit, and vexatious litigation.[54] There are several cases of note in STAC 8, including the case with the largest known composite fine for a single action, when twenty alien merchants were fined £151,500 for exporting bullion contrary to proclamation.[55] The development of libel law, in line with the burgeoning print trade during this period, can be seen from the increase in 'libel' as a subject ('defamation' in the Barnes category descriptions); over 250 such cases appear in STAC 8.[56] As the (alleged) libellous writings had to be included as evidence in the proceedings, this means that STAC 8 also contains several examples of early modern poems and songs.[57]

STAC 9 contains Star Chamber proceedings for the reign of Charles. However, this series is incomplete, only containing thirty items across two pieces. The bulk of the proceedings for Charles I's reign were kept as 'current' proceedings with the decree and order books, and as such are missing. Those records that make up STAC 9 were originally sorted with Elizabethan material, hence their survival. In 1976, four items identified as Jacobean were re-sorted into STAC 8, to be reunited with their case files.[58] At the same time, six pieces were moved to the unlisted miscellanea of the court of Requests (REQ 3), and some Caroline suits were added from the Star Chamber miscellanea in STAC 10. This miscellaneous Star Chamber

plaintiffs); STAC 8/309/29–41 (replications and rejoinders, 'W' plaintiffs).

[54] *List and Index*, i 33–6. 'Religious differences' and 'theatre' are new subjects added to Barnes's list.

[55] STAC 8/25/19 (*Att. Gen.* v *Coteel*). See, too, the chapter by S. Healy in this volume.

[56] E.g. STAC 8/5/18 (*Att. Gen.* v *Davies*), concerning a rhyming libel; STAC 8/2/2 (*Att. Gen.* v *Joanes*), concerning a libellous play called 'The Old Joiner of Aldgate'.

[57] E.g. STAC 8/138/5 (*Eliot* v *Deering*); STAC 8/100/18 (*Cunde* v *Browne*); see also A. Fox, 'Ballads, libels and popular ridicule in Jacobean England', *Past & Present*, cxlv (1994), 47–83 and the chapter by C. Egan in this volume.

[58] STAC 9/1/6 (*Nowell* v *Ashton*) transferred to STAC 8/222/22; STAC 9/1/10 (*Hastings* v *Brewen*) to STAC 8/174/13; STAC 9/1/12 (*Harman* v *Smythe*) to STAC 8/182/6; and STAC 9/1/16 (*Berrowe* v *Baggott*) to STAC 8/84/7.

series contains a further selection of Star Chamber proceedings. There are eighteen extant pieces in STAC 10, but at present only three – STAC 10/1, 2 and 4 – have item descriptions.[59] From this small sample, it is clear that STAC 10 contains records from across the court's existence.[60]

The catalogue descriptions for STAC 1–9 allow researchers to search for records by plaintiff and defendant surnames, subject, place and county. There are, however, caveats to this. Surnames, for instance, have usually not been standardized. If the bill does not survive, or is separated from its case file, it may be unclear who the plaintiff is, and if only an answer survives we do not always know how many defendants were named in the bill. Additionally, in some cases only the lead plaintiff and defendant are named; to discover the names of secondary defendants or plaintiffs, the original record needs to be consulted. Place names suffer the same spelling variants as surnames, and sometimes the only way to identify the correct place where an offence occurred is through searching the county. The county descriptions in STAC have made it possible for a number of local studies into the court of Star Chamber to be conducted, though researchers using the catalogue should be wary that in some instances abbreviations are used (e.g. Oxon or Oxford for Oxfordshire, Salop for Shropshire, etc).[61] Apart from STAC 8, which adopts the subject terminology proposed by Barnes, item descriptions vary in subject matter. For instance, not all cases of piracy are described as such. Searching for 'piracy' in the catalogue would not identify the bill of complaint brought by Peter Alves of Portugal, who complained that his ship, the *Santa Maria de Sae*, was seized en route to Barnstaple in Devon. The accused then sailed his vessel to Ireland to sell to the mayor of Cork.[62] Instead, one would have to do a broader search for the word 'ship'. Catalogue improvement work aims to rectify many of these issues, creating standardized short titles and including details such as document type in item descriptions.

The similarity in jurisdiction and procedure between the different courts of equity means that Star Chamber proceedings can be found outside of

[59] Two pieces were transferred to other series: STAC 10/20 to STAC 11/1–26; STAC 10/21 to STAC 12/1. STAC 10/19 is listed as missing.

[60] E.g. STAC 10/1/66 (*Wade* v *Pepir*, temp. Edw. IV); STAC 10/2/30 (*Savage* v *Blincow*, 1630).

[61] Notable county studies include L. A. Knafla, *Kent at Law, 1602: III. Star Chamber* (List and Index Society, Special Series 51, 2012); I. Edwards, *A Catalogue of Star Chamber Proceedings Relating to Wales* (Cardiff, 1929); *Yorkshire Star Chamber Proceedings*, ed. W. Brown, et al. (4 vols., Yorkshire Archaeological Society Record Series, 41, 45, 70, 1909–27); *A Handlist of Star Chamber Pleadings Before 1558 for Northern England*, ed. R. W. Hoyle and H. R. T. Summerson (List and Index Society 299, 2003).

[62] STAC 2/1/62 (*Alves* v *Hyre*).

the dedicated STAC series. E 111 – miscellaneous equity proceedings – encompasses all the main courts of equity at Westminster, including Star Chamber. Actions pertaining to Star Chamber can be found in this series by searching for actions brought before the council. In some cases, these records can be cross-referenced against the main series of Star Chamber proceedings. For example, a set of depositions in E 111, describing mortgaged lands in Mitcham, Surrey, relates to proceedings found in STAC 1 and STAC 2.[63] The cross-referencing on the catalogue, however, is incomplete; as catalogue descriptions improve and miscellaneous series are sorted, further Star Chamber proceedings may be identified in E 111.

Another series of note is REQ 3, containing court of Requests miscellanea. The series currently comprises forty-four boxes, each holding between 200 and 300 items.[64] At present, this series is unsorted, though a preliminary listing compiled by John Guy around 1970 identified some Star Chamber content. For example, a document in REQ 3/8 contains Star Chamber proceedings between John Bradway and Gyles Blyke.[65] Now that parts of STAC 10 have been listed on the catalogue, it is possible to connect this record to a bill addressed to Wolsey from John Bradwey, a chantry priest, who complained that master Giles Blyke, lately imprisoned by the Star Chamber for words against the king, had ever since his release threatened to kill the complainant.[66] As descriptions for both REQ 3 and STAC 10 improve, we can only hope that similar connections can be made. A more recent analysis of REQ 3 by Laura Flannigan has posited that there could be several thousand Henrician documents relating to Requests and the other conciliar courts in these unlisted boxes, which would undoubtedly link to cases in STAC 2 and identify previously unknown Star Chamber actions.[67]

Copies of Star Chamber proceedings also survive in private papers collected among the State Papers (SP 46). These private collections were often seized by the state as part of legal charges against the owners of these papers. One particularly complete set of proceedings is the matter of George Ireland versus John Daniell, heard in Star Chamber (and elsewhere) at the end of the sixteenth century, collected in Daniell's papers (SP 46/50–56). A

[63] E 111/58 (*Maydeford* v *Love*), STAC 1/1/15 (*Love* v *Maidford*), STAC 2/20/9 (*Maydeford* v *Love*). For a later example, see E 111/91 (*Vernon* v *Couper*) cross-referenced with STAC 3/7/98 (*Vernon* v *Leigh*).

[64] L. Flannigan, 'Justice in the court of Requests, 1483–1538' (unpublished Cambridge PhD thesis, 2020), p. 35.

[65] REQ 3/8.

[66] STAC 10/4/117 (*Bradwey* v *Blyke*).

[67] Flannigan, 'Justice in the court of Requests', p. 23. A qualitative search by Dr Flannigan of the first ten boxes of REQ 3 identified a large amount of material that enriches our understanding of the early Tudor conciliar courts.

copy of the 1592 bill of complaint brought by Ireland lays out the grievance at issue. Addressed to 'the quenes most excellent maiesty', Ireland's bill states that though he is entitled to the tithes of corn and grain in the lordship of Daresbury in Cheshire they were (illegally) granted to John Daniell.[68] The same volume collects Daniell's demurrer and answer, Ireland's replication and Daniell's rejoinder.[69] Both Daniell's depositions to Ireland's interrogatories, and the subsequent depositions of William and Brian Palmer to Daniell's interrogatories, are also preserved.[70] Copies of orders of the court, made by William Mill, clerk of the council in Star Chamber, describe how Daniell was unable to proceed in this action because of a prior prohibition pending in the court of Queen's Bench, while a second order appointed commissioners to hear witness statements.[71] Proceedings between the two continued throughout the 1590s.[72] This case also provides The National Archives with one of its surviving copies of Elizabeth I's second great seal. The tag attached to the seal indicates it belongs to a *dedimus potestatem* addressed to Sir William Brereton and Thomas Smith in the matter between Daniell and Ireland.[73] That this was related to the Star Chamber action is confirmed by the signature 'Cotton' on the tag. Throughout the reigns of Elizabeth I and James I, three generations of the Cotton family held the office of clerk of the process of Star Chamber, responsible for writing all of the writs issuing from the court under the great seal.[74]

Supplementing these records are documents mentioning Star Chamber proceedings, usually as part of other court cases. Exchequer depositions can refer to bills exhibited in the Star Chamber, or proceedings running concurrently with those in the court of the Exchequer.[75] So, too, do some Chancery actions refer to related Star Chamber cases.[76] Further proceedings are mentioned in PRO 30/27/16, containing records of Star Chamber and Chancery, and several other Star Chamber actions are referred to in the State Papers.[77]

The records created by the court – decrees and orders, writs and bonds – form the second key type of Star Chamber record. Although the entry books have been lost, some original drafts and copies of decrees and orders

68 SP 46/53/fo189.
69 SP 46/53/185 (demurrer and answer); SP 46/53/fo181 (replication and rejoinder).
70 SP 46/53/fo198 (Daniell's depositions); SP 46/53/fo279.
71 SP 46/53/fo267.
72 SP 46/55/fo55; SP 46/55/fo81; SP 46/53/fo62.
73 SC 13/K49R/2.
74 Barnes, 'Archival problems', p. 346.
75 E.g. E 133/3/552; E 133/10/1465; E 134/12Chas1/Trin4.
76 C 4/64/55, judgement on a bill of complaint exhibited in the court of Star Chamber.
77 E.g. SP 46/3/18.

survive. In STAC 10, a draft order of Thomas More and other councillors in the Star Chamber on 21 November 1530 gives a sense of the sort of punishments the court doled out. The barber Thomas Barley was banished from Sudbury in Suffolk after losing a case against his fellow inhabitants, instructed to leave the town and live over seven miles away by Christmas 1531. If he was found within Sudbury after that, the mayor could place him in the stocks until 'he be content to obey and observe and fulfyll this said decree and ordre in every poynte'.[78] A later original order describes how Star Chamber interacted with other courts. The order deferred a court of Wards case until the next term, because the attorney for the court was sick.[79] Based on these examples from the listed pieces, it is probable that further evidence of decrees and orders is contained within the unlisted material in STAC 10.

Chancery certifications also provide evidence of Star Chamber orders and proceedings that are now lost. A 1630 Star Chamber decree concerning the case between the Woodmongers Company and the Wharfingers and Carmen has no surviving original pleadings, but is described in the certified copies in Chancery.[80] Mentions of decrees and orders can also be found in the State Papers, either as copies brought in with private papers, or collected with conciliar material.[81]

The majority of the original records of Star Chamber process are preserved in STAC 11, the filed writs for the court, and STAC 13, containing bonds. The earliest writs in STAC 11 date from Mary's reign, though earlier writs survive attached to the proceedings for the cases they relate to in other STAC series.[82] STAC 11 contains twenty-six pieces, amounting to several hundred individual writs, largely arranged by law term within each regnal year. Writs of *subpoena ad respondendum* began the court process, requiring the appearance of the defendant on a certain day under a 'pain', a penalty for non-compliance. These writs were issued out of Chancery under the great seal, returnable before the court sitting in Star Chamber. The wording of the writs (in Latin) required those named to appear before the council at Westminster, rather than naming the court of Star Chamber itself. This alludes to when the judicial court of Star Chamber and executive Privy

[78] STAC 10/4/44 (*Inhabitants of Sudbury* v *Barley*). For other draft orders in STAC 10, see STAC 10/4/125, 130.

[79] STAC 10/4/145 (relating to the court of Wards case *Beauson* v *Chamberlaine*).

[80] C 89/17/5. A brief report of the case can be found in J. Rushworth, 'Star Chamber reports: 6 Charles I', in *Historical Collections of Private Passages of State, III: 1639–40* (8 vols., London, 1721), p. 28.

[81] E.g. SP 46/43/fo79–82A; SP 46/49/fos. 8–8d; SP 1/16, fos. 140–143; SP 1/46, fo. 221. For a list of early Tudor Star Chamber material in SP 1, see Guy, *Star Chamber*, p. 21.

[82] E.g. STAC 2/34/36 (*Grenewod* v *Smyth*); STAC 3/7/49 (*Gyll* v *Bennett*); STAC 3/7/86 (*Darcye* v *Samer*).

Council were indistinguishable from each other. If these writs failed to summon the defendant, a writ of attachment was issued into the county in which they resided. The writs in STAC 11 often contain endorsements or notes by sheriffs, explaining that they had either served them or been unable to deliver them.

When these writs were successfully delivered, the defendant entered into a bond of (usually) £20 to answer their contempt of the original summons. Upon completion of a case, these bonds were usually returned to the party; those that were not returned survive in STAC 13. Their standard form bound the named defendant on pain of forfeit until the proceedings in Star Chamber were complete. The words of obligation are written in Latin and the conditions in English, either below the obligation or on the dorse. The bonds in STAC 13 almost all date from the second half of the reign of Elizabeth I, and most are countersigned by the clerk of the council in Star Chamber (and the body of text written in his hand), at this time William Mill. To save time, batches of blank bonds were created, the details of which were filled in at a later date. This meant that in some instances the date of the bond had to be amended when it was eventually used.[83] The bonds were originally filed on a string or parchment thong, though only two pieces retain this arrangement. STAC 13/7 has a contemporary label describing its contents, which reads 'Anno 38. Bondes taken and not redelivered the whole yeare bound together' and 'M 38,39', and it contains bonds taken for the thirty-eighth year of Elizabeth I's reign, including the Michaelmas term leading into the thirty-ninth year (November 1595 to November 1596). This bundle also includes a list of over a hundred 'such persons as entred bond Anno 38 and the bonds not redelivered back'.[84] Similarly, a note on STAC 13/18, 'P' 44°', identifies the bundle as containing bonds for Easter (*Pasche*) from the forty-fourth year of Elizabeth's reign (1601/02).[85] A further twenty-two bonds for the same year are contained in Exchequer miscellanea.[86]

Financial accounts and original registers providing evidence of court business, personnel and the daily operation of the court make up the third type of record relating to Star Chamber. These records are particularly useful as they can be used to piece together information otherwise lost with the decree and order entry books. Records of fines imposed by the court can identify the outcome of some Star Chamber cases. The levying of fines was the responsibility of the Exchequer, and estreats were recorded on the king's

83 Examples in STAC 13/13.
84 STAC 13/7, no. 654.
85 STAC 13/18.
86 E 163/15/38.

remembrancer memoranda rolls.[87] Using these records, Barnes identified 122 estreats of Star Chamber fines for the period 1596–1641 and posited that enrolment of these fines occurred from at least as early as the beginning of Elizabeth's reign.[88] Fines and punishments of the court are also referred to in early modern deeds.[89] It is likely, too, that some Star Chamber exhibits are preserved in deeds series, though the associated Star Chamber action is unlikely to be marked on the record.[90] STAC 10 also contains records detailing the business of Star Chamber, including a list of active cases in Star Chamber for Hilary term 1526. Annotations note where causes were riots, how many people were involved and also whether bills had been answered, replied or examined.[91]

PRO 30/38, a set of fee books for writs issuing from Star Chamber for the period 1580 to 1633, provides further information about plaintiffs and defendants appearing in the court for the period, plus details about the court process.[92] These registers, arranged chronologically, provide names of the parties to Star Chamber actions and of those to whom commissions were issued. The name of the defendant is given first, with the date on which the writ was returnable, then the words *ad sectam* (at the suit of) and the name of the plaintiff. To enable searches of the register, Star Chamber clerks entered the first letter of the lead plaintiff's surname in the margin. In cases where writs were issued on behalf of the crown, notes in the margin identify whether it was the attorney general or the almoner working on behalf of the crown. This is significant when trying to connect these entries to surviving proceedings, as the short title will refer to the officer acting on behalf of the crown. Similarly, writs of privilege, issued on behalf of officers of the court of Star Chamber, have the word 'privilege' noted in the margin. These registers highlight much of the court process behind the records of proceedings contained in STAC 1–9. For every answer, rejoinder or witness deposition for the court of Star Chamber a writ was issued and noted in the registers. Writs of attachment have marginalia identifying the county into

87 E 159. There are also records of Star Chamber fines in the Pipe Rolls (E 372).

88 E 159/410–81. Barnes produced a typescript list of these fines, which he gifted to TNA. He also identified some original writs and estreats in E 208/26. More recently, Robert Palmer has summarized the Star Chamber fines in E 159 on the *Anglo-American Legal Tradition* website <www.uh.edu/waalt/index.php/Star_Chamber_Fines> [accessed 4 Sept. 2020].

89 E.g. E 214/1218, 1375.

90 The same is true for Star Chamber recorda files in C 260.

91 STAC 10/4/124.

92 The records in PRO 30/38 originally belonged to Thomas Saunders, clerk of the writs in Star Chamber, gifted to the Public Record Office in 1935 by Sir Giles Edward Sebright, whose family acquired them in 1688.

which the writ was issued. If the defendant had been committed to prison, these writs were instead addressed to the warden of the relevant prison.

PRO 30/38 also includes miscellanea which informs our understanding of Star Chamber personnel.[93] One such record is an indenture acknowledging that John Mayne, John Meautys and John Sybley were granted the office of clerk of the writs and process of Star Chamber by letter patent on 26 May 1631, with one Thomas Saunders receiving the benefit.[94] There were four key offices connected with Star Chamber: the clerk of the council in Star Chamber; the clerk of the process; the usher of the court; and the attorneys of the court. Three of these offices were granted by letter patent, and so the patent rolls (C 66) and their calendars can also identify personnel of the court. Attorneys were appointed by the lord chancellor or lord keeper.[95] Other items in PRO 30/38 describe the rules for Star Chamber clerks taking fees, and lists the fees for Star Chamber process.[96]

The commissions on fees, taken in the early seventeenth century, provide information about the various functions of the personnel of Star Chamber and the fees they were paid. From these commissions, we know that working for the clerk of the council in Star Chamber in 1620 were: two examiners; the register; the clerk of the affadavits and the register of the rules of the clerk (the 'under-register'); the clerk of the files and warrants; the keeper of the records; and the copying clerk.[97] The records of the commissions on fees at The National Archives (E 215) contain several records pertaining to Star Chamber, including lists of fines, reports on fees in the court and a table of fees for the officers of the court.[98] Another account in a miscellaneous Exchequer series describes how Thomas Ailway, an underclerk for the court's register, was paid 10*s* for copying forty-six sheets of decrees for a party, at the payer's discretion.[99]

With few surviving registers signifying when the court was sitting and who was present, the membership of the judges of Star Chamber must also be drawn from related accounts and registers.[100] Generally, membership

93 PRO 30/38/27.

94 PRO 30/38/27/1.

95 Barnes, 'Archival problems', p. 347.

96 PRO 30/38/27/2.

97 Barnes, 'Archival problems', pp. 347–8, citing Bodleian Library, MS. Tanner 101, fos. 58–148. For a full list of the responsibilities of these officers, see Barnes.

98 E.g. E 215/63 (28 Apr. 1633), concerning suits on fees in Star Chamber; E 215/169, a miscellaneous list of Star Chamber fines and estalled debts; and E 215/855, a table of fees for the clerk of the process, the attorneys and the ushers of the court.

99 E 165/47, pp. 269–70. For more on the fees paid to the officers of Star Chamber, see Brit. Libr., Add. MS. 48025 and Brit. Libr., Hargrave MS. 216, fos. 192b–193.

100 The manuscripts of the duke of Northumberland, held at Alnwick Castle (Alnwick

was similar to that of the Privy Council, with both often headed by the lord chancellor.[101] The chief difference between the two groups was that the chief justices of King's Bench and Common Pleas attended Star Chamber but not Privy Council. Some early accounts for the attendance of Star Chamber survive in the State Papers.[102] A draft minute book for Trinity term 1525 in STAC 10 records the councillors present in Star Chamber on particular days and whether the king was in attendance, and notes which councillors were appointed to hear particular court proceedings.[103] The most interesting surviving records detailing the membership of the court are the Star Chamber diet books, which recorded judges sitting, date of meeting and the cost of foodstuffs for the court's meals. Many of these accounts survive from across the court's existence.[104] The earliest of these were created during Thomas Wolsey's chancellorship.[105] These Star Chamber dinners were not cheap; notes by William Cecil Lord Burghley on one of these accounts baulks at the cost of these meals.[106] Later diet books for Star Chamber also mention structural work to the chamber itself.[107] As with the Privy Council registers, each account noted which judges of Star Chamber

MS.), contain a selection of Star Chamber material, including some registers of daily business. See in particular Alnwick MSS. III, V, VII, IX, X and XII.

[101] The so-called 1487 Star Chamber Act (3 Hen. VII c. 1) confirmed that the lord chancellor, lord treasurer and keeper of the privy seal (or two of them) had the power to act judicially with other members of the council.

[102] E.g. SP 1/45, fos. 298–299, describing membership of the court as: the chancellor Thomas Wolsey; Thomas Howard, the duke of Norfolk; the bishop of Bath and Wells; Thomas Boleyn, Lord Rocheforde; the two chief justices; the chief baron of the Exchequer; Humphrey Coningsby, justice of the King's Bench; and Thomas More, chancellor of the Duchy of Lancaster.

[103] STAC 10/4/123. For a similar minute book for 1636–8, see Bod. Libr., Rawlinson MS. C 827.

[104] E 407/51–5; SP 1/33, fos. 203–285; Brit. Libr., Lansdowne MS. 1/44, 49; Lansdowne MS. 58/60; Lansdowne MS. 59/41; Lansdowne MS. 69/6; Add. MS. 32117 D; Folger Library, MS. V b 179; MS. X d 98; Leeds University Library, Special Collections MS. 426. For a full transcription of Brit. Libr., Add. MS. 32117 D, see C. L. Scofield, 'Accounts of Star Chamber dinners, 1593–4', *American Historical Review*, v (1899), 83–95. A collection of unspecified Star Chamber accounts for 1594–1603, which may hold similar information, is held at Madresfield Court (National Register of Archives catalogue reference: NRA 5234 Lygon).

[105] E 407/51; SP 1/33, fos. 203–285. E 407/51 was started days after Wolsey became chancellor in December 1515.

[106] Brit. Libr., Lansdowne MS. 1/44.

[107] E 407/55, which mentions the wainscot presses that were added to the chamber in 1608. Other records relating to the structure of Star Chamber can be found in SP 1/16, fos. 35–36 and STAC 2/1/36 (*Rex* v *Alen*), which both describe how John Alen and Christopher Plommer were fined 500 marks to purchase a pardon for offences contrary to the Statute of Praemunire, used to pay for additions to the Palace of Westminster.

were present. For example, the account for 10 October 1561 noted the presence of Nicholas Bacon, chancellor and lord privy seal, William Paulet, lord treasurer, William Cecil and others.[108]

The final key types of record concerning Star Chamber are the treatises and law reports written about the court and its cases, from which we know about cases and processes that are otherwise lost. Most of these records are held outside of The National Archives, with a couple of exceptions. The most complete volume at The National Archives is an early copy of William Hudson's *Treatise of the Court of Star Chamber*.[109] William Hudson was a trained lawyer who, during his career, served as underclerk, attorney and barrister for Star Chamber.[110] His *Treatise* was a contemporary account of Star Chamber, completed in 1621. It considers the history of the court, its historic and current (in 1621) jurisdiction and how the court should function in future. Hudson's *Treatise* is notable for citing over 500 Star Chamber cases. With the loss of the court's decree and order books, these citations are often the only surviving record we have of these cases. The copy of Hudson's *Treatise* held by The National Archives is not the author's copy or the accepted most authentic text. The best extant version is thought to be one of the eighteen copies held at The British Library, which contains a 1635 memorandum claiming it to be in the handwriting of Hudson's son, Christopher, and gifting the volume to Chief Justice Sir John Finch.[111] The National Archives' copy has some corrections in a second hand, and annotations on the flyleaves suggest it was acquired by purchase, possibly for the Tower Record Office.

Two less substantial treatises on the court of Star Chamber are collected in Exchequer miscellanea series.[112] The first, a short collection of notes concerning Star Chamber, contains a copy of William Lambarde's description of the court and its jurisdiction taken from his *Archeion*, as well as detailed descriptions of Star Chamber process and the fees incurred by plaintiffs and defendants.[113] The second, a legal precedent book concerning

108 E 407/53 (Michaelmas term 1561).

109 STAC 12/1, transferred from STAC 10/21 in December 1994.

110 T. G. Barnes, 'Hudson, William (*c.*1577–1635), barrister and writer', *Oxford Dictionary of National Biography* (2004), doi: 10.1093/ref:odnb/14042.

111 Brit. Libr., Harley MS. 1226. The Honourable Society of Gray's Inn holds a manuscript copy of Hudson's treatise, which transcribes this memorandum (Gray's Inn MS. 32). I am grateful to the staff of Gray's Inn Library, particularly Abigail Cass and M. G. Jones, for their assistance in identifying this copy.

112 E 163/24/9; E 36/194.

113 E 163/24/9, containing: 'The ordinarie course of proceeding in the most ho. Court of Starr Chamber as followeth', at pp. 1r–3r; 'Annotacons of the Rules and Fees of the Court of Starr Chamber, briefly collected according as they are now used', at pp. 3r–3v; a copy of

various courts of equity, describes land law and practice in the courts of Requests and Star Chamber.[114]

The British Library holds several legal collections describing Star Chamber cases.[115] One volume, containing notes on over 1000 items, records cases from the reign of Henry VIII and is particularly complete for the period 1552 to 1596.[116] The folio reference to each order and decree book is noted against each item, which allows for a rough reconstruction of the size of the decree and order entry books for the period 1552 to 1596; eleven volumes, each containing between 250 and 500 folios.[117] The details of cases in these volumes can also be used to improve descriptions for corresponding proceedings in The National Archives' catalogue. A pilot project completed by Katie Bridger in 2020 utilized data from these law reports and cases and connected it to records in STAC.[118]

William Mill, who as clerk of the council put his signature to so many surviving records of Star Chamber at The National Archives, produced a similar set of notes on precedents and proceedings of the court at the behest of Lord Ellesmere. These volumes, along with several other records relating to Star Chamber, can now be found as part of the Egerton family papers (Ellesmere Manuscripts) at the Huntington Library in California.[119] Star Chamber records can also be found in several other US repositories.[120]

---

pages 96–224 of William Lambarde's *Archeion*, concerning Star Chamber, at pp. 4r–26r; and incomplete notes about examinations before the court, at p. 26r.

114 E 36/194.

115 Brit. Libr., Add. MS. 11764, 48057 (translation in Lansdowne MS. 620), 48061; Hargrave MS. 26, 404; Harley MS. 2143, 4022; Lansdowne MS. 639; Stowe MS. 397. For a list of British Library materials related to Star Chamber, see Scofield, *Study of the Court of Star Chamber*.

116 Brit. Libr., Harley MS. 2143, recently edited and published as *Star Chamber Reports: BL Harley MS 2143*, ed. K. J. Kesselring (List and Index Society, Special Series 57, 2018). For further details about this manuscript and the cases it notes, see the introduction to that volume, particularly pp. vii–x.

117 Barnes, 'Archival problems', p. 351.

118 E.g., using the printed *Star Chamber Reports: BL Harley MS* 2143, Dr. Bridger was able to connect STAC 5/A4/26, A9/35, A24/25, A25/14, A26/7, A30/27 and A54/5 (*Att. Gen.* v *Robinson*) to Brit. Libr., MS. 2143, nos 121 and 580 ('Justices of peace and the high sheriff fined for their negligence and partiality in not resorting to the place to appease a riot and rioters'; 'The great and rebellious riot of Drayton Bassett for which the defendants were fined and committed during the Queen's pleasure'). The National Archives is grateful to K. J. Kesselring for permission to use her published data for this pilot project.

119 Hunt. Libr., EL 2654, 2655, 2768.

120 Folger Libr., MS. V b 205 (relating to Star Chamber jurisdiction); MS. V a 133, MS. X d 336–7, MS. V b 70 (law reports); MS. V a 278 (entry book of affidavits). Harvard University Law School, MS. 1128 (law reports).

Early printed volumes, written before the loss of the auxiliary Star Chamber archive, provide us with more evidence of otherwise lost Star Chamber material. John Rushworth's *Historical Collections*, compiled while the court was still active, contains copies of over 150 entries in the decree and order books, and refers to reports for the first twelve years of Charles I's reign.[121] Other seventeenth-century publications, with either first-hand access to the court or to its surviving records, provide details about several other Star Chamber actions that have otherwise been lost.[122]

It is easy for the records of the court of Star Chamber to be defined by what no longer survives. No other court that proceeded by English bill suffered such a loss, and researchers working on Star Chamber are hampered by the hole left by the missing decree and order entry books. However, the survival of so many incidental records – of accounts, fines, law reports and treatises – means that there is a rich Star Chamber archive, albeit one spread rather more widely than those of most English equity courts. Taken together, these records help to fill the gap of the missing Star Chamber collection. This guide, and others like it, serve as a road map to these records, to advise researchers where to look for Star Chamber material and what to expect when it is found. While we wait patiently for the decree and order books to appear in some long-forgotten basement, we can take solace in the fact that thanks to the continuing work of researchers, volunteers and staff at The National Archives and other repositories, the Star Chamber archive is more complete and connected now than it has ever been.

[121] J. Rushworth, *Historical Collections of Private Passages of State, III: 1639–40*.

[122] F. Moore, *Cases Collect and Report per Sir Francis Moore* (London, 1663); W. Hughes, *An Exact Abridgement in English of the Cases Reported by Sr. Francis More, Kt, Serjeant at Law, with the Resolution of the Points in Law Therein by the Judges* (London, 1665); J. Popham, *Reports and Cases Collected by the Learned Sir John Popham … To Which are Added Some Remarkable Cases Reported by Other Learned Pens Since His Death* (London, 1656). For later publications referring to earlier reports, see J. S. Burn, *The Star Chamber: Notices of the Court and its Proceedings* (London, 1870); S. R. Gardiner, *Reports of Cases in the Courts of Star Chamber and High Commission* (Camden Society nos. 39, 1886); J. Hawarde, *Les Reportes del Cases in Camera Stellata, 1593–1609*, ed. W. P. Baildon (London, 1894).

3. Reading ravishment: gender and 'will' power in early Tudor Star Chamber, 1500–50*

Deborah Youngs

A woman's ability to wage law and petition courts in early Tudor England and Wales was compromised by the gendered roles and systems she had to negotiate. Nevertheless, historians of several major courts in England, those of Chancery, parliament and Star Chamber, have seen them as offering a more conducive environment for success than the larger common-law courts.[1] Such calculations have often been based on the proportion of women listed among their litigants, yet these figures alone cannot provide the whole picture of women's involvement in the courts, and how they fared across different types of cases. The records of Star Chamber provide an opportunity to consider more fully the female experience in court, particularly because they share with other narrative petitions the advantage of being 'more expansive' than common-law records.[2] In exploring women in Star Chamber, this chapter focuses on the suits of ravishment that came before the court in the first half of the sixteenth century. While not solely a 'women's issue', ravishment largely concerned female victims and included accusations both of abduction and rape (forced coition), which may also have featured in the proceedings as seduction, adultery and elopement. The chapter considers the framing of these narratives and the language used as it examines closely how women as litigants and victims were presented in the suits. A specific focus is the consent of the alleged abductee, her 'will', and how that was assessed both by those directly involved and in the legal counsel advising the case. The relative lack of formality in the writing up of the proceedings and in the proofs enables Star Chamber records to provide

* My thanks to Teresa Phipps, Krista Kesselring and Natalie Mears for their comments on a previous draft of this paper.

[1] For a recent summary of these arguments and discussion see C. Beattie, 'A piece of the puzzle: women and the law as viewed from the late medieval court of Chancery', *Journal of British Studies*, lviii (2019), 751–67, particularly pp. 754–6.

[2] G. Seabourne, *Imprisoning Medieval Women: The Non-judicial Confinement and Abduction of Women in England, c.1170–1509* (Farnham, 2011), p. 137.

considerable insight into the kind of fraught and furious internal family politics that have filled courtrooms across the centuries.

The sources

The chapter draws on material from the reigns of Henry VII and Henry VIII, and hence is based on research undertaken in STAC 1, STAC 2 and STAC 10.[3] At this early stage in the court's development, the council had a broad jurisdiction, and dealt with both civil and criminal cases. Its principal purpose was to investigate breaches of the peace, with suits referring to riot, assault, murder and trespass, and covering accusations relating to debt, slander, forgery, the perversion of justice or violations of royal protocol. Unfortunately, many of these records have suffered from neglect and poor archival decisions, which have led to significant losses and dispersed cases; frustratingly almost no decrees, orders or awards from the period are extant.[4] Rarely do these suits comprise a full set of pleadings and proofs. Bills of complaint are the most common survival, although on occasion much of the case has to be reimagined from an answer or replication.[5] Nevertheless, even in the early sixteenth century, Star Chamber has better prospects than Chancery for interrogatories and depositions to survive, which offer a greater range of viewpoints. The cases under discussion comprise all those where the abduction or rape of a woman was the main allegation levelled against a defendant.[6] The discussion does not account

[3] TNA, STAC 1/1 and STAC 1/2 are 2 bound volumes containing 135 cases that mainly (though not exclusively) date to Henry VII's reign. The first printed listing of these records appears to be that in J. B. W. Chapman, *List of Proceedings in the Court of Star Chamber in the Public Record Office* (PRO, Lists and Indexes, xiii, 1901, revised 1963). See too C. G. Bayne and W. H. Dunham, *Select Cases in the Council of Henry VII* (London: Selden Society, 1958). The bulk of STAC 2 records date to Henry VIII, although with cases from various reigns scattered within them. They are stored partly in 16 bound volumes organized by the plaintiff's surname (up to the letter G), with the remaining records gathered in bundles within 19 boxes. The records of STAC 10 were originally divided into 21 bundles; thus far only STAC 10/1, 10/2 and 10/4 have been fully catalogued. See J. A. Guy, 'Wolsey's Star Chamber: a study in archival reconstruction', *Journal of the Society of Archivists*, v (1975), 169–80 and his *The Court of Star Chamber and its Records to the Reign of Elizabeth I* (London: PRO, 1985) for a full discussion of the organization of the records.

[4] Guy, *The Court of Star Chamber*, p. 23.

[5] Given the incomplete nature of the records, the number of surviving cases is difficult to assess, and John Guy's estimations remains a useful guide: he calculated that around 200 cases currently survive from Henry VII's reign and around 5000 for the reign of Henry VIII: Guy, *The Court of Star Chamber*, p. 20.

[6] My starting point was to consider all those cases currently catalogued as abduction, kidnapping, rape, adultery or seduction in The National Archives, supplemented by my own research into suits where women were named as victims. I then discounted those cases

for all instances of rape and abduction found in Star Chamber records: further references may be found in the background to other suits, or as one potential offence in a broader range of misdemeanours.[7] It also cannot be known whether cases that describe women as being procured or moved to 'commytte with hym fornycation' were actually consensual acts (see below).[8] For the purposes of inclusion, what matters here is whether the plaintiff or defendant perceived the action as ravishment. On this basis, just over sixty suits have been found that fall under that label. Most of these suits (forty-two) concerned the taking away of women, which may or may not include sexual activity, while a small number (five) were sexual assault cases alone and where no abduction was mentioned. Seven involved young girls and potential wards, and there are similarly fourteen cases concerning the contested custody and abduction of boys, most of whom were wards.[9] These latter suits have been included in table 3.1 for the sake of comparison, but this chapter focuses exclusively on the forty-seven cases of female ravishment. Together they span the whole of the first half of the sixteenth century, the earliest dating to 1502 (the sole case in Henry VII's reign) while the latest is 1546/7; it also includes two STAC 2 cases where the issues began in Henry VIII's reign but where depositions continued into Edward VI's reign. While it has been possible to date thirty-three of these forty-seven ravishment cases, the surviving records of Star Chamber do not consistently provide this information. Such a small and incomplete sample makes it difficult to consider any pattern in the frequency of cases, which has been tracked in other records and for earlier centuries by Seabourne and Dunn.[10]

that came to Star Chamber as seduction or adultery cases, which did not try to recast them as abduction. It is worth noting that while bills of complaint do not use the English terms abduction or kidnapping, TNA cataloguers appear to have labelled a case 'kidnapping' when the person taken had not returned from her abductors: see *Piott* v *Meverell* STAC 2/27/138.

[7] I have excluded from the sample STAC 2/34/18, where reference to the abduction of a young girl features among the interrogatories concerning the violent quarrels between the Herberts and Morgans in South Wales. There are no pleadings to indicate whether this was central to the bill of complaint or any further information to put it into context. Nor have I included the case where rioting and murder had occurred during an attempt at mediation following the ravishment of Kathryn, daughter of Llewellyn ap Thomas of Cyfeiliog (Powys): TNA, STAC 2/18/92.

[8] For example, TNA, STAC 2/24/3.

[9] It is difficult to be precise because the question of whether someone was a ward could be deliberately obscured in a suit. For examples of cases triggered by the potential or actual marriage of male wards, see, e.g., TNA, STAC 2/26/401; STAC 2/30/45. There is also one case of the abduction of an apprentice, an under-explored subject: STAC 2/16, fo.374.

[10] Seabourne's analysis of the plea rolls show a significant drop in cases in the second half of the 15th century: *Imprisoning*, pp. 121–2; C. Dunn, *Stolen Women in Medieval England: Rape, Abduction, and Adultery, 1100–1500* (Cambridge, 2013), pp. 89–90. Whether this

What can be said is that, setting aside the single suit in Henry VII's reign, cases gradually increased as the volume of Star Chamber proceedings expanded, and they averaged around one to two cases a year.

Table 3.1: Suits and their plaintiffs

Type of case	Number	Single female plaintiff	Married female plaintiff with husband	Female plaintiff with male relative	Male plaintiffs only	Unknown
Abduction of female	42	4	7	1	29	1
Abduction of male	14	2	0	0	12	0
Rape	5	4	1	0	0	0
Totals	61	10	8	1	41	1

Sources: TNA, STAC 1, STAC 2, STAC 10

The litigants

Table 3.1 records those who brought the suits, or at least in whose name(s) the bills were composed; it should not be overlooked that plaintiffs might have been persuaded into petitioning or completely unaware of a suit pursued in their name (as a number of defendants argued).[11] They share the characteristics of Star Chamber litigants more generally in that they came from a broad spectrum of society, albeit with some access to resources. Landed gentry feature prominently, but suits were also generated by a yeoman, a husbandman and a shoemaker, while a few of the alleged victims were in service, such as Mary Trotter who was apprenticed to be a silkwoman. Though late medieval statutes against abduction were written with elite concerns in mind, these examples reinforce the view that suits did not come solely from the upper echelons of society.[12]

It is immediately evident that more men brought suits claiming abduction than the female victims themselves. Of the forty-seven cases in the sample, just seventeen (36%) included a female plaintiff: eight as the sole petitioner and nine alongside a male relative, usually the husband. There are also only nine cases where a woman petitioned her own abduction: eight as a single female plaintiff and one alongside her husband. In the remaining

reflects a fall in the number of abductions or a drop of interest in suing in the central courts is unclear.

[11] E.g. *Burges* v *Brandon* TNA, STAC 2/7, fo. 148. See S. McSheffrey, 'Detective fiction in the archives: court records and the uses of law in late medieval England', *History Workshop Journal*, lxv (2008), 72.

[12] Seabourne, *Imprisoning*, p. 124.

nine, women pleaded on behalf of their daughters.[13] This is to be expected for several reasons, not least because male litigants dominated in all legal jurisdictions. A search through the records of STAC 1, STAC 2 and STAC 10 more broadly reveals approximately 735 cases that contain at least one female plaintiff, or around 14% of the surviving material.[14] Similar statistics have been calculated for other jurisdictions, largely reflecting women's legal limitations, especially if married and subject to coverture, when a woman's legal identity was covered by her husband's.[15] More specifically relevant here is that, in common law, women could bring appeals only for their rape, not their abduction, and the legal process was gruelling.[16] Late medieval statutes also gave greater motivation and opportunity for men to prosecute the abduction of their female kin. By the early sixteenth century, not only did the nearest male relatives of the abducted women have the right to sue for felony, but they could also recover any property gained by the ravisher if a subsequent marriage had been solemnized, or any other obligations a woman had consented to under duress.[17] As a consequence, the majority of plaintiffs in Star Chamber were a group of fathers, stepfathers, male guardians and husbands who sought redress from the loss of power over the abductee's body and, through it, control over inherited property and chattels.

It is a familiar pattern found across all records of abduction. Where women petitioned Chancery concerning an abduction it was mostly in relation to their children or other relatives.[18] Mark Ormrod identified thirty-three

[13] If the ravishment of boys is included in these statistics, increasing the sample to 60, then an additional two female plaintiffs can be included. The figures would then show 18 female plaintiffs: nine as sole petitioner and nine alongside a male relative.

[14] D. Youngs, '"A besy women … and full of lawe": female litigants in early Tudor Star Chamber', *Journal of British Studies*, lviii (2019), 1-16.

[15] M. F. Stevens, 'London women, the courts and the "Golden Age": a quantitative analysis of female litigants in the fourteenth and fifteenth centuries', *The London Journal*, xxxvii (2012), pp. 74, 81 and the appendix on p. 84. For the application of coverture see *Married women and the law: coverture in England and the common law world,* ed. T. Stretton and K. J. Kesselring (Montreal, 2013); *Married women and the law in premodern northwest Europe,* ed. C. Beattie and M. F. Stevens (Woodbridge, 2013).

[16] Seabourne, *Imprisoning*, p. 129.

[17] W. M. Ormrod, *Women and Parliament in Later Medieval England* (Basingstoke, 2020), p. 97; E. W. Ives, '"Agaynst taking awaye of women": the inception and operation of the abduction act of 1487', in *Wealth and Power in Tudor England: Essays presented to S. T. Bindoff,* ed. E. W. Ives, R. J. Knecht and J. J. Scarisbrick (London, 1978), p. 23; S. McSheffrey and J. Pope, 'Ravishment, legal narratives and chivalric culture in fifteenth-century England', *Journal of British Studies*, xlviii (2009), 822–4.

[18] J. Pope, 'Abduction and power in late medieval England: petitions to the court of Chancery, 1389–1515' (unpublished MA dissertation, Concordia University, 2002), p. 39. In

cases of rape and abduction in late medieval parliamentary petitions, of which twenty-two had male petitioners.[19] Nevertheless, as in parliament, so in Star Chamber, the presence of female plaintiffs in a third of these cases is a notably higher proportion than seen elsewhere. Ormrod's suggestion that this figure reflected parliament's status 'as a place of special refuge for those, including women and the poor, who claimed that the common law could not protect them' can also be applied to Star Chamber.[20] During the early Tudor period it became seen as a court to which plaintiffs turned to circumvent the limitations of common law and, as a prerogative court, it was less formulaic and more flexible and could be appealed to for help when other remedies had failed.[21]

Of the female plaintiffs who saw an opportunity in Star Chamber over half were single women, a number bolstered by the cases of rape, which four petitioners sued alone. Among these plaintiffs we might have expected to see a large proportion of widows, a common occurrence in other courts and other types of cases. Dunn's statistics show that widows were more likely than maidens to initiate their own abduction prosecutions, relying less on family members. She suggested this was because widows were more independent and, conversely, more likely to be victims of bride-theft if wealthy.[22] This is not the pattern in Star Chamber, however, where only three cases were brought by widow-plaintiffs, of which two were for their own taking away. Wife-plaintiffs feature more prominently, but rarely sued for their own abduction; the sole exception is a case of attempted rape where a married woman petitioned alongside her husband. This is to be expected because a wife would not be able to sue the perpetrator if he became her husband following an abduction.[23] The marriage could be challenged, but it would require the involvement of the ecclesiastical court for it to be dissolved. As in Chancery, therefore, the majority of abduction cases pursued by wife-plaintiffs were those involving remarried women who were appealing alongside their current husbands concerning the abduction of children borne of a previous marriage.

---

her sample of fifty petitions concerning abduction cases she found thirteen female plaintiffs (26%). See too G. Walker, '"A strange kind of stealing": abduction in early modern Wales', in *Women and Gender in Early Modern Wales*, ed. S. Clarke and M. Roberts (Cardiff, 2000), p. 51.

[19] Ormrod, *Women and Parliament*, p. 97.

[20] Ormrod, *Women and Parliament*, p. 99.

[21] J. A. Guy, *The Cardinal's Court: The Impact of Thomas Wolsey's Star Chamber* (Hassocks, 1977), pp. 52-3; Seabourne, *Imprisoning*, p. 130; Ives, 'Agaynst taking awaye of women'.

[22] Dunn, *Stolen Women*, pp. 94, 96.

[23] Seabourne, *Imprisoning*, pp. 117–18.

There are nevertheless instances in Star Chamber where women forced into marriage petitioned the court against their abductor-husband, refusing to accept that they were espoused.[24] Margaret Kebell is the best-known example thanks to her lengthy and tenacious battle against her abduction and forced marriage in 1502 by Roger Vernon of Wirksworth. Margaret had originally appealed her abductors of felony at assizes in Derbyshire and Staffordshire and pursued three civil actions in King's Bench and another in Common Pleas. She failed in all of them because she was married and she struggled to prove the marriage had occurred under duress.[25] She therefore turned to the king and his counsel, submitting a formal bill against members of the Vernon family.[26] Here she presented herself as a widow, using her deceased husband's surname, and hence able to sue her own case; yet her opponents' first line of defence was to assert she was married to Roger Vernon, not named in the bill, and therefore the suit should 'abate'.[27] That the counsel continued to investigate is a good example of the flexibility in approach that married women could experience in Star Chamber.

Building a case

In petitioning Star Chamber, plaintiffs needed to attract the attention of its judges, and to have their cases seen as suitable for the court's consideration. Much has been written on the crafting of legal petitions and how their construction was a product of the particular jurisdiction and action taken.[28] Accounts of abduction were partly shaped by legal, statutory requirements, which plaintiffs and their counsel needed to meet in order to indicate an offence had taken place. The most recent legislation on abduction had been issued in 3 Henry VII (1487) – the 'Acte against taking awaye of women against theire willes' – which reaffirmed that abduction was a felony and stipulated not only that those who took 'any woman against her will' were committing a crime, but so too their procurors, abettors and receivers. Like previous legislation, notably the anti-ravishment statutes of 1382 and 1453,

[24] See too Pope, 'Abduction and power', p. 41.

[25] TNA, KB 27/979, mm.44, 50; /980, mm.65, 65d; /981, m.109; /983, mm.17, 29d; /984, m.26; /987, m.27d; /980, m.20. A full account of Kebell's case can be found in Ives, 'Agaynst taking awaye of women', pp. 21–44.

[26] TNA, STAC 1/17/2. Related Star Chamber documents can also be found in STAC 2/19/71, STAC 2/22/18, STAC 2/23/4, STAC 2/24/305, STAC 2/25/68 and STAC 10/8/373–82.

[27] TNA, STAC 2/22/18.

[28] T. Stretton, *Women Waging Law in Elizabethan England* (Cambridge, 1998), p. 13; J. Bailey, 'Voices in court: lawyers or litigants?', *Historical Research*, lxxiv, no. 186 (2001), 392–408, at p. 393; C. Beattie, '"Your oratrice": women's petitions in the late medieval court of Chancery', in *Women, Agency and the Law*, ed. Kane and Williamson, p. 20.

it was more concerned with abductions for forced marriage than sexual assault more generally. Significantly, the 1487 act also had the practical effect of making kidnapping – or abduction for any reason – a felony.[29]

The terminology used was important. One of the challenges for historians working on medieval 'ravishment' records has been the use in the Latin and French sources of *raptus* and *ravissement*, which were often employed interchangeably to mean both rape as sexual assault and abduction.[30] This is less apparent in the English-language petitions that went to Chancery, parliament and Star Chamber. They were more varied in their use of phrases and less ambiguous in their choice of verbs; they were far less likely to conflate rape and abduction.[31] The writers of early Star Chamber bills commonly used the phrases 'taken', 'led', 'carried' or 'conveyed away', with the regular refrain of 'against her will' echoing closely the terminology of the 1487 act. The verb 'to ravish' features on far fewer occasions, but it is instructive to note the specific contexts in which it appeared: in cases where rape was alleged; where plaintiffs wished to indicate that a sexual act had occurred following the abduction (as in 'ravished and carnally knew her'); and where wards or children under twelve had been taken, resonating with the formulation 'ravishment of wards'.[32] An example can be found in the suit of Kathryn Robert of Neath in 1529, which claimed that her assailant had 'felonously ravished her and toke and caried her away' and forced her to marry.[33] The bill refers to Kathryn's failed attempt to appeal a case of rape in the town court at Neath, which suggests that 'ravished' had been deliberately chosen in the Star Chamber bill to indicate sexual assault alongside her abduction. The English term 'rape' was rarely deployed, although its presence in another Welsh case shows that it was still being used to mean abduction in the sixteenth century. While the bill of complaint in Jane Howell's abduction suit described her as being taken

[29] Ives, 'Agaynst taking awaye of women', pp. 25–6.

[30] E. Hawkes, '"She was ravished against her will what so ever she say": female consent in rape and ravishment in late-medieval England', *Limina*, i (1995), 47; C. Dunn, 'The language of ravishment in medieval England', *Speculum*, lxxxvi (2011), 79–116; Dunn, *Stolen Women*, p. 43.

[31] Dunn, *Stolen Women*, pp. 44, 47–8; Pope, 'Abduction and power', p. 86.

[32] For pleas of *rapuit et abduxit* in relation to wards see S. S. Walker, 'Common law juries and feudal marriage customs in medieval England: the pleas of ravishment', *University of Illinois Law Review*, iii (1984), 705–18, particularly p. 709, n. 20. On modern historians using 'ravishment' to describe abduction cases see McSheffrey and Pope, 'Ravishment', p.835.

[33] TNA, STAC 2/26/105; D. Youngs, '"She hym fressely folowed and pursued": women and Star Chamber in early Tudor Wales', in *Women, Agency and the Law, 1300-1700*, ed. B. Kane and F. Williamson (London, 2013), pp. 73–85.

away against her will, those sent to investigate the events referred to it as a rape. This included an enraged Bishop Rowland Lee, who described the incident as a 'case of rape', when referring to how her abductor had forcibly carried away 'a wedowe against her will out of a churche'.[34] The suit itself does not suggest that a sexual assault had taken place, so the ambiguity and connotations from those who wished to see a conviction are likely to have been deliberate.

Around these phrases, narratives were constructed to indicate a person's unwillingness to go with her abductor. Statutory law remained a determining factor, but we also see the influence of other literatures as compelling accounts were written to tug on the readers' emotions.[35] There were regular motifs. In its proceedings Star Chamber's familiar tales of riotous behaviour could be used to underline forceful acts, while in the interrogatories witnesses were asked about broken windows or doors and other kinds of destruction that signified unlawful entry or harassment.[36] Signs of suspicious behaviour, such as approaching a house after dark, were seized upon, as was any type of disguise. Witnesses to the supposed abduction of Maud and Dorothy Barry, for example, were questioned over the face coverings of the accused; Margaret Barley responded that one of the abductors had something over his face, either a hood or a visor, while another had a kerchief on his head.[37] Similarly, there was a focus on where a person was conveyed. Travelling to multiple places was suspicious behaviour and an indication that individuals were trying to cover their tracks.[38] The case could be made stronger if the places travelled were in marginal lands, or indeed 'wild' lands that were perceived as out of the way and potentially beyond the scope of local jurisdictions. Those living in English counties in the Marches of Scotland or Wales might see abductees taken across the borders.[39] The manner of their travelling also came under scrutiny. Being taken away on a horse was a

[34] TNA, SP 1/129, fo. 124; TNA, STAC 2/20/223 (bill of complaint); STAC 2/26/394 (list of interrogatories); STAC 2/24/34 and STAC 10/4/82 (depositions); D. Youngs, '"A vice common in Wales": abduction, prejudice and the search for justice in the regional and central courts of early Tudor society', in *The Welsh and the Medieval World*, ed. P. Skinner (Cardiff, 2018), pp. 131–53.

[35] McSheffrey and Pope, 'Ravishment', 820.

[36] E.g. in *Habington* v *Blount*: TNA, STAC 2/21/141; STAC 2/21/155.

[37] TNA, STAC 2/21/141; STAC 2/21/155.

[38] E.g. TNA, STAC 2/21/33.

[39] S. A. Sinclair, 'The "ravishing" of Isabel Boteler: abduction and the pursuit of wealth in Lancastrian England', *The Ricardian*, xi (1997–9), 552, 555; Seabourne, *Imprisoning*, p. 137; Ives, 'Agaynst taking awaye of women', pp. 40–1.

common trope, but it made a difference whether the woman rode behind or in front of her abductor, and whether she was bound while spirited away.[40]

What were not so well detailed were acts of personal violence inflicted on women. Early Star Chamber bills themselves have been read as documents rarely focusing on the suffering of women. For C. G. Bayne, writing on Star Chamber cases in Henry VII's reign, 'accusations of cruelty to women' were noticeably few and far between.[41] Bills can indeed be perfunctory in describing the suffering of the alleged victims, and while the situation was regularly described as riotous and violent, it often seems more to provide an explanation of why male onlookers were not able to rescue a woman rather than the threat to the woman herself. At most, interrogatories asked if the abductee had 'cried out' or showed some physical signs of resistance,[42] and crying more generally features when describing those who failed to stop an abduction rather than the emotional response of the abductee. Yet it needs to be remembered that the absence of detailed violence in these bills was largely because it was superfluous to constructing the case. Such was the focus on consent in late medieval English abduction laws, that all the bill had to specify was that the taking away was with force or against her will, however that was enacted.[43] Where more detailed descriptions of physical violence were required, then they were recorded, and it is noticeable that these occurred in the rape cases rather than abduction claims. Isabel White's assailant clamped his hand over her mouth while holding her down; Elizabeth Bransby, widow, of Bardney (Lincs) suffered a miscarriage in her rough handling; Agnes Typlary was thrown to the ground, causing her leg to break in the fall. When Joan Stanton accused her master, Hugh Fenne of Chigwell, of raping her in Waltham Forest she maintained he had beaten her, broken her head and left her with a limp. That the interrogatories focused on whether Joan's smock had been covered in blood on her return from the forest reflects the legal procedures in determining a physical sexual rape.[44] The modulation in the use of violence was, therefore, that of the creators of the bills and not the supposed assailants. This means that where we do find more detailed forcefulness in abduction suits, it is worth noting. Anne Salwayn's abduction was unusually brutal in that her attackers apparently

[40] E.g., the abduction of Dame Anne Salwayn: TNA, STAC 10/4/55. For other tropes see J. Goldberg, *Communal Discord, Child Abduction and Rape in the Later Middle Ages* (Basingstoke, 2008), pp. 137–8.

[41] Bayne and Dunham, *Select Cases,* p. cxxxviii.

[42] E.g., TNA, STAC 2/24/59.

[43] Pope, 'Abduction and power', p. 56.

[44] TNA, STAC 10/1/21 (White); STAC 2/6, fo.277 (Bransby); STAC 2/18/15 (Typlary); STAC 2/18/228; STAC 2/25/27 (Stanton).

dragged her out of the house by her leg and laid her on the back of a horse 'lyke a sak of vyle burdeyn', binding her with cart rope.[45] However, whether such an image was the product of overly zealous abductors or of the plaintiff's counsel is unknown.

Jurisdiction and types of cases

In explaining why these matters should be considered by the king's council in Star Chamber, the petitioners regularly recounted why they were unsuitable for the common law courts. This was usually expressed on the grounds of the poverty of the plaintiff; the relative wealth and powerful reach of the defendant; or the threat or exercise of violent action; reasons also regularly seen in Chancery and in parliament.[46] Similarly, many of the suits going to Star Chamber had already been considered in other courts or were still being pursued there.[47] References were made to cases heard in local town or borough courts and in county sessions, while allusions to perpetrators languishing in gaol intimate earlier actions. These often came with complaints about the ineffectiveness or misconduct of officials, and there was some stated dissatisfaction with the enforcement of remedies in the regular courts and in gaining access to them. Kathryn Robert's bill recounted how her bid to see her rapist tried at the town court in Neath had been derailed by his supporters, and so she had followed her accused to London where she had him arrested and put in the gaol at Bread Street.[48]

It would be wrong, however, to see these cases as all arising from a stated failure of the local or lower courts. Some litigants had also faced (or were still facing) each other in the Court in the Marches of Wales or in Chancery, using Star Chamber to countersue. Not surprisingly, given the centrality of marriage, fornication and adultery to many abduction cases, there were several references to the ecclesiastical courts under whose jurisdiction these issues usually fell. By recasting marital issues such as desertion and non-cohabitation as abduction, petitioners could make them fit within the purview of the secular courts.[49] There are not a large number, suggesting that Star Chamber was not inclined to encroach regularly on the jurisdiction of the ecclesiastical courts when issues of marriage – its

[45] TNA, STAC 2/26/452.

[46] Seabourne, *Imprisoning*, pp. 133–4, 136; Beattie, 'A piece of the puzzle', p. 752.

[47] J. H. Baker, *The Oxford History of the Law of England, vol. VI. 1483–1558* (Oxford, 2003), p. 118.

[48] TNA, STAC 2/26/105.

[49] Examples include the abduction of Agnes Leom, a case first heard at the ecclesiastical courts in York before being taken to Chancery (TNA, C1/435/12) and then to Star Chamber: TNA, STAC 2/10, fos. 186–187.

formation or dissolution – were under scrutiny.[50] Nevertheless, Star Chamber could still be seen as a potential mechanism to challenge their judgements. Indeed, in one instance, an accusation of abduction was levelled at the legal counsel. Robert Howard of Tilney, Norfolk, accused Edmund Bonner (the future bishop of London) of instructing his servant, John Hubberd, to abduct Howard's wife, Margaret, and convey her to Bonner's house in Stoke Newington, where she was kept for several weeks before marrying Hubberd.[51] Bonner, by then a doctor of civil law, responded by explaining that he had been assigned the counsel for Hubberd by Wolsey's court of audience in a suit against Margaret, and Hubberd had won his case. Hubberd and Margaret had married and were together until Robert Howard, by unlawful means, had taken possession of Margaret once again. In other words, the Star Chamber case reads as one where the couple, or at least the ex-husband, had refused to accept the legal divorce decreed by the ecclesiastical court. Bonner was clearly not happy at having his actions examined too closely by another court. While he provided an answer, he was not willing to be subjected to further questioning. When the interrogatories were put to him, he stated that he had given a response and was not bound to say anything more unless it could be shown that his answer was wrong.

These suits had also reached Star Chamber because petitioners and their counsel saw their circumstances as ones where common law or statute law could not be applied. This might be because the victims were not heiresses or women of substance; because husbands wanted to recover property and goods taken when their spouses were abducted; or because they wanted restitution of the abducted women, which was not possible under common law.[52] They were complex and difficult cases, or at least they could be made to appear so. As might be expected, many were the result of internecine disputes over marriage formation, legitimation and dissolution. They included fathers or remarried mothers and spouses trying to get (step) daughters back or prevent their marriage; husbands trying to recover their wives; remarried mothers contesting rights of guardianship; and fathers and husbands battling over which man had married a woman first.

It is also the case that while legislators appear to have specific scenarios or events in mind when drawing up their statutes, those plaintiffs pursuing a case of ravishment in Star Chamber might do so for various reasons. Like Chancery, this was a court that dealt with a large number of petitions concerning property matters, and accusations could arise in the course of

[50] Seabourne, *Imprisoning*, p. 160; Ormrod, *Women and Parliament*, p. 99.
[51] TNA, STAC 2/21/33.
[52] Seabourne, *Imprisoning*, pp. 132–3; Ormrod, *Women and Parliament*, p. 98.

disputes or proceedings over land, with the stealing of women part of a wider quarrel or attempt at revenge.[53] At times, a suit was a bid to force someone to take particular actions unconnected to marriage. A case in point is that of George Habington of Suckley, Worcestershire, who accused John Blount of Bromyard and other men of breaking into his house and, with force, having 'toke & caryed away felonyously' his wife Elizabeth against her will.[54] Subsequent pleadings and interrogatories reveal that Blount was Elizabeth's son and he had a case pending against her at the Court in the Marches of Wales.[55] This had resulted in letters commanding Elizabeth to appear before its commissioners in Shrewsbury. Blount claimed that it was but a series of coincidences that saw his servant present when the letters were delivered to Elizabeth, and him travelling at the same time as his mother when she made the journey towards Shrewsbury, including an overnight stay at Leominster. Once Elizabeth had delivered her answers, she had left of her own free will. While laws of abduction were not developed to cover a son frogmarching his mother to court, Habington saw it as an appropriate action with which to sue Blount.

Will and consent

Cases like Habington's illustrate the differing ways women can appear in abduction cases; sometimes as a silent victim, sometimes as a navigator of competing family factions. Yet in its focus on a woman's personal and real property, and through whom these might descend, we see the familiar drivers behind almost all abduction cases. An argument can be made that litigants, and the statutes to which they referred, gave little thought to the welfare of the female victim and were more concerned with the potential loss of property, or in Dunn's words, 'with patrimony than matrimony'.[56] As women lost control of their real and personal property on marriage, statutes appear to reflect 'the increasing emphasis on the damage which could be caused through women, rather than the damage caused to them'.[57] This

[53] See Dunn's table in *Stolen Women*, p. 170: reasons included revenge, property, malicious, and a previous quarrel.

[54] TNA, STAC 2/23/253 for bill and answers. A list of interrogatories for Blount's servant is STAC 2/24/59.

[55] It is likely that this relates to the issue that prompted Blount to initiate a case in Chancery concerning the forgery of a conveyance document in Elizabeth's name for several manors in Herefordshire and Shropshire (1532 x 38): TNA, C1/751/1.

[56] Dunn, *Stolen Women*, p. 97.

[57] Seabourne, *Imprisoning*, pp. 128, 141.

offers up a reading where male voices are dominant, and female will and consent is irrelevant.[58]

This should not be taken too far, however. Historians have pointed to the emotive language used in pleas of ravishment, and political society's 'general revulsion of unreasonable violence towards women'. Ormrod's reading of discussions in parliament convinced him that the Commons did not simply see the crime as a matter of property rights.[59] As mentioned above, cursory comments in Star Chamber should not be taken as a sign of indifference to the extent of harm inflicted on women and young girls; abducted women were also not simply passive units of exchange. One of the more interesting aspects of abduction cases, as Garthine Walker has clearly shown, is that they 'often depended on the agency of the women supposedly stolen away'. It is where rape and abduction cases differ, because victims of the latter were more often described as strong-willed.[60] This was partly in response to the need to show resistance (against her will), and to avoid all suspicion of collusion. Late medieval statutes against abduction had been particularly concerned with women who consented to their own abduction; legislators had tried to ensure no benefits were conveyed by rulings that included barring dower to those women considered co-conspirators. Most of these anxieties reflected male fears of having daughters and widows stolen away, and historians have become sceptical about claims that there were widespread elopements. They argue that there were far fewer cases of collusive actions than medieval ruling classes imagined.[61]

Star Chamber cases suggest a broad spectrum of 'realities' behind abduction claims, including those we might consider consensual. Some alternative readings can be detected in the bills themselves, notably those where adultery cases seem to be masquerading as wife-abductions. Ieuan ap Hugh ap Robert of Denbigh, North Wales, accused John Holland of taking away his wife Alice, as well as goods and chattels, on 18 June 1531, yet he asked for the subpoena to be issued to both John and Alice.[62] In other instances, answers and depositions provide different versions of the events described in the plaintiff's bill. While it is not possible to know how many suits proceeded beyond the

58 Walker, 'Stealing', p. 51; Hawkes, 'She was ravished against her will', pp. 48, 51.

59 Ormrod, *Women and Parliament*, pp. 104–7, quotation on p. 104; Hawkes, 'She was ravished against her will'; Pope, 'Abduction and power', pp. 64–5.

60 Walker, 'Stealing', pp. 51, 63, 66.

61 Dunn, *Stolen Women*, ch. 4; Seabourne, *Imprisoning*, ch. 7.

62 TNA, STAC 2/29/21. This suit had already gone to the Council in the Marches of Wales and involved lands and tenements in Kinmel, Denbighshire. Another example can be found in TNA, STAC 2/13, fo. 273. For discussion of similar cases see S. Butler, 'Runaway wives: husband desertion in medieval England', *Journal of Social History*, xl (2006), 337–59.

bill stage, and bearing in mind archival losses, there are still around thirty suits, nearly two-thirds of the total, where a response from the defendants is known. These range from brief denials and tenuous defences to robust responses that appear to offer an equally convincing narrative of events. We see scenarios where girls have run away with lovers; consensual marriages have taken place; tussles between 'husbands' on who married a woman first; and debates over wardship in which both sides accuse each other of ravishment. All illustrate the difficulties, then as now, of deciding whether an abduction had actually occurred.

Nonetheless, what is particularly noteworthy is how central the woman's will was in the court's attempt to understand what had happened. This does at times appear to move beyond the legal narratives of abduction, as relayed in the bills, to the actual, more complicated and potentially malleable issue of consent as recounted by female abductees. In these instances direct testimony was crucial and, as elsewhere in Europe, such declarations appeared to give the woman 'a conscious and active role'.[63] In the Star Chamber cases these statements may have been received in direct response to interrogatories drawn up for investigating commissioners or through witness statements garnered in previous legal proceedings: for example, jurors testified that Jane Howell had declared her collusion before them at the sessions in Gloucester.[64] More frequently, where the suit turned on the legitimacy of marriage, female abductees had been questioned by church authorities as to their intentions; free consent, of course, was central to the Church's laws on marriage. Mary Trotter was examined by the bishop of Chester, president of the Council of Wales, as to her age and her motivations.[65] Agnes Browne made her confession to Harry Mote, curate of St Margaret's, London. Mote had stated that he would not marry Agnes and her intended, William Johnson, until they had been examined by Dr Barber, doctor of law and commissary of the abbot of Westminster in his peculiar jurisdiction.[66] Similarly, deponents in the case of Denise Bolt claimed that she had confessed contentment at her marriage during her examination before the ordinary, which was then written down under his seal.[67] The stories these women told were often emotionally driven and

[63] In Brabantine cities the distinction between an abduction and elopement hinged on an official declaration in front of aldermen: C. Delameillieure, '"Partly with and partly against her will": female consent, elopement, and abduction in late medieval Brabant', *Journal of Family History*, xlii (2017), 351–68.

[64] TNA, STAC 2/24/34.

[65] TNA, STAC 2/3, fos. 152–153, 288.

[66] TNA, STAC 2/18/191; STAC 2/22/55; STAC 2/22/105; STAC 2/24/7.

[67] TNA, STAC 2/7, fos. 148, 75–87, 89–92 and 199–202.

conformed to romantic notions of love and chivalry. The reported speech in the cases of Agnes Salwayn, Jane Howell, Agnes Browne and Jane Barrenton produced similar narratives involving secret assignations and requests to lovers for assistance. Jane Barrenton stated that she had pleaded to be taken away because she had been evilly treated by her husband's household and made to do all the drudgery, but mainly because she could not find it in her heart to love her husband. When she left with her alleged abductor, she did so with her 'owne volentary mynde'.[68]

How one interprets these women's confessions is challenging. What this 'will' or 'volentary mynde' meant, and what was understood as consent, is problematic. As Seabourne has pointed out, modern researchers need to be cautious in reading what a medieval lawyer or legislator saw as a consent case, commenting that there was a 'whole spectrum between wholehearted agreement and active refusal'.[69] It should be remembered, as Margaret Kebell found in the common-law courts, that marriage in itself was seen as evidence for assent or collusion. Women may well have subsequently accepted their marriage because they had no alternatives: a decision made after the event rather than before it.[70] In addition, Delameillieure has found cases in medieval Brabant where women declared their consent despite the record stating that the abduction was against their will. She suggests that women's consent may have been prompted by concepts of sexual purity and a desire to save their honour, and argues against the potential 'slippage between consent and choice', seeing the former as a 'passive form of acquiescence'.[71]

These are important considerations in reading female consent, but such a focus places the sole responsibility on the will of the woman, whether she was expressing her true feelings or acting as a mouthpiece for others. Yet, as the Star Chamber evidence shows, consent was hardly a straightforward issue in the early sixteenth century. Nor was it a question only for women, but something debated and mulled over by men and by those who carried out the crime. Abduction was, after all, a felony, and high risk for all involved. How was a lover to respond when asked by a woman to be 'rescued'? Was the often-provided chivalric narrative merely a predictable retort to justify predatory actions or hot-headed desire? Such defence statements usefully show that deliberation and perhaps reluctance on the side of an abductor could be considered mitigating factors, and some sought reassurances to this effect before taking action. One such example can be seen in the answers

68 TNA, STAC 2/24/107; STAC 2/26/436; STAC 10/4/71.

69 Seabourne, *Imprisoning*, pp. 145, 151, 154, 160.

70 Ives, 'Agaynst taking awaye of women'; McSheffrey and Pope, 'Ravishment', p. 834.

71 Delameillieure, 'Elopement and abduction', pp. 359–61.

and depositions of those accused of assisting Peter Hering in abducting Jane Barrenton. Their defence was that Jane had desperately wanted to leave her new husband and had asked Peter Hering, a regular visitor to the house, to carry her away.[72] Peter Hering was a young lawyer at Clifford's Inn, and undersheriff of Hertfordshire, and therefore in an ideal position to consult with associates at Clifford's Inn and the Temple along with two doctors at the Arches – Dr Lyell and Dr Leson – concerning the legalities of such actions.[73] He was apparently told that the law would support the case if no carnal copulation had taken place – addressing questions about the legality of the marriage – and, so long as it was not against her will, he could convey her away and it would not be unlawful. He admitted, however, that he had married her hurriedly, without licence; no doubt the reason why his witnesses comprised four men from Clifford's Inn and one from Temple. Such advice did not prevent Peter from being pursued by the law, or his associates ending up in the Fleet, but it shows he was sufficiently aware of the dangers arising from his actions.

The abductor-lover's motivation was the prize of marriage, but what of those who supported him? As mentioned earlier, allies in an abduction had been targeted from the early fifteenth century, and the 1487 statute had pronounced that accessories were henceforth to be 'judged as principals'.[74] Family and friends could find themselves inadvertently caught up in abduction cases for providing shelter to an offending couple. Others, like those assisting Peter Hering, may have thought they had right on their side, but that did not save them from gaol. Many of those named in abduction suits argued their innocence by presenting countersigns that their actions were in accordance with a woman's will. We would expect deponents to have received some coaching on what to say, but they do at least show a popular understanding that asking a woman about her intentions was a useful defence. There are several examples where accessories claimed to be responding to a woman's request as much as the man they were assisting. In the depositions of those accused of taking away Anne Salwayn, they claimed that they had been told by Stephen Miles that Anne had wanted to be fetched and she had written letters to that effect. When Anne had been led from her chamber 'with a mery countenaunce', one of the men

[72] TNA, STAC 10/4/71.

[73] Among those he consulted at Clifford's Inn was Thomas Hanchett of Braughing (Herts) who was a Hertfordshire attorney (will dating to 1577: PROB 11/59/635). Richard Lyell was an advocate of the arches from the 1530s: C. J. Kitching, 'The probate jurisdiction of Thomas Cromwell as vicegerent', *Historical Research*, xlvi (1973), 104. William Leson was also a master in the Chancery, and a doctor of the arches: TNA, C1/886/62.

[74] Dunn, *Stolen Women*, pp. 202–3; Ives, 'Agaynst taking awaye of women', p. 24.

had specifically asked her if she was 'contente to go with Stephen Myllys or no' and she had confirmed that she did for 'why shuld I have sent for hym ells'.[75]

Buoyed by the abductee's statement, these men had carried out the abduction. Others, however, chose to step back and call on legal assistance. Again, men knew they had to make a choice in committing an abduction. A notable example comes from those accused of abducting Denise Bolt in the winter of 1512. They deposed that they had been asked by their master, Sir Robert Brandon, to bring Denise to him, whom he claimed was his ward, but to do so quietly and not to break down any doors (which would have shown unwanted entry). By stealth, they managed to enter the house unobserved and found Denise in the hall. She tried to avoid their attempts to apprehend her, but she was finally taken out into the yard. The defendants conceded that there was much 'ado': Denise and her friends made great lamentation; a neighbour attempted to defend Denise with a bat, while a priest held on to her; weapons were drawn. These were recognizably signs of force around which a case could be made. The accused admitted that they knew at that point she had been taken out of the house unwillingly and realized that she would not go quietly 'but aygenste her wyll & with vyolenc'. As a result, all parties agreed to deliver Denise to the local constable. She was taken on his horse peacefully to Sir Robert's house, alongside her mother and stepfather. In Brandon's own deposition, he stated that he could not say whether she was taken against her will, but he pointed to the presence of the constable and her parents as mitigating evidence.[76] Brandon's servants, therefore, had stepped back from using force and invited the law to step in.

Conclusion

Ravishment suits provide excellent examples of the kind of complex cases that found their way to Star Chamber in the early sixteenth century, and the evidence of associated issues of consent and female agency with which such suits were concerned. Their multiple viewpoints ensured that both parties had the opportunity to present convincing and conflicting narratives of an abductor's or abductee's intentions. Plaintiffs had either tried at other courts or felt that they had a better option in Star Chamber; this might be to expedite a matter or to prolong an already long-running dispute. The bills also demonstrate that while the listed litigants are important and tell us much

[75] TNA, STAC 10/4/55.

[76] TNA, STAC 2/7, fos. 75–87, 89–92, 148 and 199–202 (quotation on fo. 79); STAC 2/26/309.

about the drivers behind the suits, they alone are never the whole story. The proceedings and proofs provide insights into earlier actions and accusations that led to the suit being filed, and show the different motivations lying behind the complaints of abduction. The 1487 act allowed a broad range of possibilities in relation to women, and claims of ravishment could be deployed against anyone taking away someone's next of kin for any reason. While for males, only dependants, largely wards, could be ravished, with female abductees age did not matter as there was never a sense that women would reach a point where they had full control over their bodies.

Nevertheless, women had choices. These are sometimes visible in their involvement as litigants, but more often in the various instances where they were accused of acting against the wishes of family or friends. Some Star Chamber suits were very likely elopements. Historians have recently downplayed the number of these cases, countering the ravishment statutes' implications of widespread consensual abduction. Yet there is sufficient evidence from Star Chamber to show that women were not simply positioned as passive victims, or ones without a voice, and various motivations were attributed to them: the loveless marriage, a fear of a forced marriage, romantic notions, or too much housework. These were all positions from which they needed to negotiate an alternative life, to engineer a solution. A consensual abduction did not necessarily mean one entirely freely entered; a choice can be between a rock and a hard place. But there was a recognition that the will of the woman was crucial to advancing or defending an abduction suit. While it might be a subordinate consideration to family desires, a woman's will was not immaterial. The deliberations of the men who initiated or joined an attempt to spirit women away also knew this, which adds to our knowledge of the popular understanding of the law. Some planned their movements more carefully than others and ensured compliance could be demonstrated before they acted; others may have clutched at straws afterwards. Yet the Star Chamber records, particularly the proofs, illustrate the extent to which consent mattered in late medieval and early Tudor England and Wales, and that it was an issue for both men and women alike.

4. Sir Edward Coke and the Star Chamber: the prosecution of rapes at Snargate, 1598–1602*

Louis A. Knafla

The Attorney General v *Harwood et al.* was unusual in that rape cases were seldom prosecuted in the early modern era.[1] It was also unusual in that Sir Edward Coke decided to take it on and then, after a lengthy intermission, put all his weight behind the prosecution in Star Chamber. The assaults at the core of the case involved several women caught in a series of brutal attacks that lasted well into the night of 6 October 1598, in the victualling house of John Grigsby in the Romney Marsh village of Snargate, Kent. After drinking for some time, seven yeomen became disordered, prompting neighbours to summon the village constable and minister. They entered the house and asked the men either to leave or keep better order. Nonetheless, the disorder continued and led to more violence throughout the evening. By the end of the night the men had assaulted Joan Grigsby, wife of the house, and her maidservants Elizabeth Crouchman, Agnes Horn and Mary Gamby. Local authorities had refused to prosecute the men who were accused of the atrocities, but eventually Coke stepped in.

* The author wishes to thank Krista Kesselring, Natalie Mears and David Chan Smith for their meticulous suggestions on the manuscript, and Sir John Baker for useful comments on a few matters.

[1] For the literature in this era, see N. Bashar, 'Rape in England between 1550 and 1700', in *The Sexual Dynamics of History*, ed. London Feminist History Group (1983), pp. 34–40; B. J. Baines, 'Effacing rape in early modern representations', *English Literary History*, lxv (1998), 69–98; M. Chayter, 'Husband[ry]: Narratives of rape in the seventeenth-century', *Gender and History*, vii (1995), 378–407; C. Herrup, *House of Gross Disorder: Sex, Law and the 2nd Earl of Castlehaven* (Oxford, 1999); L. Gowing, *Domestic Dangers: Women, Words and Sex in Early Modern London* (Oxford, 1996); M. Ingram, 'Child sexual abuse in early modern England', in *Negotiating Power in Early Modern Society*, ed. M. Braddick and J. Walter (Cambridge, 2001), pp. 63–84; and G. Walker, 'Rereading rape and sexual violence in early modern England', *Gender and History*, x (1998), 1–25; *Crime, Gender and Social Order in Early Modern England* (Cambridge, 2003); and 'Everyman or a monster? The rapist in early modern England, *c.*1600–1750', *History Workshop Journal*, lxxvi (2013), 5–31. There is also a long line of pamphlets and chapbooks on this subject; see most recently *Stories of True Crime in Tudor and Stuart England*, ed. K. MacMillan (London, 2015).

L. A. Knafla, 'Sir Edward Coke and the Star Chamber: the prosecution of rapes at Snargate, 1598–1602' in *Star Chamber Matters: An Early Modern Court and Its Records*, ed. K. Kesselring and N. Mears (London, 2021), pp. 61–78.

It is difficult to understand why Coke, already an icon of the common law, decided to put so much effort into this cause from one of the most quiet and forlorn areas in the kingdom. Evidence reveals that it was two godly ministers who attained his confidence and persuaded the women, along with numerous local people of non-gentle status, to give testimony. The men charged with the offences had as their attorneys two prominent local landowners, lawyers and justices of the peace (JPs), Matthew Hadd and Robert Edolph. Coke, however, became relentless in his search for information as the men at first fled into France and elsewhere. His pursuit eventually won him the verdict he sought: the three chief perpetrators were fined the financially crippling sums of £200 each, and three lesser ones £40 each. The case reveals an interesting side of the attorney general as well as an unusual insight into the prosecution of sexual offences in the Star Chamber.

Because so many of the region's disputes were resolved by arbitration, and because its world was largely beyond the purview of the central courts, it is by accident – as with Carlos Ginzberg's miller – that we find an entry point into the lives of Kent's marsh society.[2] The point is a series of case files in the Star Chamber records for the reign of Elizabeth I (STAC 5), which comprise a crown prosecution by the future chief justice of England of seven men of Romney Marsh plus a JP. The case is exceptional for several reasons. Coke generally focused on civil matters at common law in search of unravelling their legal intricacies. He also typically kept his efforts to great matters of state, involving conspirators such as Dr Lopez, the earl of Essex, Sir Walter Raleigh and the perpetrators of the Gunpowder Plot. Thus, it is unusual to find him bringing a bill of complaint on 1 May 1600 against six yeomen of Romney Marsh and another of Sussex for alleged rapes which took place nineteen months earlier, privileging the allegations made by the maidservant Agnes Horn.

The attorney general's action against John Harwood of Brookland, his brother-in-law John Yealding of Battle, Sussex, and Thomas Tookey, Nathaniel Rayner, William Elderton, Robert Bladen and Thomas Allen – all of Brenzatt[3] – and against William Lamb,[4] Brookland's bailiff and JP, began poorly.[5] The bill was vague, alleging unlawful assembly, assaults,

[2] C. Ginzberg, *The Cheese and the Worms: The Cosmos of a Sixteenth-Century Miller* (London, 1992).

[3] The National Archives of the UK, STAC 5/A35/38, A37/39.

[4] TNA, STAC 5/A16/15.

[5] On a personal note, Coke had married the flamboyant Lady Elizabeth Hatton on 22 Nov. 1598, and until their daughter Frances was born on 21 Aug. 1599, his colleagues on the Queen's Bench considered him up and down 'as a dead man' in those months, where he often wept, and in which he had also taken ill with a fever that re-occured in 1601: see

misdemeanours and outrages committed at Grigsby's house by seven yeomen against four women on a Sunday after evening prayer in October 1598. Few specifics were given. The alleged crimes lacked conviction in their telling, and not all of the names were spelled correctly.[6] Coke struck first at Lamb, who was also the first to answer, for his failure to prosecute. Lamb held that Agnes Horn did not allege rape or attempted rape, nor any serious injuries. He called her a 'runagate' and maintained that the problem was her master who often allowed young men to resort to his house, drink their fill and show what contemporaries observed as 'tricks of youth'. In a preliminary examination of the house, he made no attempt to examine the men. Riding to Snargate to investigate Mr Grigsby, Lamb learned that he had left town. So too had most of the other defendants, whose being beyond his jurisdiction allowed him to end his work. Later, he admitted that he may have erred in not pursuing the matter, pleading ignorance in law and begging forgiveness. He closed with the comment that hopefully his neighbours, and the country, would think well of him.

Lamb gave his deposition just four days after his answer, where he offered little additional information to the range of questions which were designed to pursue his handling of the matter and his possible culpability. He said that he did not know Agnes's name, and that the 'misdeeds' were 'lewd parts' which the young men 'played' with her. The worst, he said, was when one of them put a stick up her dress and others 'shouldered' her down the stairs. Because her complaint was uncertain and informal, he did not bind over the accused and told her to make no formal accusations as the men had played such tricks there before.[7]

In their answers of 26 May to 8 June 1600, the defendants to the main charges denied all. Their joint answer was vague, made no factual statements and gave nothing away for their later defences.[8] With a bill nineteen months after the event lacking specifics, and defendants who denied all charges, it is equally surprising that a set of interrogatories and depositions exist which are dated nearly another year later, from 30 January to 8 June 1601.[9]

C. D. Bowen, *The Lion and the Throne* (London, 1957), pp. 106–9. It should also be noted that he could become violent with young women, as in his later life with Lady Hatton and their daughter: Bowen, *The Lion and the Throne*, pp. 144–7, 344–55.

[6] E.g., Bladen is given as 'Blodwell' throughout Coke's pleadings, but we know it is 'Bladen' from his own deposition.

[7] TNA, STAC 5/A16/15, dated 30 May 1600. Lamb may have been unlearned in the law, as he makes a mark instead of a signature on the last page of his deposition.

[8] TNA, STAC 5/A35/38, dated 28 May 1600. Their answer was made by 'Altham', probably the same John Altham who was soon to become a baron of the court of Exchequer.

[9] *Kent at Law 1602: The Court of Star Chamber*, vol. III, ed. L. A. Knafla (London, 2012),

A detailed description of the facts of the night was not put into writing until the deposition of Agnes Horn and Mrs Joan Grigsby several months after the defendants' answers, on 30 January 1601, by two local preachers, Henry Stafford of New Romney and Nicholas Gear of Snargate. Their accumulative evidence was gruesome and contested Lamb's deposition. They deposed that the seven men came to the house after evening prayer, between about 5:00pm and 6:00pm, to eat the venison pasties they brought with them with beer and bread. The men took a room in the loft and shouted for beer. When Agnes, aged thirty-five, came up, Tookey threw her on Yealding's lap and then pulled up her clothes. Rayner hit her on the thigh with his stick and threatened to have her, but she escaped. They then took to shouting and stomping on the floor, which caused dust to fill the rooms below and the noise to bother neighbours. Joan Grigsby, aged thirty, begged Agnes to go up again; at first, Agnes refused, but then agreed. As soon as she went up, Yealding grabbed her and threw her on Rayner's lap, who thrust a stick under her clothes and then threw her down the stairs, causing great injuries.

At one point Mary Gamby, aged fourteen, went up and was thrown on the bed by Yealding and Tookey, who laid on her and made a 'great mess'. She cried for help, bringing up Joan with her baby who ordered them to leave. They said they would not leave as they were bent on sex. While this was occurring, other men downstairs left the house. (Mr Grigsby had left sometime earlier.) Then Harwood came down and told Agnes, who was in the parlour, not to refuse them because as men of property they would make amends 'for any doings'. He then tried to rape her, and left her for Tookey, who came in and closed the door. Rebuffed, he went into the buttery, where Joan was with her baby, and pushed up against her for the same. Joan grabbed a knife on the table behind her and threatened to put it through him. When Agnes heard Joan's and the baby's cries, she tried to go into the buttery, but was grabbed by Harwood. When Agnes said that she would go to the minister to make a complaint, Yealding responded that he should have the priest's wife as well as her. He then tried to rape Joan's sister Elizabeth.

At this point, about 8:00pm, Harwood blew out the candles, stamping the fire and causing the embers to spread, almost burning the house down before buckets of water were thrown on the cinders. When Joan confronted him for his actions, he threw her on the ground and plucked out the hairs from her 'privities'. They offered forcible violence upon the maids, who

items 30–66 for an extensive calendar of the proceedings. Cited hereafter as *KAL Star Chamber*.

fled into a chamber and locked the doors. The men broke through and attempted to ravish the maids by force but failed by their resistance. Mrs Grigsby was attacked when she had a child in her arms which she had taken from the cradle to succour. Mary Gamby was left in dire straits, assaulted by three men who left her for dead. When the men could not have their way with Agnes Horn, they beat her about the body with a cudgel and a staff three feet long. She was hurt so badly that she would become permanently lame. Finally, the men left around 11:00pm.

Later that night, Agnes went to minister Gear's house intending to make a complaint. But Yealding followed her on his horse and threw her on the ground. In her words, he held a hand over her mouth and 'set upon me most unseemly, and with great violence pinched me about those parts of the body (which are not to be mentioned) with such considerable pain that fire seemed to splash out of my eyes'.[10] The next morning Agnes went to the two parish ministers, Stafford and Gear, who told her to make an official complaint to the Romney Marsh parish JP William Lamb. She went that morning to Lamb's house and related her story. Lamb shunned her, referring to her inferior social background, and tried to put the blame on Mrs Grigsby for allowing such disorders in her house. He told Agnes that the assault was 'but a trick of youth'. Then he investigated the other women individually, who declined to make specific accusations. Meanwhile, it was reported that the men had left the area for 'vacations' and fled into France.

More than six months after the event, on the morning of Easter Day (8 April 1599), a little before morning service, Rayner went to the house of Henry Stafford, minister of New Romney, saying that he would attend the service and receive communion. Stafford, having heard of his outrages and misdemeanours, told him not to come because he had to confer with him further. When Rayner pressed him as to why he was not allowed to take communion, Stafford replied, in front of several witnesses, that it was because of the rape in Snargate. Rayner then brought an action upon the case in the court of Queen's Bench for speaking such words, requesting damages of £200 and putting Stafford to charges for his defence.[11] He also threatened the minister, saying that if he spoke anything of his alleged offences, he (Rayner) had chased a priest already and would have Stafford as well.[12]

The six defendants and ten character witnesses, from the neighbouring parishes of Brenzatt, Snargate, New Romney, Dymchurch and Hythe, all

[10] TNA, STAC 5/A37/39, p. 4v, modernized in *KAL Star Chamber*, item 43, article 12.

[11] TNA, KB 29/236 and 237, and KB 27/1356/1 and 1357.

[12] TNA, STAC 5/A35/38.

described as yeomen, deposed on 30 May 1600 that no threats, disorders, outrages or rapes had occurred. Their statements, however, were full of inconsistencies, and Coke directed his examinations on 8 June 1600 to the four men who were the principal actors – Tookey, Rayner, Harwood and Bladen. Coke wanted specifics from each man: who got them together, when they arrived at the house, in which rooms they met whom, what happened when and where, and when they left. Their replies were not well orchestrated. Their departure time ranged from 8:00pm to 10:00pm, while all the women and neighbours agreed on 10:00pm to 11:00pm, and closer to 11:00pm. But several other matters incriminated the defendants. Lamb, the JP who deposed four days after his pleading and before any of the other defendants pleaded, said the women did not tell him the full story originally, and lacking knowledge of law he did not know what to do. Allen, a sub-bailiff and one of the last men to depose, was found to have been Lamb's servant at the time of the assaults, but soon afterward left his employment.

The fact that Coke did not attempt to examine any of the women at this time suggests that he may have been looking for what we might call a 'smoking gun' on which to hang a successful prosecution. Somehow, he had to find a way to end the community's silence. The men denied attempting the chastity of the women, of closeting themselves with any of them or causing any violence. But they were good friends, all living within three miles of each other and of Snargate.[13] Allen had organized the meeting at Brenzatt Wall just after evening prayer with news that Elderton had a venison pasty for them and they needed drink – hence a short journey to Grigsby's house at Snargate. Their accounts of who was where and when, and who did what to whom, all differed. Apart from those differences, Harwood and Bladen said they went out to see an affray at Arrowhead, a mile away, from 5:30pm to 7:00pm. Allen, who deposed six days later, identified Elderton as the ringleader and said that Yealding was armed. He denied the allegations of Agnes, that Mary Gamby was there or that any complaint was made to Lamb. Obviously he had been coached to lessen whatever damage the others did to themselves in their depositions.

Mary Gamby had died in August or September 1599 – possibly from the lingering effects of the assault – and in October, Stafford and the puritan lawyer and mayor John Ming[14] of New Romney conducted their

[13] Tookey, a yeoman, lived in Hinxsfield; Rayner, a yeoman, at Kenardington; Harwood, a husbandman, at Brookland; and Bladen, a butcher, at Brenzatt. Note that their official designations above for the proceedings are more generic, reflecting the practice that J. S. Cockburn has observed for the assizes: Cockburn, *Calendar of Assize Records, Home Circuit Indictments, Elizabeth I and James I: Introduction* (London, 1985), pp. 73–87.

[14] Ming was a puritan leading the movement to reform the parish. For his work and that

own investigation of the women and Grigsby's neighbours. Their action was prompted by Stafford's hearing of Agnes's permanent incapacity from his own personal examination of a witness who had accompanied Rayner to visit her at Southwark. There is a mention in the proceedings of a bill in the ecclesiastical court to try the offenders, but the bill has not been found in the records at Canterbury.[15] Since Stafford and his colleague Gear were puritan preachers dedicated to the moral and spiritual reformation of the parish, they may have tried to proceed against the culprits in the ecclesiastical court because of the wall of silence that had been established among the older ruling families. A suspicion is that Stafford, having failed in this task, forwarded his and Ming's information to Coke, a known supporter of moderate puritans in these years as well as a known opponent of violent youths. This may help to explain why Coke brought his bill in May 1600 after conducting his own investigation. He had a public reputation at that time for securing punishment for violent offenders.

Lamb's confession to the fact that these events may have occurred and that he may have erred gave Coke the opportunity to pursue an interrogation of the parties under oath. There was, however, an eight-month delay in the preparation of the interrogatories. The delay might have arisen from the attorney general's heavy workload on national affairs. It may have been due to a statement by Joan Grigsby that no harm was done (to protect her husband's house and her employment of victualling), the subsequent disappearance of her husband John or a separate investigation by the new mayor of New Romney – the conservative William Thurbarne – and jurat Robert Oakman. Internal evidence states that Thurbarne and Oakman examined the three young women and concluded that no abuses were committed.[16] Therefore, the door for prosecutions may have appeared to be closed.

That Coke proceeded to the final stage was due perhaps to his learning that Rayner had visited Agnes in Southwark in December 1600, where she was living incapacitated, and paid her 20*s* for her fall, along with another 20*s* at a later visit. This information was given away by one of the witnesses for the defendants, John Godderd of New Romney, aged twenty-four. Thus the stage was set for Agnes's depositions of 30 January 1601, which formal evidence led to the interrogatories drawn for the other parties on 20 February. The prosecution and the defence each called thirteen witnesses. The depositions for the defence were virtually useless with their vague

of similar leaders see T. J. Tronrud, 'Dispelling the gloom. The extent of poverty in Tudor and early Stuart towns: some Kentish evidence', *Canadian Journal of History*, xx (1985), 1–21.

15 Canterbury Cathedral Library, Prerogative Court of Canterbury, cause books 1600–1.

16 *KAL Star Chamber*, items 59–60.

testimony, while the depositions of parties and witnesses for the prosecution read like modern documentary evidence. The case files ended there.

The two puritan ministers who had approached Coke were in the process of creating a New Jerusalem for this marginal marsh society. The records of the borough courts of New Romney and Romney Marsh are replete with prosecutions against drunkenness, lewd speech, disorders and offences against morals.[17] Perhaps the events on the night of 6 October 1598 at Snargate were seen as a lightning rod for action – one to mobilize the community to recognize the evils of its ways and call for God's judgement against what their local lawyer and historian William Lambarde called 'the evil doers' who lead society into the abyss. For once, a few lay and spiritual leaders of the marsh were willing to go beyond their borders, to call upon the most fearsome institution of the central state and one of its most outstanding legal practitioners, to make an example of these wild youths of prominent local social status who defiled women and threatened the advent of a new world order.

The Star Chamber judgements in these years have not weathered the passage of time. But the Fine Rolls of the Exchequer reveal that on 25 February 1602, nearly a year after the last depositions in this case, six of the defendants were fined.[18] Elderton, who was not identified with any of the actions, and Yealding, who escaped into Yorkshire and was not found, did not provide answers to the bill and were not interrogated. But Lamb and Allen were fined £40 each, a sizeable sum given that a family of five in the area lived on wages of £9 12*s* a year. The real hammer, however, fell on Harwood, Rayner, Tookey and Bladen, who were fined £200 each. Since the average yeoman of the area was worth a net £160, in essence they were made bankrupts. The hefty fines were due in part not only to Coke's vigilance, but also to Lord Keeper Sir Thomas Egerton's aphorism that great malefactors should pay the greatest amounts.[19] In addition to the fine, the convicted were also charged to pay the costs and fees of the court, 'and so it was ordered'.[20]

[17] *Kent at Law 1602: Local Jurisdictions: Borough, Liberty and Manor*, ed. L. A. Knafla (2 vols., London, 2011), ii (part I), pp. xxxv–xxxvii, xxxix–xl; and ii (part II), pp. 259–97, 334–44.

[18] TNA, King's Remembrancer Rolls (James I), E159/422.

[19] His original phrase was '*dignitas delinquentis auget culpam*', quoted in J. Hawarde, *Les Reportes del Cases in Camera Stellata 1593 to 1609*, ed. W. P. Baildon (London, 1894, repr. 2008), p. 288.

[20] Cited contemporaneously in W. Hudson, 'A treatise of the court of Star Chamber', in *Collectanea Juridica*, ed. F. Hargrave (London, 1792, repr. 1986), pp. 134–5.

***

The men were not without their pasts. In the month prior to their attacks, Nathaniel Rayner was indicted for assaulting Clement Ellesmore, a petty chapman of Maidstone, at Warehorne on 21 September 1598.[21] There is no record of its outcome. Harwood was indicted for a trespass on the case later in April 1602.[22] He did not appear and was in mercy three times for non-appearances. Eight months later on 13 December he came to an agreement with the plaintiff.[23] But before that case was resolved he was indicted for another trespass on the case on 29 November, was in mercy twice for non-appearance, and came to an agreement on the same day as the previous prosecution.[24] That summer he was on a coroner's inquest for the killing of a man and was a surety for a glover prosecuted for slanderous words. He appeared no more in the extant local court records of the day until a gaol calendar entry of 19 March 1610, in which he was listed as a prisoner in Canterbury gaol, where he later died.[25]

One of the puritan ministers was not without his foibles either. Henry Stafford's servant Anthony Rhodes was accused of fathering the child of a servant, Elizabeth Bingham, aged twenty-three, on Sunday, 22 September or 6 October 1601, in a field behind a barn of mayor John Thurbarne.[26] She deposed that she had a ring and other things from Rhodes in her custody. He was accused of 'going to the Devil' with Mr Stafford, but Stafford put things right. Rhodes was convicted and ordered to pay the town overseers 12*d* weekly until the child reached age eighteen.[27] Stafford was also involved in pleas of trespass upon the case in 1602.[28] His servants continued their misdemeanours, as John Reke and William Wind were accused of stealing a

[21] Centre for Kentish Studies, Quarter Sessions Indictments, QM/SI 1599/1; he was joined in the assault by Robert Durborne of New Romney.

[22] The documents appear in *Kent at Law 1602: Local Jurisdictions: Borough, Liberty and Manor*, vol. 2, part II, before the New Romney Hundred Court, items 2693, 2785, 2796, 2814. Cited hereafter as *KAL Local Jurisdictions*.

[23] *KAL Local Jurisdictions*, item 2831. The plaintiff was William Brockman.

[24] *KAL Local Jurisdictions*, also before the New Romney court, items 2806, 2823, 2839. The plaintiff was Nicholas Archer.

[25] *Calendar of Assize Records: Kent Indictments, James I*, ed. J. S. Cockburn (London, 1980), item 450.

[26] *KAL Local Jurisdictions*, items 2928 and 2929, in the New Romney Hundred Court Sessions of the Peace, Examinations, numbers 46 and 46v, 11 Apr. 1602.

[27] *KAL Local Jurisdictions*, item 2758. Rhodes claimed that he was not the father. The judges ruled that he would have to bring the father to the mayor.

[28] *KAL Local Jurisdictions*, item 3370, 2 Sept. 1602, the agreement on 21 Apr. 1603.

turkey and five hens in the spring of 1602.[29] With regard to Nicholas Gear, he does not appear in any of the court records of the county.

Whatever the failings of Stafford's own household, he and Gear had been able to interest the attorney general in taking on the case not just on behalf of the formidable Agnes Horn but also on behalf of the godly cause of reform. Coke, the attorney general who was soon to become chief justice of the Common Pleas, had made his point, and the ministers of God had a precedent with which to work their transformation of this marginal marsh society. By the English civil wars of the 1640s, Romney Marsh was thoroughly puritan and in the vanguard of the revolution that brought down King and Court.

It is interesting that Stafford and Gear brought to Coke allegations of disorder centred on rape when it was a crime denounced in the abstract but not much prosecuted in practice. According to major legal writers such as Sir Anthony Fitzherbert, in law the crime of rape was considered as the most heinous after that of murder.[30] Other law writers such as Lambarde, Michael Dalton and Sir Henry Finch gave it little discussion, however. Ferdinando Pulton's authoritative 1609 treatise on crime and the criminal law considered an assault as rape only if the woman did not become pregnant, and then it was important to have evidence distinguishing it from ravishment.[31] Coke himself, writing later in his *Commentaries*, defined rape as 'unlawful carnal Knowledge and abuse' against a woman's will, citing clauses from Westminster I and II and statutes from Henry VI through Edward VI. Evidence of penetration and semen were crucial, and Coke closed with a 'holy history' of this heinous crime.[32]

The crime was in the public eye as it was well represented in the theatre through the plays of Thomas Heywood, Thomas Middleton and William Shakespeare. Puritans in particular spoke and wrote vehemently against rape among all sexual crimes. But few cases of rape or attempted rape were prosecuted, either in the ecclesiastical courts or the common-law assizes, and fewer succeeded. Some prosecutions focused on 'assault', not 'rape'. According to Cynthia Herrup, the reaction of the offenders in the Snargate case was typical: most such perpetrators fled the scene, and the difficulty at trial was providing credible witnesses as well as uncontroverted facts.[33]

[29] *KAL Local Jurisdictions*, item 2959, 9 March 1602. They were noted clearly as Mr Stafford's 'men'.

[30] Sir A. Fitzherbert, *The Newe Boke of Iustices of the Peas* (London, 1538), p. 19.

[31] F. Pulton, *De Pace Regis et Regni* (London, 1609), fos. 133r–134r. Ravishment was the unlawful taking of a woman with force, which was required for the crime of rape.

[32] Sir E. Coke, *The Third Institute* (New York, 1644, repr. 1979), ch. 11.

[33] Herrup, *House of Gross Disorder*, pp. 25–32, 37–8, 59–62, 134–6, 148–54. See also Bashar,

Few depositions were ever taken, and few women were willing to speak afterwards of their ordeals. M. Chayter has argued that depositions in rape cases for the Northern Circuit were dictated by the JPs, thus challenging the victims' original voices.[34] But there appears to be no such suggestion for Coke's deponents in the Star Chamber where, presumably, we have a higher standard of evidence. Even in politically charged cases of riot, the voices of local inhabitants in Star Chamber materials were strong.

Bernard Capp provides several general insights into neighbourhood dynamics that are pertinent. First, local communities often witnessed disputes between young women and men of the propertied class, and churchwardens often complained of unruly behaviour committed by young men. Such complaints were often brought before the ecclesiastical consistory courts, where they usually expired due to the non-appearance of parties and witnesses, in spite of a crusade in Kent against immoral and sexual behaviour by the Archdeacon of Canterbury. Second, courts in metropolitan London were quick to protect maids who had been abused by their masters or customers. Finally, husbands who found their wives raped would often seek immediate vengeance upon the culprit.[35]

The age of victims mattered, too. According to Martin Ingram, the sexual exploitation of children to the marriage age of twelve, and for youngsters aged twelve to fifteen, was considered 'abuse' by contemporaries in the sixteenth and seventeenth centuries, but as with sexual assaults more generally, only a fraction of such cases came to the authorities. The age of consent for marriage was twelve, though the 1576 act (18 Eliz. I c.7) made carnal knowledge of any child under ten rape regardless of 'consent', as well as refusing the plea of clergy for all such perpetrators. Ingram also cites evidence that there were no explicit cases in Essex church courts from 1560–1680, though some in London's Bridewell, and that ravishing a girl aged seven brought an acquittal because she was considered too young to have been so molested, but not at age nine.[36] Garthine Walker's examination of

'Rape in England between 1550 and 1700', and Baines, 'Effacing rape in early modern representations'.

[34] Chayter, 'Husband[ry]: narratives of rape', pp. 387–407.

[35] B. Capp, *When Gossips Meet: Women, Family, and Neighbourhood in Early Modern England* (Oxford, 2003), pp. 135–6, 144–6, 225–66. See also P. Collinson, 'Cranbrook and the Fletchers: popular and unpopular religion in the Kentish weald', in *Reformation Principle and Practice*, ed. N. Brooks (London, 1980), pp. 171–202, and see the Canterbury court records at the Canterbury Library Archives, Canterbury, fonds X 1–10. About two-thirds of those cited did not appear (Collinson, 'Cranbrook and the Fletchers', pp. 177–8).

[36] Martin Ingram, 'Child sexual abuse in early modern England', in *Negotiating Power in Early Modern Society*, ed. Michael J. Braddick and John Walter (Cambridge, 2001), pp. 64–6.

the depictions of rapists as 'everyman' or as 'monsters' makes several observations on their motives and methods, ranging from importunity and harassment to lust and sweet-talking their young female victims. Sexual harassment and coercion were routine aspects of daily life, and such routine forms were seldom if ever prosecuted. It was the act of violence and bodily harm that might bring such matters to the courts, and here is where the 'monster' appeared.[37] There is, however, no such rhetoric in the descriptions of the rapes at Snargate – rather, drunken male lust and disorder that required a message to be sent into this local community.

Table 4.1: Victims of alleged rape in the home county assizes, 1558–1625[1]

	Children[2]	**Teens**[3]	**Wives**	**Spinster/ Widows**	**Women**[4] **Unspecified**	**TOTAL**
Elizabeth I:						
Essex	6 – 1	6 – 0	2 – 0	3 – 1	10 – 4	27 – 6
Herts	0 – 0	1 – 0	0 – 0	1 – 0	1 – 0	3 – 0
Kent	9 – 1	3 – 1	2 – 1	3 – 1	7 – 0	24 – 4
Surrey	15 – 1	2 – 0	1 – 0	1 – 0	5 – 3	24 – 4
Sussex	2 – 1	1 – 0	0 – 0	2 – 0	6 – 3	11 – 4
TOTALS	32 – 4	13 – 1	5 – 1	10 – 2	29 – 9	89– 18
James VI & I:						
Essex	6 – 3	2 – 2	2 – 0	0 – 0	2 – 1	12 – 6
Herts	2 – 0	3 – 0	0 – 0	0 – 0	1 – 0	6 – 0
Kent	0 – 0	0 – 0	0 – 0	0 – 0	1 – 1	1 – 1
Surrey	7 – 2	1 – 0	0 – 0	0 – 0	2 – 0	10 – 2
Sussex	0 – 0	1 – 0	0 – 0	0 – 0	1 – 0	2 – 0
TOTALS	15 – 5	7 – 2	2 – 0	0 – 0	7 – 2	31 – 9
GRAND TOTALS	47 – 9	20 – 3	7 – 1	10 – 2	32 – 11	120–27

Source: Works cited in note 38.

Notes:

[1] The first numbers are cases, the second number following the dash are persons slated for execution. For simplicity, not guilty, clergy, remanded and at large conclusions are not segregated here, and 'slated for execution' means a verdict to hang without information on that outcome.

[2] Children are aged 12 and under; no other ages are given for victims named 'children'.

[3] Teens include daughters who are not listed as children.

[4] 'Women Unspecified' includes for Elizabeth's reign three servants of Essex (accused deemed not guilty) and one of Sussex, for which the accused was found guilty and hanged.

[37] Walker, 'Everyman or a monster?'.

The extant assize court records from the reign of Elizabeth I through that of Charles II also provide instructive context. As most prosecutions for rape as such were tried at the common law at the county assizes, we can examine those for the Home Counties in the reigns of Elizabeth I and James I from the prodigious calendar of assize records produced for those counties by the late Professor James Cockburn.[38] The results of those cases are presented in the table above.[39]

Of the 119 cases, eighty-nine come from Elizabeth's reign and thirty from James's. What is striking is that about 40% of the cases are of children aged two to twelve, and in only nine of those cases (19%) did the culprit face hanging. Overall, excluding children, the rate of men sentenced to hang was 25%. While the annual number of child cases did not change from one reign to the other, the hanging sentence rate for all cases changed from 20% in Elizabeth's reign to 30% in James's, but in children's cases from 12.5% to 33%. The latter figures suggest that sentencing for such cases increased significantly in the reign of James. Whether these cases were rape, ravishment or sexual molestation is unclear; it is difficult to explain such a sharp increase in sentencing.

Several cases in the Home County assize records address some of the issues that shaped prosecutions. While a wife was considered something akin to the property of her husband, one case suggests that a similar view prevailed for men and their lovers, as John Davey, shoemaker, raped his 'mistress' Agnes Wood and was found not guilty.[40] Incestuous attacks differed: Edmund Hammond, yeoman, raped his daughter Anne, aged eighteen, and was sentenced to hang.[41] Evidence does not appear to be a factor in all cases. For example, Nicholas Nicholas, shoemaker, assaulted Elizabeth, wife of Thomas Riffe, with a bearing-bill and a dagger; her husband Thomas, a weaver, and Richard Baker, a husbandman, gave evidence but Nicholas was found not guilty.[42] When John Vivvars, labourer, was charged with raping Catherine Belgrave, aged ten, three men (two farmers and a baker)

[38] The series edited by J. S. Cockburn: *Calendar of Assize Records: Essex Indictments, Elizabeth I* (London, 1978); and the following edited volumes: *Essex Indictments, James I* (London, 1982); *Hertfordshire Indictments, Elizabeth I* (London, 1975); *Hertfordshire Indictments, James I* (London, 1975); *Kent Indictments, Elizabeth I* (London, 1979); *Kent Indictments, James I* (London, 1980); *Surrey Indictments, Elizabeth I* (London, 1980); *Surrey Indictments, James I* (London, 1982); *Sussex Indictments, Elizabeth I* (London, 1975); *Sussex Indictments, James I* (London, 1975). What follows builds upon work done by Bashar, 'Rape'.

[39] There is a similar tabulation by Martin Ingram for the Home Counties 1558–1625, but only for prosecutions by reign and victim age groups: Ingram, 'Child sexual abuse'.

[40] *Surrey Indictments, Elizabeth I*, item 733.

[41] *Essex Indictments, James I*, items 460, 462, 511–12.

[42] *Surrey Indictments, Elizabeth I*, items 42, 45.

gave recognizances to give evidence on behalf of their wives, along with Catherine's father (a farmer), mother and herself, but he was found not guilty.[43] One could also avoid prosecution: Edward Sharp, brewer, charged with raping Elizabeth Withers, aged nine, on 1 November 1580, stood mute and was sentenced to the ancient sanction of *peine forte et dure*.[44]

But prosecution was still feared. That factored into the dread of being summoned for a rape as witnessed by Anthony Cass, labourer, who in a coroner's inquest was found guilty of murdering Judith Smith, a servant girl, out of fear she would reveal that he had 'ravished' her; he took her into a field, broke her neck and threw her into a pond.[45] Sometimes a murder investigation also revealed a previous rape that had not resulted in charges, as in Richard ap Bevan, petty chapman, who appeared before a coroner's inquest for the murder of Agnes New, aged six; he raped her on 17 November 1599 and she 'lingered' and died of the injuries on 17 March 1600.[46] Sentencing was not always according to the criminal law, as judges often used their discretion. For example, Gerson Gerard, labourer, was found not guilty on charges that he had raped a woman aged twenty, but was sent to the House of Correction for a month.[47] John King, yeoman, charged with raping Joan Taylor, aged five, was found not guilty but bound over for good behaviour.[48]

Several offenders were charged with multiple rapes. Henry Walker of Southwark, joiner, was charged with assaulting Mary More, aged six, daughter of a joiner's family, on 28 August 1611, and Gartred Wastall, aged five, daughter of a similar family of Southwark, on 30 August 1611, but found not guilty of both.[49] Richard Jackson, husbandman, raped Mary Goodlad, aged ten, Rachel Bonner and Liddia Duke, both aged eleven, on 2 February 1619, and then raped Elizabeth Dagnett, aged twelve, on 10 January 1620; prosecuted at the time of the last assault, he was convicted and hanged.[50] A more complex scenario was that of John Rich, miner, accused of raping his servants Elizabeth Harris on 26 June 1566 and Catherine Burrell on 10 June 1567; tried for the latter, he was found guilty and hanged. John Smith,

[43] *Surrey Indictments, James I*, item 1305.
[44] *Surrey Indictments, James I*, item 1256.
[45] *Essex Indictments, Elizabeth I*, items 2264, 2270–1.
[46] *Sussex Indictments, Elizabeth I,* item 1929.
[47] *Essex Indictments, James I*, items 1258, 1302–3.
[48] *Surrey Indictments, James I*, items 234, 241–2.
[49] *Surrey Indictments, James I*, items 424, 421–42.
[50] *Surrey Indictments, James I*, items 1450, 1454, 1457.

another miner at Ashburnham, was accused of raping Catherine, who was Smith's servant, on 10 June 1567, but found not guilty.[51]

In Kent, there is the case of John Henshaw of Deptford, tailor, who allegedly raped Elizabeth Rowson, aged eight, on 3 February 1583; Alice Keeling, aged six, on 28 August 1584 at the house of Richard Halpeny; and then Agnes Keeling, aged seven, in the same house on 28 August 1584; he was found not guilty on all counts.[52] Prosecutions of rape in Kent continued, albeit at a slower pace, in the succeeding sixty years. The assize records for 1625–85 document thirteen cases in the reign of Charles I (0.5 yearly), twelve in the Interregnum (1.0 yearly), and nineteen in the reign of Charles II (0.76 yearly). Clearly the prosecutions increased between 1650 and 1685, while the number of prosecutions for assaults on children declined dramatically. Instead, most of the alleged victims were wives, spinsters and widows. A major change occurred with regard to outcomes. In Elizabeth's reign no accusations were thrown out by grand juries as *ignoramus* or unfit for trial. Most of the accused were deemed to be at large (78%). Things changed in the Interregnum, when seven accusations were found *ignoramus* and four of the accused not guilty, and in the reign of Charles II twelve were found *ignoramus* and only three not guilty. Obviously grand juries preferred to make no finding rather than to send these accusations to trial, which suggests a view to ignore them.[53]

Generally, then, rape was not much prosecuted. But turning to the socio-economic and religious background in Kent and the adjoining Home Counties around the time of the Snargate assaults provides context for the unusual decision to pursue this case with rigour and in Star Chamber.[54] The year 1597 brought a plague to the region, where a major decline in the cloth industry led to an unstable economy and a fall in property values. It also contributed to a rise of religious non-conformity in rural country parishes.[55] The region had been a breeding ground of Lollards from the 1420s, later supporting 'sacramentarianism' and its vernacular heresy in the 1550s; many Marian exiles hid in the marshes of Kent; and John Foxe's files reveal

[51] *Sussex Indictments, Elizabeth I*, items 239, 248, 250.

[52] *Kent Indictments, Elizabeth I*, items 1351, 1369, 1371.

[53] The later volumes of Cockburn's *Calendar of Assize Records* for Kent: *Kent Indictments, Charles I* (London, 1995); *Kent Indictments, 1649–1659* (London, 1989); *Kent Indictments, Charles II 1660–1675* (London, 1995); and *Kent Indictments, Charles II 1676–1688* (London, 1997).

[54] See in general, A. Kussmaul, *A General View of the Rural Economy of England, 1538–1840* (Cambridge, 1990).

[55] A. Everitt, 'Nonconformity in country parishes', in *Land, Church and People*, *Agricultural History Review* supplement, xviii (1970), 174–6.

inhabitants who denied Christ's divinity and the doctrine of the Trinity.[56] It was considered a 'sickly and contagious country' because of its marsh fog or 'vapors' that made it a 'sink hole', had a population that comprised about ten persons and hundreds of sheep per square mile.[57]

The view of Patrick Collinson is instructive: this was an expanding community of sin where puritans were accelerating their work.[58] While towns such as New Romney and Rye were puritan by the 1590s, the *classis* movement in the Church was promoting puritan ministers in rural parishes and even a printer – John Stroud at Smarden. Puritan efforts extended into the realm of education and the schools, where Thomas Good of Cranbrook taught a reformed church. A flurry of non-traditional forenames such as Comfort, Faintnot, Freegift, Mercy and Wellabroad began to fill the parish registers. Such activities mirrored the scene in Coke's homeland, and he must have seen the resemblance.

A remaining question is: where does Coke fit into this mosaic? For background, he spent much of his twenties and thirties as a lawyer in defending puritans and puritan sympathizers in slander cases – many of which he lost through technicalities.[59] Afterwards, he did the same as a crown prosecutor riding the Norfolk assize circuit on horseback from 1576 through 1602, and as recorder of Norwich and London from 1591, where he was the judge of its criminal courts of oyer and terminer and gaol delivery.[60] As attorney general in the late 1590s, he led vigorous prosecutions of Catholics such as Dr Lopez and Edward Squire, and the Jesuits John Gerard and Henry Walpole. He also staked out a corner of Gray's Inn Fields to trap Italian courtiers who served the Roman Catholic establishment. His prosecutorial energy continued in the Star Chamber, where, as attorney general between 1584 and 1606, he preferred more cases than any other Elizabethan official.[61]

Coke was also a man of religion and emotion. He was the eldest of ten children, of whom eight were female. Most of his sisters became puritans or separatists, including his favourite sister Ann. Ann married the puritan Francis Stubbs, a college friend of Coke, whose sister married the puritan Thomas Cartwright. A light of Coke's life, his sister Ann raised puritan

56 Everitt, 'Nonconformity', pp. 176–86.

57 W. Lambarde, *A Perambulation of Kent* (London, 1570), pp. 104–17.

58 Everitt, 'Nonconformity', pp. 186–9.

59 A. D. Boyer, *Sir Edward Coke and the Elizabethan Age* (Stanford, 2011), pp. 59–78.

60 Boyer, *Coke*, pp. 189–93, 215–18.

61 *KAL Star Chamber*, where in 1602 Coke prosecuted cases involving purveyance, engrossing and riots, pp. 4–10. For his role on the court, see pp. xix–xx, xxiv–xxvi. The cases of attorneys general are derived from my search of the records.

children, catechized her servants and sponsored Calvinist preachers. She viewed the Scriptures not as men's words but as tongues from the heart.[62] Coke went to Trinity College, Cambridge with Thomas Cartwright, who preached hotly on the primitive Church and whom he befriended. Coke's law chambers at the Inner Temple were those of the earl of Leicester, and many of his clients were puritans of East Anglia.

Coke was outwardly conventional in matters of religion and a defender of the Anglican Church as he dedicated his life to serving God and continuing the reformation of the established Church.[63] Privately, his sister and cousins married into puritan households, and the ministers he patronized and placed into Church livings wore no surplices, omitted ceremonies and taught Protestant theology in unlicensed schools. He attracted sermons from 'Godly divines' who characterized him as one of the 'Elect'. Thus he railed against priests, spoke well of Lollards, found church livings for the children of relatives and instructed his children on the sins of bribery, simony, usury and avoidance of physical excesses. He held such views emotionally, wept when honoured, and was seen weeping when sentencing criminals to death and crying at executions.[64] Therefore, he took his religion and emotions seriously, which also may account for his long delays at Star Chamber proceedings when he was examining the earl of Essex and the men in his revolt.

Professionally, Coke's litigation of cases was known as plodding. A man who began work at 3:00am, he was pedantic, would leave no stone unturned and would not be rushed by the press of time. This may explain why there was so much time in between his moves in prosecuting this rape case. But when it came down to the evidence, his examinations of the culprits and witnesses were seldom matched in the court's proceedings. The strength of his work was all the more impressive as he was very short-sighted by 1602, and most of his reading and writing had to be done in daylight or by candle. He would maintain this prodigious workload for another thirty-odd years, which is a testament to his fortitude.

That Coke would listen to the appeals of two puritan ministers in the marshlands of Kent and work their case into his busy schedule for the state is thus not as surprising as it first seems. He was noted for his zeal against troublesome youth and a hatred of physical violence. In Henry Stafford he had an ally with similar goals – the reformation of the Church and stamping

[62] Boyer, *Coke*, pp. 6–24, 172–5.

[63] See in general D. C. Smith, 'Sir Edward Coke: faith, law and the search for stability in Reformation England', in *Great Christian Jurists in English History*, ed. M. Hill and R. H. Helmholz (Cambridge, 2018), pp. 93–113.

[64] Boyer, *Coke*, pp. 184–8, 204–6.

out the activities of violent youths. Stafford was becoming a landowner, and by 1606 owned marshland in Romney and was the clerk and vicar of the town and port of New Romney, which had become a puritan centre of the region.[65] He was also noted as the town clerk.[66] There was an environmental connection, too. The administrative hundred where Coke began his landed empire in the marshy region of central Norfolk, raising sheep and cattle for the London market, was not dissimilar.

In conclusion, there are a number of threads which can be woven to reveal how this future chief justice of England stepped into Romney Marsh, a region defined by contemporary observers as 'Evill in Winter, grievous in Sommer, and never good', in the midst of high affairs of state, to place his standard on the behaviour of aspiring young men of local landed society, behaviour of a sort not often prosecuted in the regular criminal courts. With several privy councillors sitting as judges in Star Chamber, they could not but be impressed by the work Coke had undertaken and the slew of effective evidence he presented, which left no room for anything but heavy sentences.

While Coke would go on to become a lynchpin for the future of the common law,[67] in this case he sent a stirring message to the people of Romney Marsh via his efforts in Star Chamber. The courts of early modern England were a matrix of jurisdictions, often overlapping. This multiplicity allowed prosecutions of actions in more than one court, with people who found themselves unable to get justice in one court free to turn to another. The value of Star Chamber was that it allowed prosecutions of amorphously defined wrongs; in this instance, a brutal case of multiple sexual assaults that could at least be tried as violent disorder, pushed forward by puritan reformers and the ally they found in Coke. Star Chamber's value laid in part in that court's broad power to enforce its investigatory processes and to make extensive use of written examinations for testimony – testimony that would be preserved for posterity. Because of that fact, our study of its history enables us to respond to Frederick William Maitland's plea to discover 'The Shallows and Silences of Real Life'.[68]

[65] *Kent at Law 1602, Volume VI. The Court of Wards and Liveries*, ed. L. A. Knafla (London, 2016), a court suit at item 8.

[66] *KAL Local Jurisdictions*, item 3370, a suit before the Romney Marsh Court of Civil Pleas.

[67] The recent major study of his legal career by D. C. Smith, *Sir Edward Coke and the Reformation of the Law: Religion, Politics and Jurisprudence, 1578–1616* (Cambridge, 2019).

[68] L. A. Knafla, '"Sin of all sorts swarmeth": criminal litigation in an English county in the early seventeenth century', in *Law, Litigation and the Legal Profession*, ed. E. W. Ives and A. H. Manchester (London, 1983), pp. 50–67, at p. 66.

5. 'By reason of her sex and widowhood': an early modern Welsh gentlewoman in the court of Star Chamber*

Sadie Jarrett

In 1608, Dame Margaret Lloyd (1565–1650) sued her younger brother, John Salesbury (1575–1611), in the court of Star Chamber. John was the head of the Salesbury family and the owner of their estates at Rhug in Merionethshire and Bachymbyd in Denbighshire, North Wales. Margaret, a widow, accused John of assembling armed men and instructing them to enter her house in Denbighshire with force and threaten the lives of those in the household. John countered that Margaret lived in the house illegally and that she had abducted her young son from his rightful guardian. This is a classic example of a forcible entry case, and Margaret presented herself as a woman maintaining the boundaries of her home.[1] However, Margaret's suit also provides a rare insight into the relationship between a Welsh gentlewoman and her male relatives at a time when Wales was adapting to laws which sometimes conflicted with Welsh gentry society's established views on women. Margaret's suit demonstrates perceptions of acceptable female behaviour in early modern Wales, and how the male kindred responded to perceived transgressions. The case is particularly pertinent in early seventeenth-century Denbighshire, a former marcher lordship of North Wales that was only two generations removed from Welsh laws which limited a woman's ability to hold land, and where custom still preferred male kinsmen over mothers as the guardians of a deceased man's children.

* This chapter appears in S. Jarrett, '"Of great kindred and alliance": the status and identity of the Salesburys of Rhug and Bachymbyd, *c.*1475–*c.*1660' (unpublished Bangor University PhD thesis, 2020). I am grateful to Huw Pryce and Shaun Evans for their comments and suggestions on previous drafts.

[1] For a detailed analysis of Welsh women's involvement in forcible entry cases at Star Chamber, see N. Whyte, '"With a sword drawne in her hande": defending the boundaries of household space in seventeenth-century Wales', in *Women, Agency and the Law, 1300–1700*, ed. B. Kane and F. Williamson (London, 2013), pp. 141–55.

S. Jarrett, '"By reason of her sex and widowhood": an early modern Welsh gentlewoman in the court of Star Chamber' in *Star Chamber Matters: An Early Modern Court and Its Records*, ed. K. Kesselring and N. Mears (London, 2021), pp. 79–96.

This chapter uses the example of Margaret Lloyd to highlight the role of widows in Welsh gentry society. Importantly, although Margaret Lloyd ostensibly had limited agency, she was able to access Star Chamber and had recourse to sue her brother. Deborah Youngs has noted the untapped potential of the records of Star Chamber to understand the ability of early modern women to access justice.[2] After a brief assessment of the limited historiography on early modern Welsh women, this chapter begins with a consideration of the cultural perceptions of women in late medieval and early modern Wales. Next, it examines the effects of the Acts of Union (1536 and 1543) on people's access to justice in Wales. It then looks at widowhood in early modern Wales and the Salesbury family itself to demonstrate Margaret's position within the family and wider society. Finally, it presents a critical analysis of Margaret's Star Chamber suit and John Salesbury's answer to her bill, and places their respective arguments within the context of Welsh gentry society. Although John unsurprisingly claimed he was not guilty, there are notable gaps in his account where he did not deny Margaret's story, including the threats of violence. The chapter argues that the constructed stories within the suit, truthful or not, provide valuable evidence of Margaret Lloyd's relationship with her male kindred.[3] The suit presents Margaret Lloyd as a confident agent within the constraints of a patriarchal society.

The history of women at all levels of society in early modern Wales lacks much comprehensive research. In Michael Roberts's words, 'men loom very large' in early modern Wales.[4] In 2004, Christine Peters surveyed the historiography of early modern women in Britain and found little work on Wales.[5] Katharine Swett comments that, although there are rich enquiries into early modern English women and a burgeoning interest in the Welsh gentry, studies of early modern women in England do not include Welsh women, and studies of the early modern Welsh gentry do not include women at all.[6] John Gwynfor Jones's pioneering 1998 book on the Welsh gentry focuses almost entirely on men, even when discussing the family and the household, areas of gentry life which might reasonably be

[2] D. Youngs, '"A besy woman … and full of lawe": female litigants in early Tudor Star Chamber', *Journal of British Studies*, lviii (2019), 735–50, at p. 736.

[3] For the usefulness of constructed accounts, see N. Z. Davis, *Fiction in the Archives: Pardon Tales and their Tellers in Sixteenth-Century France* (Oxford, 1988).

[4] M. Roberts, 'Introduction', in *Women and Gender in Early Modern Wales*, ed. M. Roberts and S. Clarke (Cardiff, 2000), pp. 1–13, at p. 1.

[5] C. Peters, *Women in Early Modern Britain, 1450–1640* (Basingstoke, 2004).

[6] K. W. Swett, 'Widowhood, custom and property in early modern Wales', *Welsh History Review*, xviii (1996), 189–227, at p. 189.

expected to include women.[7] To an extent, this lack of research on early modern Welsh women stems from an absence of easily available sources: men dominated administrative and legal life in Wales and women often appear in the historical record only at the time of their marriage and after their husband's death. Simone Clarke notes the 'scarcity ... of anecdotal accounts and personal papers written by women or about women [in pre-modern Wales]'.[8] Medieval and early modern Welsh poetry, a potentially important source of information on the lives of women, presents them as 'girls' or 'mothers', linguistic stereotypes which hint at their expected role in society.[9] The poetry also emphasizes women's expected roles in the household, with a focus on providing hospitality and charity.[10] It is a challenge to find women in many of the surviving sources of early modern Wales, and the current historiography of early modern Welsh women is limited.[11] This is in stark contrast to the many studies of early modern women at multiple social levels in England, and it is all too easy to assume that the experiences of Welsh women were identical to those of their English counterparts.[12]

This is a mistaken approach because early modern Wales was distinct, culturally and socially, from its neighbour. As such, one should be open to the ways in which the roles of women in Welsh society differed from those of their English counterparts. The medieval Welsh legal system had significantly limited women's right to hold or inherit land, and society

[7] J. G. Jones, *The Welsh Gentry 1536–1640: Images of Status, Honour and Authority* (Cardiff, 1998, repr. 2016), ch. 6. However, Jones also contributed one of the few existing studies of early modern Welsh gentlewomen (J. G. Jones, 'Welsh gentlewomen: piety and Christian conduct, *c.*1560–1700', *Journal of Welsh Religious History*, vii (1999), 1–37).

[8] S. Clark, 'The construction of genteel sensibilities: the socialization of daughters of the gentry in seventeenth- and eighteenth-century Wales', in *Our Daughters' Land: Past and Present*, ed. S. Betts (Cardiff, 1996), pp. 55–79, at p. 56.

[9] M. Roberts, 'Gender, work and socialization in Wales *c.*1450–*c.*1850', in Betts, *Our Daughters' Land*, pp. 15–54, at p. 24.

[10] See D. Johnston, 'Lewys Glyn Cothi, Bardd y Gwragedd', *Taliesin*, lxxiv (1991), 68–77; and S. Davies, 'Y ferch yng Nghymru yn yr Oesoedd Canol', *Cof Cenedl*, ix (1994), 3–32.

[11] This contrasts with the burgeoning historiography of women in Wales before the Acts of Union (1536 and 1543). See, e.g., S. M. Johns, *Gender, Nation and Conquest in the High Middle Ages: Nest of Deheubarth* (Manchester, 2013); the work of E. Cavell, including 'Widows, native law and the long shadow of England in thirteenth-century Wales', *English Historical Review*, cxxxiii (2018), 1387–419; and the work of D. Youngs, including '"For the Preferement of their Marriage and Bringing Upp in their Youth": the education and training of young Welshwomen, *c.*1450–*c.*1550', *Welsh History Review*, xxv (2011), 463–85.

[12] For an overview of the historiography on women in early modern England, see Peters, *Women in Early Modern Britain*. Recent research includes L. L. Peck, *Women of Fortune: Money, Marriage, and Murder in Early Modern England* (Cambridge, 2018); *Women and the Land 1500–1900*, ed. A. L. Capern, B. McDonagh and J. Aston, (Woodbridge, 2019).

prioritized the importance of the male kindred.[13] Under Welsh law, land ultimately belonged to this kindred and, after a man's death, his holdings transferred to his nearest male relatives within four generations. Inheritance was partible, rather than primogenital.[14] Parts of the Welsh legal system remained in use until the sixteenth century and there is also evidence of later, unofficial survival, particularly in inheritance practices which continued to provide for younger sons.[15] Women did hold land in medieval Wales: heiresses were crucial to the establishment of the Mostyn family, for example.[16] Nevertheless, women were significantly disadvantaged by Welsh law and, although the Welsh legal system officially ended in 1536, it continued to exert cultural power.[17] However, in a gentry society which valued ancestry over wealth, Welsh women had significant cultural importance.[18] For instance, the Welsh gentry depicted their ancestors in '*achau'r mamau*', elaborate pedigrees in the maternal line which traced their mothers' descent from important figures in Welsh history and legend.[19] Welsh bards praised women for their illustrious ancestors and importance within the household. For example, when Rhys Cain praised Katherine ferch Ieuan, the wife of Robert Salesbury (d. 1550) of Rhug and Bachymbyd, he described her as the '*merch gwyrwallt marchog euraid*' ['yellowish-red-haired daughter of a golden knight'] and warned Robert '*cadw'r lloer i gadw'r llys*' ['to guard the beautiful woman (lit. moon) to guard the court'].[20] This emphasized that a wife was central in a gentry *plasty*, loosely translated as country house; Katherine's presence was vital for the continued success of the household. Culturally, as demonstrated in praise poetry, gentlewomen were valued as wives and mothers, but also as fulcrums of the *plasty*.

[13] R. R. Davies, 'The status of women and the practice of marriage', in *The Welsh Law of Women*, ed. D. Jenkins and M. E. Owen (Cardiff, 1980), pp. 93–114, at pp. 100–1.

[14] See T. M. Charles-Edwards, *Early Irish and Welsh Kinship* (Oxford, 1993), ch. 4.

[15] R. R. Davies, 'The twilight of Welsh law, 1284–1536', *History*, li (1996), 143–64; G. Owen and D. Cahill, 'A blend of English and Welsh law in late medieval and Tudor Wales: innovation and mimicry of native settlement patterns in Wales', *Irish Jurist*, lviii (2017), 153–83.

[16] A. D. Carr, 'The Mostyn family and estate, 1200–1642' (unpublished University of Wales PhD thesis, 1975), pp. 1–2.

[17] S. Parkin, 'Witchcraft, women's honour and customary law in early modern Wales', *Social History*, xxxi (2006), 295–318; Owen and Cahill, 'A blend of English and Welsh law'.

[18] J. G. Jones, 'Concepts of order and gentility', in *Class, Community and Culture in Tudor Wales*, ed. J. G. Jones (Cardiff, 1989), pp. 121–57, at p. 126.

[19] See B. Guy, 'Writing genealogy in Wales, *c.*1475–*c.*1640: sources and practitioners', in *Genealogical Knowledge in the Making: Tools, Practices, and Evidence in Early Modern Europe*, ed. J. Eickmeyer, M. Friedrich and V. Bauer (Berlin, 2019), pp. 99–125, at pp. 103–4.

[20] A. L. Hughes, 'Noddwyr y beirdd yn Sir Feirionnydd' (unpublished University of Wales, Aberystwyth MA thesis, 1969), p. 584.

In 1536, the 'Act for Laws and Justice to be Ministered in Wales in like form as it is in this Realm', more commonly known today as the 1536 Act of Union, extended the English legal system to the whole of Wales. Coupled with the supplementary 1543 act, the Acts of Union officially swept away the remaining vestiges of Welsh law. The daily administration of Wales was now overseen by the Council in the Marches, which also acted as a court of law for Wales. However, Welsh litigants could also access the central courts in London. This included the court of Star Chamber, where Margaret Lloyd sued her brother. In 1929, Ifan ab Owen Edwards calendared many of the Welsh cases in Star Chamber and emphasized the court's importance to the Welsh gentry: they used it as a court of appeal away from the influence of their rivals.[21] The legal jurisdictions of the Council in the Marches and Star Chamber overlapped: both dealt with issues of corruption, oppression and violence, and inhabitants of Wales and the Marches could start a suit in both or either court.[22] It is a matter of debate whether the Welsh gentry were more or less inclined to use Star Chamber than their English counterparts; they are often described as litigious, but statistical analysis is not helped by the process of suit and countersuit, as well as the tendency for plaintiffs to begin suits on the same matter in the various courts available to them, or indeed the wrong court for the matter in question.[23] Social and political factors affected the likelihood of the Welsh gentry choosing to plead their suit in Star Chamber; Howell Lloyd calculates that Denbighshire, accounting for 9.9% of Wales's population, provided 16.9% of Wales's Star Chamber suits and highlights a marked increase in Welsh cases at Star Chamber during the dispute between the earls of Pembroke and Essex in the 1590s.[24] Suits involving women were rare, and Tim Stretton believes they comprised just 8.5% of cases during the reign of James I.[25] Thus, it stands to reason that suits involving Welsh women were even rarer. Using Deborah Youngs's calculations, for the 190 or so Welsh cases brought to Star Chamber during the reign of Henry VIII, sole women, predominantly widows, were complainants in 7% of cases, or 0.28% of the estimated 5,000 total suits.[26]

[21] I. ab Owen Edwards, *A Catalogue of Star Chamber Proceedings Relating to Wales* (Cardiff, 1929), p. iv.

[22] See P. H. Williams, 'The Star Chamber and the Council in the Marches of Wales, 1558–1603', *Bulletin of the Board of Celtic Studies*, xvi (1956), 287–96.

[23] H. A. Lloyd, *The Gentry of South-West Wales, 1540–1640* (Cardiff, 1968), pp. 167–9.

[24] H. A. Lloyd, 'Wales and Star Chamber: a rejoinder', *Welsh History Review*, v (1970), 257–60, at pp. 258–60.

[25] T. Stretton, *Women Waging Law in Elizabethan England* (Cambridge, 1998), p. 40, n. 80.

[26] D. Youngs, '"She hym fresshely folowed and pursued": women and Star Chamber in

The Salesburys of Rhug and Bachymbyd were an early modern gentry family with their powerbase in northeast Wales.[27] They were one of the many cadet branches of the Salusburys of Lleweni, who moved from the English estates of Henry de Lacy, earl of Lincoln, to settle in his new marcher lordship of Denbigh, created after Edward I's conquest of Wales in 1282/3. From the 1470s, John, a younger son of Thomas Salusbury of Lleweni, began purchasing a small estate at Bachymbyd, near Ruthin, and his son Piers acquired the Rhug estate in Merionethshire through his marriage to Margaret Wen, a Welsh heiress. By the mid sixteenth century, the Salesburys of Rhug and Bachymbyd also owned much of the land in the valley between their two estates, a distance of about fifteen miles. With estates in both Merionethshire and Denbighshire, the Salesburys had access to political offices in two counties, as well as a large network of relationships through their tenants and servants. The Salesburys were also part of an extended kindred, one of the multiple branches of the Salusbury family in North Wales, and fully embedded in Welsh gentry society. Within their local community, the Salesburys were powerful, wealthy and conscious of their status. This status was based on their pedigree, the illustriousness of their ancestors, which gave the Welsh gentry a God-given right to own land and hold authority. In early modern Wales, the gentry were also increasingly influenced by European humanist ideals, filtered through their own cultural understanding of their role in society.[28] The Salesburys were embedded in the world of the early modern Welsh gentry, established in their position by the late fifteenth century and connected to other families through extensive marriage and kinship bonds. The Salesburys understood the ideals and expectations of Welsh gentry society, even if they did not always abide by them.

Margaret Lloyd was born in 1565, the eldest child of John Salesbury (1533–80) and his wife, Elizabeth Salusbury (d. *c.*1584) of Lleweni (see figure 5.1).[29] When John Salesbury died in November 1580, he named three

---

early Tudor Wales', in *Women, Agency and the Law, 1300–1700*, ed. B. Kane and F. Williamson (London, 2013), pp. 73–85, at p. 75.

[27] For existing work on the family, see W. J. Smith, 'Introduction', in *Calendar of Salusbury Correspondence, 1553–c.1700*, ed. W. J. Smith (Cardiff, 1954), pp. 1–19; E. G. Jones and W. J. Smith, 'Salusbury, Salesbury family, of Rug and Bachymbyd', in *Dictionary of Welsh Biography* (1959) <https://biography.wales/article/s-SALU-RUG-1525> [accessed 8 June 2020]; and S. Jarrett, 'Credibility in the court of Chancery: Salesbury v Bagot, 1671–1677', *The Seventeenth Century* xxxvi (2021), 55–79, doi: 10.1080/0268117X.2019.1694060. The spelling 'Salesbury' reflects the family's own practice, though Salusbury was common among other branches.

[28] Jones, *Welsh Gentry*, ch. 2.

[29] North East Wales Archives, Ruthin (Denbighshire Record Office), DD/DM/1647, fo. 26r.

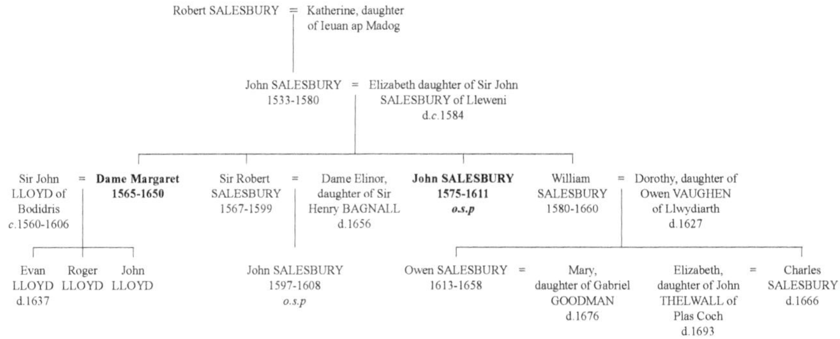

Figure 5.1: Key members of the Salesbury family.

children in his will: the future Sir Robert (1567–99), John and Margaret.[30] He also included his posthumous child, a third son called William (1580–1660). Sir Robert was the heir and received the Salesbury patrimony; John, the second son, received the park and township of Segrwyd, Denbighshire; and Margaret received a marriage portion of £800 from the profits of the Salesbury estates.[31] Not long after the death of her father, Margaret married the future Sir John Lloyd (*c.*1560–1606) of Bodidris, Denbighshire. Like most of the Salesbury women, little survives of Margaret's time as a wife. However, the marriage created or confirmed a successful alliance. Sir John Lloyd was a close associate of Margaret's brother, John Salesbury, and they served as soldiers together, both participating in the earl of Essex's 1601 revolt.[32] The two men were also joint antagonists of the Salesburys' cousins, the powerful Salusburys of Lleweni, and they supported the candidacy of their ringleader, Sir Richard Trevor of Trevalyn, against Sir John Salusbury of Lleweni in the schismatic Denbighshire parliamentary election of October 1601.[33] Sir John Lloyd died in 1606 in Newry, Ireland, where he held land, and Dame Margaret Lloyd became a widow. Their eldest son, Evan Lloyd (d. 1637), inherited the family estates and divided his time between North Wales and Ireland.[34] Meanwhile, Margaret's brother and the Salesbury heir, Sir Robert Salesbury, died of an illness in 1599, leaving the estates to his young son, John.[35] The boy died aged ten on 1 January 1608 and his uncle,

[30] The National Archives of the UK, PROB 11/63/70.

[31] National Library of Wales, Bachymbyd Letters 48.

[32] A. H. Dodd, 'North Wales in the Essex Revolt of 1601', *English Historical Review*, lix (1944), 348–70, at pp. 366–8.

[33] J. E. Neale, 'Three Elizabethan elections', *English Historical Review*, xlvi (1931), 209–38, at pp. 218–27.

[34] R. Morgan, *The Welsh and the Shaping of Early Modern Ireland, 1558–1641* (Woodbridge, 2014), p. 118.

[35] TNA, PROB 11/96/125.

John Salesbury, inherited the family estates and became the patriarch of the Salesbury family.[36] In the same year, Margaret sued John in the court of Star Chamber.

Widowhood could be a dangerous time for a gentry family. It risked alienating the widow's land from the estate for an unknown and potentially lengthy number of years, with the added threat that a widow could remarry and temporarily subsume the land into another family's estate. On the other hand, gentry families also contained daughters who could be potentially widowed, and it was in a family's interest to negotiate a good settlement in the event of their son-in-law's death. Under English common law, a widow received a dower, a life interest in a third of any freehold land her husband had possessed during marriage, while manorial law made provision for widows to receive a proportion of their husbands' copyhold land. From the sixteenth century, the growing practice of jointure, commonly agreed in a marriage settlement along with the wife's portion size, provided a widow with an interest in property or an annuity from property that might be less than a third, replacing her right to dower in a manner that left her husband's freehold land free of traditional encumbrances.[37] Under ecclesiastical law, a widow was entitled to a third of her husband's moveable goods, or half if they had no children.[38] In contrast, reflecting the limitations on women holding land under medieval Welsh law, Wales retained customary provision for widows which entitled them to a proportion, usually a third, of their husband's moveable goods, but no land. This proportion increased to a half under the custom of North Wales. The Acts of Union did not affect customary widowhood provision, and Wales retained the custom of a widow's entitlement to part of her husband's moveable goods until 1696.[39] Widows ostensibly had a right to claim dower from the thirteenth century, following Edward I's attempts to compel dower provision throughout Wales in the 1284 Statute of Rhuddlan. However, there remained a distinction between Welsh and English land tenure, with only the latter dowered.[40] After the Acts of Union, all land was held under English tenure and widows could claim dower in addition to the customary provision of moveable goods. The receipt of a jointure, however, forfeited any customary entitlement, a

[36] NLW, Bachymbyd 490.

[37] A. L. Erickson, *Women and Property in Early Modern England* (London, 1993, repr. 2002) pp. 24–5.

[38] Erickson, *Women and Property*, p. 28.

[39] For a detailed exploration of early modern widowhood provision in North Wales, see Swett, 'Widowhood, custom and property'.

[40] Davies, 'The status of women', pp. 101–2.

more advantageous situation for a gentry estate as the heir received all its moveable goods not bequeathed by last will and testament, which included livestock. A widow's entitlement to livestock challenged the gentry's efforts at estate-building, and it was in the estate's interest to provide a jointure to women who married into the family. The jointure enabled a woman to support herself as a widow and the land would be subsumed back into the estate after her death. It was also possible for families to use Welsh or English widowhood provision in different circumstances. For example, Katharine Swett sees the decision of Sir John Wynn (1553–1627) of Gwydir to use the English practice of jointure for his sons' marriages and Welsh customary provision for his daughters' marriages as a father tailoring marriages in his children's best interests.[41] However, Christine Peters challenges her interpretation, suggesting it shows only that Sir John had different levels of negotiating power when he organized marriages with English families.[42]

The Salesburys of Rhug and Bachymbyd rapidly adopted the practice of jointure: from the late sixteenth century, they settled jointures on their wives, with its inheritance secured for the couple's legitimate children. Margaret Lloyd's oldest brother, Sir Robert (d. 1599) provided a jointure for his wife, Elinor Bagnall, who died fifty-seven years after Sir Robert in 1656.[43] In 1608, when Margaret Lloyd sued her middle brother, John, in Star Chamber, part of John's estates was therefore reserved for their widowed sister-in-law, Elinor, and it would not return to the Salesburys' control for almost fifty years. After John Salesbury's death in 1611, the estates passed to Margaret's youngest brother, William (1580–1660). In 1617, William settled the entirety of the Rhug estate on his wife, Dorothy (d. 1627), for her jointure and afterwards to their eldest son, Owen, then in tail to William's heirs, first his sons, then his daughters, then his right heirs.[44] This was a generous grant during a time of financial trouble for the Salesbury estates, and it demonstrates particularly well how marriage settlements protected a wife's interest in property, as well as the interests of the couple's children.[45] A jointure could protect a family's future and it often gave gentlewomen control of significant amounts of land as widows. In 1645, William and his younger son Charles (d. 1666) agreed a marriage

[41] Swett, 'Widowhood, custom and property', p. 207.

[42] Peters, *Women in Early Modern Britain*, p. 39.

[43] Gwynedd Archives, Caernarfon, XD2/494.

[44] NLW, Bachymbyd 729.

[45] See A. L. Erickson, 'Common law versus common practice: the use of marriage settlements in early modern England', *Economic History Review*, 2nd series, xliii (1990), 21–39.

settlement with John Thelwall, the father of Charles's future wife, Elizabeth (d. 1693). Among other holdings, the settlement provided the Pool Park estate, an extension of the Salesburys' estate at Bachymbyd, as Elizabeth's jointure. It was secured for the term of Charles and Elizabeth's lives, then to Charles and Elizabeth's sons, then their daughters, then William's right heirs.[46] In the seventeenth century, there was an expectation that widows of gentlemen would have access to land. In 1635, William's eldest son, Owen (1613–58), married Mary Goodman (d. 1676) without William's consent and thus they did not have a marriage settlement. However, Mary, a wealthy heiress of both her father and uncle, had control of at least the Plas Isa estate, Denbighshire, after Owen's death, which she leased out with her mother.[47]

Before the development of jointure, the Salesburys' provision for their widows was less cohesive. When Robert Salesbury died in 1550, he bequeathed his wife Katherine a third of all his lands, tenements and hereditaments with appurtenances in the counties of Denbighshire, Flintshire and Merionethshire for the term of her life 'in full recompence of her dower ... if she will so accept'. Most of the Salesbury estate at this time was copyhold and thus governed by manorial law.[48] The proportion of copyhold land allocated to a widow varied between manors; it could be a third of the land or even the entire estate.[49] However, the risk that Katherine might refuse the bequest suggests that Robert hoped to persuade Katherine to accept a third of all his land rather than insist on the North Wales custom of moveable goods as well. If Katherine refused to accept the land and claimed her full dower, then Robert voided his bequest. Dower provision was never particularly common in Wales and, only a decade or so after the Acts of Union, Robert's bequest reflects that the Salesburys historically held land converted to English tenure.[50] Robert and Katherine's son, John (1533–80), also used a dower to provide for his wife, Elizabeth (d. *c.*1584), although he augmented the dower with a grant of either Clocaenog Park or Pool Park.[51] There was clearly a degree of administrative continuity in the family, with land set aside from the main estate to provide for widows; John's son, Sir Robert Salesbury, also granted Clocaenog Park to his wife, Elinor, and it

[46] NLW, Bachymbyd 342.

[47] Gwynedd Archives, XD2/799; XD2/800.

[48] TNA, WARD 9/103/82, fo. 83r.

[49] A. Wood, *The Memory of the People: Custom and Popular Senses of the Past in Early Modern England* (Cambridge, 2013), pp. 298–301.

[50] Swett, 'Widowhood, custom and property', p. 204.

[51] NLW, Bachymbyd 484; TNA, PROB 11/63/70. The sources disagree over the name of the land granted to Elizabeth; they may have been considered one park at this time.

was very close to Pool Park. Robert's will suggests that Katherine had some agency in her widowhood provision: she will receive the lands 'if she will so accept'. Almost certainly, Katherine received advice from her male relatives, but Robert's will places the decision entirely on Katherine: it is her choice. This fits with contemporary complaints that women were knowledgeable of their rights as widows and they were willing to challenge in court for them. George Owen (*c.*1552–1613) of Henllys, Pembrokeshire, criticizing women as gossips and mocking their learning, wrote that 'the women of our country would erect an Inn of Court and study the law to defend their common cause, wherein I think they were like to profit, for that there are of them many ripe wits and all ready tongues'.[52] While this does not present a favourable image of women, it does suggest that they could be confident defenders of 'their common cause', to men's disapproval. Women were the main plaintiffs or defendants in a quarter of all Chancery suits, highlighting the extent to which women were willing to protect their rights to property as well as the willingness of others to challenge those rights.[53] These legal records present some of the most visible accounts of early modern Welsh gentlewomen, including Dame Margaret Lloyd.

Margaret was described in her bill of petition as 'of Bersham', near Wrexham, Denbighshire, and this may have been her jointure or dower land.[54] However, by the time of the incident portrayed in her Star Chamber suit, Margaret had moved to Llanrhaeadr-yng-Nghinmeirch, Denbighshire to stay at a messuage belonging to her son, Roger of London, a minor. Roger and his grandmother, Elizabeth Lloyd, bought the land, including a garden and orchard, from Harry ap Harry of Llanrhaeadr-yng-Nghinmeirch for £100 on 12 June 1605, as well as further parcels of land from Richard Heaton of Llanynys, Denbighshire. Roger received the land by right of survivorship when his grandmother died in 1606, and Margaret and Roger went to live there together.[55] Margaret said that she was Roger's guardian and 'tutrix' and they lived peaceably at Roger's house in Llanrhaeadr-yng-Nghinmeirch. The messuage was at the centre of the dispute between Margaret and her brother, who both presented slightly different accounts of the incident which caused Margaret's Star Chamber suit.

In her bill of petition, Margaret said only that her underage son, Roger, received the land in question after his grandmother's death with no further details about the inheritance. The joint answer to the bill, given by John

[52] B. Howells, *Elizabethan Pembrokeshire: The Evidence of George Owen* (Haverfordwest, 1973), p. 7, quoted in Peters, *Women in Early Modern Britain*, p. 40.

[53] Erickson, 'Common law versus common practice', p. 28.

[54] TNA, STAC 8/201/24, bill of petition.

[55] TNA, STAC 8/201/24.

Salesbury, Piers Salesbury, Henry Underwood and John Anwyll, is from John's perspective; he is described as 'this defendant'.[56] In his answer, John contested Margaret's version. John agreed that Elizabeth Lloyd, Roger's grandmother, bought the messuage, but claimed that she organized a loan of £120 with interest from Sir Thomas Myddleton (*c*.1556–1631) of Chirk, even though the land only yielded £9 a year. According to John, when the grandmother died and Roger inherited the land, Margaret did not want Roger responsible for paying the debt. Margaret asked John, their cousin Edward Thelwall, and Margaret's eldest son, Evan, to buy the land and discharge the debts. In return, Evan also agreed to pay Roger £200 for the land when Roger reached his majority at the age of twenty-one. Margaret asked Evan to be responsible for Roger's education and 'bringing up', and Evan agreed out of 'duty' to his mother and 'love' for his brother. Evan duly discharged the debt and entered into the lands, leasing it to a tenant called Edward ap Robert since 1606. Evan also 'tooke his ... brother [Roger] into his charge and kept him at schoole'. However, when Evan was away from North Wales, John claimed that Margaret 'inveigled' Roger from his rightful guardian, 'takeing opportunity of the absence of [Evan Lloyd]'. John said that Margaret knew that Roger was in North Wales while Evan was away; given Roger's description in Margaret's bill as 'of London', he was presumably sent to boarding school there and was not usually resident in the locality. John himself was also incapacitated because he was 'sickly and lately recovered of a dangerous and desperate sickenes'. John's answer implies that Margaret knew John had the ability to influence the situation, to protect his nephew Evan's land and constrain his sister's actions.

After abducting Roger, Margaret then proceeded to seize the messuage leased to Evan's tenant, Edward ap Robert. According to John, Margaret had no lawful claim on the messuage where she lived with Roger, and she went from her house in Bersham to take it from the tenant. Edward ap Robert lived with his wife's family and thus 'the premisses was but slenderly defended and that onely with a mayd servant and one child'. On the night of 7 May 1608, Margaret and her accomplices 'did breake downe the dore of the said house and did also breake the lock of the said dore'. When Edward arrived at the house the following morning, he 'found his Cattell impounded' and Margaret refusing to let him inside the house. Margaret's servants, 'as this defendant [John Salesbury] was credibly enformed', 'drew their swords and weapons' upon the 'pore tenant'. In the absence of his landlord Evan Lloyd, the tenant went to John Salesbury for aid. John was living at his

[56] TNA, STAC 8/201/24, answer.

Bachymbyd estate, two miles from Llanrhaeadr-yng-Nghinmeirch. After Edward ap Robert 'acquainted him with the outrages', John says he 'sent Robert Salusbury gentleman [Margaret's] uncle' and 'Pyers Salusbury' her third cousin 'to entreat' Margaret to return the messuage to the tenant. Although initially she refused to leave, 'afterwarde the said Dame Margaret Lloyd was perswaded to depart the said house'. John himself did not go to the property; he was 'farre of from the said house', presumably still recovering from his illness. John did not explain how the men persuaded Margaret to leave the house.

Margaret gave a different account.[57] She accused her brother of assembling armed men at Bachymbyd, including 'Piers Salusburie his servante in liverie who is a Commone drunkarde and was herefore detected of willfull murther'; Harry Salusbury, a former soldier; Simon Salusbury; Piers Salusbury, the son of Hugh Salusbury; Robert Salusbury of Pant Glas, gentleman; Robert Salusbury of Maes Cadarn, gentleman; and around fourteen other named men, 'all of them beinge the servantes followers and retainers of [John Salesbury] … beinge moste desperate and dissolute people and att all times readie to execute any willfull violente and unlaweful acte which [John Salesbury] shall Commaund or directe them to doe'. Margaret said that there were around thirty men in total and they went from Bachymbyd to Llanrhaeadr-yng-Nghinmeirch. According to Margaret's account, the men intended to take the land forcibly from Margaret and her son, 'well knowinge' that Margaret and Roger could not withstand an attack due to 'the tendernes of his age [and] by reason of her Sex and widowhood'. Margaret was inside the house, 'muche affrighted', and she, along with the local constable, 'entreated' the men 'to keepe your Majesties peace'. Margaret told them that there were lawful means to claim title to the land. However, the men retorted that 'they Cam thither by the said John Salusburie his expresse Commaundemente to pull [Margaret] out of the house either alive or dead'. The men proceeded to attack the house: they 'Suddenlie therewith then and there with greate violence pulled downe A beame and parte of the said house'. With drawn weapons, the men broke down the door and attacked Margaret and her three servants, who were 'in verie greate danger of their lives'. The men pulled them out of the house though they were 'greviouslie wounded'. In her bill of petition, Margaret complained that the men now had possession of the house and lands 'without any Colour of title'. According to Margaret, John 'hath afterwardes given out speeches that he hadd appointed the aforesaid Riotous persons to

57 TNA, STAC 8/201/24, bill of petition.

Comytt the outrages ... and that he would beare them out and save them harmles for the same whatsoever it should cost him'.

Margaret took her case to Star Chamber very soon after the incident, a court far from the influence of her brother and son. John and his fellow defendants gave their joint answer on 4 July 1608, less than two months after the alleged attack. Although the emphasis and interpretation are different, the two accounts are not incompatible. Margaret and John agree that Roger was living with her on 8 May 1608, they agree that her male relatives came to take Roger away, they agree that Margaret resisted them. However, there are no further records concerning the case. There is no judgement and no indication of what happened to Margaret or Roger. Margaret's Star Chamber suit is a fleeting, constructed insight into the life of an early modern Welsh widow and it presents interestingly contradictory accounts of her character. In her version, Margaret is a widowed mother living with a handful of servants and caring for her young son, subject to violent mistreatment by her male relatives at the instigation of her brother. In John's version, Margaret is a subversive and unreliable woman, breaking her agreement with her eldest son, overstepping the boundaries of acceptable female behaviour and in need of correction by her male kin. Margaret's Star Chamber case highlights the problematic nature of widowhood when early modern Welsh society privileged the male kindred. At a time when women marrying into the Salesbury family acquired the security of jointure and marriage settlements, Margaret's case shows that widows required more than just land and they could be disadvantaged when they contravened custom.

The absence of other records relating to the case makes it impossible to know which version was closest to the truth. Margaret implies that John had no reason to assemble men and remove Roger and her from the messuage. John does not explain how Margaret came to leave the property. Both accounts are filtered through the strong, emotive language of Star Chamber, peppered with stock phrases such as men 'beinge armed arraied and weaponed in warlike manner', suggesting that both parties adjusted their accounts to adhere to the court's conventions.[58] Still, the case presents important insights into Margaret's position as a widow in early modern Welsh gentry society. In John's account, Margaret was a woman whose actions required the intervention of her male relatives. When the tenant, Edward ap Robert, went to John Salesbury for assistance, John was both his landlord's uncle and his assailant's brother. Whether John's story is true or not, it was credible to argue that the tenant was aware John would be able to help him in Evan Lloyd's absence. Llanrhaeadr-yng-Nghinmeirch

[58] TNA, STAC 8/201/24, bill of petition.

is only two miles from Bachymbyd, and the Salesburys were a prominent local family. John's answer does not elaborate on why Edward ap Robert chose to go to John Salesbury for help, but his relationship to Margaret as well as Evan was surely important. In his answer, John emphasizes the familial connection to Margaret. In the absence of Margaret's oldest son, John, as Margaret's brother and the head of the Salesbury family, organized his own kinsmen to curb Margaret's behaviour and protect Evan's tenant. These kinsmen were, of course, also Evan's kinsmen through his mother, an important connection in a society which valued kinship. In his answer, John only mentions two of the kinsmen, his uncle Robert and cousin Piers, but Margaret names twenty men, six of whom – more than a quarter – were kin of some sort. Given the preponderance of various Salusbury branches in early modern Denbighshire, it is difficult to identify their precise relationship to John and Margaret, but they were clearly part of the wider kindred, followers and retainers of the Salesbury patriarch. John himself identifies Piers as their third cousin, showing both the longevity of kinship ties and the distant degree of recognized kin relationships. The other half of the group consisted of yeomen and craftsmen, including John Foulk, a smith, and John ap Ieuan, a miller, with some names, such as Richard ap Robert and Thomas ap Morris, included in a 1601 list of tenants on the Bachymbyd estate.[59] It is realistic to conclude that they all had some sort of tenurial or patronal relationship with John. The composition of the group of armed men suggests they were John's *plaid*, or retinue, which the Welsh gentry used to reinforce their power in the local area. *Pleidiau* were vital demonstrations of status in later medieval Wales, but similar patronal relationships survived into the early modern period.[60] Regardless of whether or not the *plaid* attacked her house, there is credibility in Margaret's account that John had a *plaid* consisting of the Salesbury kindred and his tenants.

Margaret's bill gives a lengthy description of the men's attack on the house. John's answer instead focuses on Margaret's transgression: her broken deal with her eldest son that he would have the land for himself and raise Roger. John says only that Margaret 'was perswaded to depart the said house'. 'To persuade' someone could encompass a whole range of possibilities and certainly does not preclude Margaret's version of what happened on 8 May 1608 at Llanrhaeadr-yng-Nghinmeirch. It is clear from John's answer that he believed Margaret's behaviour transgressed the boundaries of acceptable female behaviour. He said that Margaret is his 'naturall and sole sister' and

[59] The Huntington Library, Ellesmere MS. 1782e.

[60] A. D. Carr, *The Gentry of North Wales in the Later Middle Ages* (Cardiff, 2017), pp. 20–1; Jones, *Welsh Gentry*, pp. 115–17.

brought the bill 'not of her owne discrecione but by the instigation ... of some others', whom John does not name. In his answer, John does not permit Margaret sufficient agency to sue her brother, yet presents her as a conniving and underhanded woman, working to undermine her eldest son. Margaret's actions were premeditated; she acted 'takeing opportunity of the absence of [Evan Lloyd]', ascertaining that Roger was home from school and that the messuage was 'slenderly defended', and that John Salesbury was still recovering from his illness. Her eldest son, meanwhile, is a paragon of gentlemanly behaviour, nobly discharging his younger brother's debts at Margaret's behest and agreeing to pay him £200 after Roger's twenty-first birthday, despite the low value of the land in question. Evan also spent around £247 on Roger's education and keep, before Margaret 'inveigled him away'. The case particularly emphasizes the difficult position of a widow in early modern Welsh gentry society. On the one hand, Margaret still had access to land and wanted control of her underage child. On the other hand, her eldest son now controlled the family estates and Margaret was a threat to his position.

As a Welsh widow, Margaret's actions were further constrained beyond primogeniture by the boundaries of Welsh custom. The estate archives of prominent North Wales gentry families, as well as legal records and wills, demonstrate that North Wales custom gave the guardianship of children to male kin, not mothers. Although similar expectations existed in England, Katharine Swett argues that the Welsh cultural focus on male kinship created particularly restrictive conditions of guardianship for widowed mothers.[61] Margaret's behaviour thus transgressed not only her alleged agreement with Evan, but the received expectations of Welsh society that male kin raised children upon their father's death. Garthine Walker has demonstrated that abduction was a common accusation levied by men at widowed mothers who took their children away from appointed legal guardians, and the existence of such cases suggests that placing children with male kin after their father's death could cause considerable distress, whether to the mother, the children or both. For example, George Owen of Henllys related the abduction by her mother of thirteen-year-old Jennett Thomas; her mother claimed she took Jennett from her guardian because he neglected her and Jennett asked to leave.[62] It is clear from John and Margaret's accounts that Roger was living with Margaret on 8 May 1608, whether by Roger's choice or Margaret's duplicity. However, regardless of

[61] Swett, 'Widowhood, custom and property', p. 219.

[62] G. Walker, '"Strange kind of stealing": abduction in early modern Wales', in Roberts and Clarke, *Women and Gender in Early Modern Wales*, pp. 50–74, at pp. 57–9.

the alleged agreement between Margaret and Evan, Margaret evidently wanted to raise Roger herself and, if the agreement existed, she desperately wanted to remove him from Evan's guardianship.

It is worth remembering too that the suit occurred at a time when Wales was still adjusting to legal change, just two generations after the Acts of Union. Margaret's suit highlights a clash between the principles of the early modern Welsh gentry and the principles of English law. In Welsh gentry society, Margaret's behaviour was transgressive, and John acted properly by organizing her male kindred to correct her. According to English law, however, it was John who acted in a transgressive manner, using violence to force a woman and her child out of a house. John accused Margaret of acting against custom, and Margaret accused John of acting against the law. Margaret's Star Chamber suit is therefore not just a microcosmic study of a Welsh gentlewoman or a revealing portrait of male and female relations in a Welsh gentry family; it is also indicative of Welsh gentry society adapting to different and occasionally conflicting behavioural standards. Margaret Lloyd was a product of the same society as her brother. She knew the behavioural standards expected of her as a Welsh gentlewoman and a widowed mother. These standards emphasized obedience to the male kindred and recognition of a man's position as head of the family. Margaret's account, however, presents a greater responsibility to her child. Margaret's suit thus reveals the intensely patriarchal nature of gentry society in early modern North Wales, but the very fact that Margaret took her case to Star Chamber in the first place demonstrates that Welsh gentlewomen were willing to defend their interests against their male kindred. For Margaret Lloyd, the law provided legitimate defence against a society which privileged male relatives over mothers.

On 8 May 1608, there was a dispute over the ownership of a messuage in Llanrhaeadr-yng-Nghinmeirch, Denbighshire. There may have been armed men who forcibly entered the house and removed the inhabitants, or there may have been reasoned persuasion. The bill of petition and the defendants' answer presents a constructed account of the relationship between a widow and her closest male relatives, but the documents agree that some sort of incident occurred. However, there remain questions about the purpose of the suit. On 15 September 1610, John Salesbury leased a substantial amount of his land in Denbighshire to his sister, Dame Margaret Lloyd. The lease was for a term of twenty-one years and an annual rent of *6d*; the consideration was £10 and the natural love and affection held by John for Margaret and her younger children, especially a younger son called John.[63] By this time John

[63] North East Wales Archives, Hawarden (Flintshire Record Office), D/PT/397.

Salesbury was significantly in debt, and the lease to Margaret was almost certainly part of his desperate attempt to raise money by alienating parts of his estate, although, depending on the value of the land, it is possible that John genuinely wanted to provide for his nephew. Nevertheless, it is clear that the dispute raised in Star Chamber did not irrevocably harm the relationship between brother and sister. If John did send his *plaid* to remove her from the messuage, Margaret was not sufficiently aggrieved to refuse to lease land from him. This might indicate that the dispute over the messuage was routine; perhaps the suit was fundamentally a means of establishing who had right title to the land. Even so, within Margaret's bill of petition and John's answer, there is revealing evidence of how a widowed Welsh gentlewoman should act and how she should behave in relation to her male kindred. This is not to say that Welsh gentlewomen always or often met these expectations, but that the suit presents an ideal within Welsh gentry society. It is revealing, however, that Margaret Lloyd had sufficient confidence and knowledge to take her suit to Star Chamber within two months of the incident. Of course, she may well have received advice from her kin, and a lawyer constructed her case for her, but Margaret was willing to engage with the legal process and challenge her brother in court. For the Welsh gentry, the ideal widow was obedient to her male kindred, but Dame Margaret Lloyd's suit in Star Chamber demonstrates that widows had considerable agency and the ability to defend against perceived violations of their interests.

6. Consent and coercion, force and fraud: marriages in Star Chamber*

K. J. Kesselring

Many people now deem child, early and forced marriages to be violations of human rights, a significant change from centuries past. After long debate, recent United Nations General Assembly resolutions identified 'gender inequality' as a root cause of practices that usually count girls and women as their most direct victims, but which have many harmful outcomes for societies more generally, ranging from lower levels of education to higher levels of poverty and violence. As such, the sustainable development goals support a growing bureaucratic machinery premised on reducing the estimated 12 million child, early and forced marriages that still take place every year.[1] Early and forced marriages persist within some communities in Britain today, with community workers and women's rights activists struggling to have existing laws against these practices better enforced, against a backdrop of racist and post-imperial assumptions that paradoxically hinder their efforts.[2] While such marriage practices are sometimes assumed to be novel imports, community activists can try to have existing laws better enforced precisely because child, early and forced marriages are by no means new or foreign to the history of England and Wales.

* My thanks to Sara Butler, Gwen Seabourne and Deborah Youngs for reading earlier versions of the chapter, and to both Helen Good and Amanda Bevan for assistance in locating some of the court cases discussed here. My thanks, too, to the Social Sciences and Humanities Research Council of Canada for funding the research from which it derives.

1 See, e.g. <https://www.ohchr.org/EN/Issues/Women/WRGS/Pages/ChildMarriage.aspx> [accessed 7 Nov. 2020].

2 See, e.g., A. Wilson, 'The forced marriage debate and the British state', *Race & Class*, xlix (2007), 25–38. On nineteenth-century discussions of the age of consent for sexual relations and on child marriage in their imperial contexts, see the recent collection of articles in the *Law and History Review*, xxxviii (2020), e.g., I. Pande, 'Vernacularizing justice: age of consent and a legal history of the British Empire', 267–79. For more recent debates on establishing a universal minimum age of marriage, tied to efforts to eradicate slavery, see A. Tambe, 'The moral hierarchies of age standards: the UN debates a common minimum marriage age, 1951–1962', *American Historical Review*, cxxv (2020), 451–9.

K. J. Kesselring, 'Consent and coercion, force and fraud: marriages in Star Chamber' in *Star Chamber Matters: An Early Modern Court and Its Records*, ed. K. Kesselring and N. Mears (London, 2021), pp. 97–114.

The balance between consent and coercion in the making of marriage continued to be reset well into the era in which modernity took shape. Individuals could be forced into marriages by would-be spouses or by their own parents. Medievalists have paid spousal abduction some attention, tracing both the Church's insistence upon the necessity of consent to create binding unions and the efforts of secular authorities to limit the seizing of wealthy brides.[3] Early modernists have attended rather less to the subject of marriage-by-capture, though, at least outside of Wales,[4] perhaps swayed by a sense that such marriages had become too rare to matter or by a belief that parents' accusations of their daughters' abductions masked collusive elopements. Indeed, in so far as early modernists have paid attention to forced marriage, they usually see the parents in the role of aggressor. But as Gwen Seabourne and Chanelle Delameillieure have argued for the late middle ages, the distinction between abduction and elopement can

[3] On medieval canon law re: consent, see J. A. Brundage, *Law, Sex, and Christian Society in Medieval Europe* (Chicago, 1987) and R. H. Helmholz, *Marriage Litigation in Medieval England* (Cambridge, Mass., 1974). For abduction, see, e.g., S. M. Butler, '"I will never consent to be wedded with you!": Coerced marriage in the courts of medieval England', *Canadian Journal of History*, xxxix (2004), 247–70; S. S. Walker, 'Common law juries and feudal marriage customs in medieval England: the pleas of ravishment', *University of Illinois Law Review*, iii (1984), 705–18 and 'Punishing convicted ravishers: statutory strictures and actual practice in thirteenth and fourteenth-century England', *Journal of Medieval History*, xiii (1987), 237–50; J. B. Post, 'Ravishment of women and the Statutes of Westminster,' in *Legal Records and the Historian*, ed. J. H. Baker (London, 1978), pp. 150–64 and 'Sir Thomas West and the Statute of Rapes, 1382', *Bulletin of the Institute of Historical Research*, liii (1980), 24–30; J. Goldberg, *Communal Discord, Child Abduction, and Rape in the Later Middle Ages* (New York, 2008); S. McSheffrey and J. Pope, 'Ravishment, legal narratives, and chivalric culture in fifteenth-century England', *Journal of British Studies*, xlviii (2009), 818–36; C. Dunn, *Stolen Women in Medieval England: Rape, Abduction, and Adultery, 1100–1500* (Cambridge, 2013); G. Seabourne, *Imprisoning Medieval Women: The Non-Judicial Confinement and Abduction of Women in England, c.1170–1509* (Farnham, 2011); C. Delameillieure, '"Partly with and partly against her will": female consent, elopement, and abduction in late medieval Brabant', *Journal of Family History*, xlii (2017), 351–68.

[4] G. Walker, '"Strange kind of stealing": abduction in early modern Wales', in *Women and Gender in Early Modern Wales*, ed. M. Roberts and S. Clarke (Cardiff, 2000), pp. 50–74, analysing 38 Welsh abduction cases heard in Star Chamber, 1558–1640. See also E. W. Ives, '"Agaynst taking awaye of women": the inception and operation of the Abduction Act of 1487', in *Wealth and Power in Tudor England*, ed. E. W. Ives, R. J. Knecht and J. J. Scarisbrick (London, 1978), pp. 21–45; B. Harris, 'Aristocratic women and the state in early Tudor England', in *State, Sovereigns and Society in Early Modern England*, ed. C. Carlton, et al. (Stroud, 1998), pp. 3–24. H. Brewer, *By Birth or Consent: Children, Law, and the Anglo-American Revolution in Authority* (Chapel Hill, 2005) pays the subject brief but illuminating attention in ch. 8. See, too, A. Capern, 'The heiress reconsidered: contexts for understanding the abduction of Arabella Alleyn', in *Women and the Land, 1500–1900*, ed. A. Capern, B. McDonagh and J. Aston (Woodbridge, 2019), pp. 100–26.

be difficult to draw and anachronistic as well: consent did not necessarily indicate free choice.[5] We may sometimes be too quick to see love lurking behind the fictions in the archives: violence remained not just a product of many marriages but also, at times, a factor in their formation.

This chapter examines one facet of that early modern story: the regulation of marriage in the court of Star Chamber. Most basically, it makes a case for adding Star Chamber to our list of courts that dealt with marriage and for adding marriage to our list of Star Chamber's areas of responsibility. It suggests that we ought to look beyond the church courts alone to understand the post-Reformation remaking of marriage and, indeed, to look beyond the regular common-law courts to trace the longer history of secular authorities' attempts to direct the trade in women in ways conducive to public order.[6] More substantially, it highlights evidence from Star Chamber of wide-ranging discussions of the nature and limits of consent in marriage formation: whose consent, given in what circumstances, sufficed to make a binding union? Star Chamber built upon precedents from both clerical and common-law histories of marriage regulation, then creating precedents of its own in turn. Suitors brought to the court all sorts of claims on behalf of themselves or their children, alleging the use of drink, drugs, enchantments and other deceits alongside the traditional narratives of force in trapping people into marriages. In a set of reported Star Chamber cases, the court's judges responded to some such complaints by extending notions of improperly secured marriage beyond the remit of medieval abduction statutes with their focus on property to include both boys and girls who were not heiresses, deeming any marriage of a minor without parental approval 'evil in itself'. The court also grappled with issues of consent and coercion in ways that extended beyond force to include fraud as well.

Star Chamber grew from medieval roots in the judicial capacities of the King's Council, acquiring clear institutional definition in the sixteenth century. Often depicted as a laudable element in the Tudor effort to 'tame the nobility', the court was nonetheless eventually attacked as having acted illegally, and was abolished by parliament in 1641. It operated somewhat outside the common law, without juries and with royal councillors as its judges. By the second half of the 1500s, its focus had shifted from civil to criminal causes, and its judges then included the justices of King's Bench and Common Pleas as well. In that later manifestation, it focused on charges of 'force and fraud' – a fact that made it an ideal venue for marriage cases.[7]

[5] Seabourne, *Imprisoning* and Delameillieure, 'Elopement and Abduction'.

[6] The first of these arguments is set out more fully in a book on divorce and separation being co-authored with Tim Stretton.

[7] For the court's innovations in respect to fraud, see T. G. Barnes, 'Star Chamber and

Indeed, marriage by 'sleight or force' was one of the few offences for which Star Chamber had explicit statutory authority to act.

In doing so, Star Chamber built upon a long history of interventions into forced marriages by both ecclesiastical and secular authorities. Throughout Europe, the medieval Church had countered Germanic practices of bridal abduction and aristocratic forced marriage with canon law that insisted upon the necessity of free consent. Then, as the theology of the spiritual and sacramental qualities of marriage developed, canonists decided (somewhat problematically) that consent and consent alone made a valid, binding union. Drawing upon Roman law and assessments of the age at which youths were able to take on the duties of marriage, canon law set the age of marriage at twelve for girls, fourteen for boys. While marriages could be arranged for younger children, they were voidable without consent subsequently given at that age. Church teaching allowed that marriages could be annulled based on claims that one party was not what they had been thought to be, that an 'error of person' or of 'condition' invalidated a union. Church courts also allowed annulments based on evidence of duress, though typically requiring 'force and fear' sufficient to sway a 'constant' man or woman.[8] As thin and hedged about as this consent might now seem, canonists had to fight doggedly for even this much in societies where bridal abduction and paternal arrangements had long prevailed.

The frequency of child marriages and of unions made without the consent of brides or grooms after centuries of such teaching is impossible to know, but in his study of matrimonial litigation in the consistory court of the archbishops of York, Charles Donahue found that 12% of cases in the fourteenth century and 16% of cases in the fifteenth alleged either forced or underage marriage, or both.[9] Such cases seem to have become less common over the sixteenth century, but with regional variations. The cause papers for the archbishopric of York include proceedings on 116 annulments and separations in the 1500s, of which forty-four were for nonage or force.[10] In his samples of records from the diocese of Norwich, Ralph Houlbrooke identified only three annulments for coercion or youth; Martin Ingram

the sophistication of the criminal law', *Criminal Law Review* (1977), 316–26 and H. Mares, 'Fraud and dishonesty in King's Bench and Star Chamber', *American Journal of Legal History*, lix (2019), 210–31.

[8] Helmholz, *Marriage Litigation*, p. 91.

[9] C. Donahue, Jr., 'Female plaintiffs in marriage cases in the court of York in the later middle ages', in *Wife and Widow in Medieval England*, ed. S. S. Walker (Ann Arbor, 1993), pp. 183–213, at pp. 187, 189.

[10] Searches on *Cause Papers in the Diocesan Courts of the Archbishopric of York*, comp. P. Hoskin, et al., <https://www.dhi.ac.uk/causepapers/> [accessed 5 May 2020] .

counted similarly low numbers in Chichester and Wiltshire.[11] Johanna Rickman, in contrast, found at least four or five annulments of child marriages each year in records that survive from Chester's church courts in the 1560s, comprising just over 50% of the courts' matrimonial business. While demographic studies suggest an average age of first marriage for both women and men in their twenties by the late sixteenth century if not sooner – part of a broader northwestern pattern of late marriage compared to early marriages elsewhere – child marriage had certainly not disappeared.[12]

English secular law, meanwhile, had sought to regulate forced marriage from concerns for order, status and property. It tied abduction and forced sexual intercourse closely together, with a statute making 'raptus' a felony in 1285.[13] 'Ravishment' could refer either to carrying a woman away for rape, as we understand it, or to abducting a person under someone else's guardianship with no implication of sexual violation.[14] It could apply to voluntary elopements without the guardians' consent as much as to forced marriage against a person's will. Both girls and boys could be forced into marriage, but the problem was particularly acute for young women, given the patriarchal provisions of coverture which gave husbands ownership or control over their wives' property. A measure in 1382 sought to deal with collusive abductions and to minimize the temptation to abduct an heiress and then compel her 'consent' to a union: thereafter, any such ostensibly consensual marriage following an abduction disabled the woman from inheriting, thus denying her wealth to her abductor-spouse.[15] (As one Tudor legal commentator later noted, this was a 'shrewd statute'. Until this time, a ravisher might hope for mercy from the woman ravished, persuading her to agree to the union, but thereafter she dared not be merciful, 'lest she be cruel to herself. Therefore now men look on fair gentlewomen, heirs, and

[11] R. Houlbrooke, *Church Courts and the People During the English Reformation* (Oxford, 1979), p. 73; M. Ingram, *Church Courts, Sex and Marriage in England, 1570–1640* (Cambridge, 1987), pp. 172–3.

[12] J. Rickman, '"He would never consent in his heart": child marriages in early modern England', *Journal of the History of Childhood and Youth*, vi (2013), 293–313, at p. 296. See also Brewer, *By Birth or Consent*, pp. 294–5, esp. fn. 7, for suggestions that the averages presented by demographers might be too high, given their exclusion of data suggesting marriages under the age of 15, shaped by modern norms of child sexuality and possibly by ideologically driven assumptions that England had not had a history of child marriage.

[13] This survey of medieval legislation follows Ives, Dunn and Seabourne, cited above.

[14] McSheffrey and Pope, 'Ravishment', p. 818.

[15] 6 Richard II, st. 1, c. 6. A subsequent measure addressed abductions followed by forced bonds to sign over wealth. 31 Henry VI, c. 9 (1453).

widows, as the cat looketh at a fish in the water: she would fain be dealing, but is loath to go wetshod'.[16])

As shrewd as the 1382 statute may have been, legislators eventually thought they needed more. Renewed attention came in 1487, early in Henry VII's reign, alongside acts against murder and aristocratic disorder. The 1487 abduction act made it a capital felony to take any maiden, wife or widow 'having substance ... against her will unlawfully', noting that the resulting marriages worked to the 'disparagement of the said women and utter heaviness and discomfort of their friends'.[17] Unusually, the act treated accessories as principals and was, for a time, interpreted as making abduction of a woman of wealth a felony in itself, regardless of any subsequent forced marriage or intercourse. A judicial decision in 1557 lessened its force, however, by finding that abduction would only count as capital felony if accompanied by sex or marriage.[18]

Perhaps prompted by this judgement, in 1558 parliament passed a new law related to forced marriages, one that allowed abduction alone to be prosecuted either at common law upon indictment or in Star Chamber by bill of complaint. The act did not just fill a hole opened by the 1557 judicial decision, though. It also marked out new directions, perhaps in part responding to Reformation-era discussions about age of marriage and a desire to protect parental consent, discussions that led to secular encroachments on the church courts' marriage jurisdiction elsewhere.[19] The 1558 act did not deal with all women of substance but focused on young heiresses, on maidens under the age of sixteen who had wealth or claims upon it, who by force or 'sleight' were taken from their parent or guardian to their own disparagement, their parents' discomfort and the displeasure of God. According to the act, anyone who took from a father or other legal guardian an unmarried girl of means under the age of sixteen might be punished with two years' imprisonment or a fine assessed in Star Chamber. If the offender sexually assaulted or married the girl, a penalty of five years' imprisonment or a fine in Star Chamber applied, with half of the fine going to the injured parties. If a girl between the ages of twelve and sixteen 'consented' to such an unlawfully arranged union, her inheritance was to

[16] T. E., *Lawes Resolutions of Women's Rights* (London, 1632), p. 383.

[17] 3 Henry VII, c. 2.

[18] W. Dalison, *Les Reports des Diverse Special Cases* (London, 1689), p. 22.

[19] In 1557 (1556 o.s.) the French issued their first secular marital edict to extend parental control over children's marriages, up to ages 30 for men and 25 for women, partly in response to discussions at the Council of Trent. See S. Hanley, '"The jurisprudence of the arrêts: marital union, civil society, and state formation in France, 1550–1650', *Law and History Review*, xxi (2003), 1–40, at pp. 12–13.

pass to the person who would acquire it if she had died.[20] As Garthine Walker has noted, 'despite the Act's emphasis upon paternal authority, the distinction it drew between forced and consensual marriage meant that female consent was not elided'.[21] Like others, Walker also suggests that the Marian act weakened the earlier Henrician measure, in downgrading the crime from felony, but prosecutions could thereafter proceed under either statute.[22] The Marian measure was distinctive not just because it focused only on young maidens of substance and offered a punishment for abduction alone (though less than death), but also for extending beyond force to include 'flattering, trifling gifts, and false promises'.

Unusually, too, the Marian measure allowed prosecutions in the court of Star Chamber. And plaintiffs brought many tales of illegitimately secured marriages to the court. Some of these complaints seem as if they could have gone to the church courts instead, but perhaps hoping to shore up litigation being advanced elsewhere, appreciating the looser criteria for gaining a hearing in Star Chamber than in other courts, or being attracted by its alternative remedies, some plaintiffs turned here. The Elizabethan records include some such cases but as yet have no subject index, making a comprehensive survey prohibitively difficult.[23] But Thomas Barnes's index of the 8228 Jacobean files identifies nearly 100 suits that alleged abduction.[24] Bills came from every county in England and Wales save for Bedfordshire and Northumberland. Most of the Jacobean cases centred on the marriages of young women, but at least twenty-nine of the bills focused on the disputed marriages of young men. Most arose from the marriages of orphans and wards, a sign of their vulnerability as well as the lure of inheritances to potential spouses (and their worth to the guardians). Many of the marriages behind these cases appear to have arisen from elopements and may well have had the consent of both parties, but some seem to be just what the plaintiffs said: marriages secured through 'sleight or force'.

In many of the cases it appears that the young person did at least initially consent to the union that alarmed the guardian. The plaintiffs sometimes then picked up on the statutes' language of 'disparagement' to argue against

[20] 4&5 Philip and Mary, c. 8.

[21] Walker, 'Stealing', p. 52.

[22] Walker, 'Stealing', p. 53. See, too, 39 Elizabeth I, c. 9 (1597/8) which reiterated the 1487 statute and barred principals and accessories before the act from claiming benefit of clergy.

[23] But see forthcoming work from Chloë Ingersent, who is working through samples of the Elizabethan files.

[24] T. G. Barnes, *List and Index to the Proceedings in Star Chamber for the Reign of James I (1603–1625) in the Public Record Office, London, Class STAC 8* (3 vols., 1975), ii. 215–17, now supplemented by The National Archives of the UK's Discovery catalogue, thanks to work by Amanda Bevan, Megan Johnston, et al.

the propriety of the union, but most relied instead, or as well, on allegations of impediments to free consent.[25] Bills alleged various frauds, deceits or intoxicants had impaired the young person's ability to decide. One bill maintained that Nicholas Prideaux's would-be father-in-law had inveigled the young man's affections by giving him spending money, tobacco and sweetmeats, and also by 'excessive and immeasurable drinking of wine'. He had had the young man toast his companions with eight 'healths' in strong wine, 'far too much for any of his tender years'. Through 'overmuch carousing and drinking of wine forced upon him', Nicholas did not understand what he did when he took Elizabeth Carmynow in marriage. The next day he awoke to bewail his fate and said that rather than live with Elizabeth as his wife, 'he would be contented to live as a pilgrim all the residue of his days'.[26] One disappointed father maintained that his sixteen-year-old son had been lured into an improper marriage only after imbibing 'strange intoxicated drinks which produced a kind of frensy in his brain'.[27] Joan Cartwright's guardian alleged that the eleven-year-old had married Edward Holloway only after drinking 'a great quantity of hot waters and other strong and heady drink mingled with hot spices and other intoxicating powders'.[28] Some bills suggested that unnatural intoxicants had been used: one referred to 'enchanted potions and drinks', while another alleged that a suitor gave his intended 'certain rolls made of sugar and some other things therewith mixed and composed by enchantment or witchcraft or other unlawful or unhonest devise to make the said Elizabeth to love him'.[29]

Some parents argued that their children were too young to agree to a marriage, whatever the law might say about the age of consent. Hester Onslowe acknowledged that her daughter Mary had initially given herself willingly in marriage and that as a sixteen-year-old she was legally free to do so. But Hester emphasized several times Mary's 'very small stature and growth', called her a 'very simple girl and easily allured and drawn by reason of her childishness', and insisted that she was 'utterly unfit yet to contract' herself in such a way, let alone to a man of 'forty years, light and unthrifty'.[30] Frances Cresswell admitted that her daughter Frances was of legal age but

[25] For a brief discussion of the language of disparagement in these bills, see Kesselring, 'Disparaging marriage in early modern England', *Legal History Miscellany* <https://legalhistorymiscellany.com/2020/01/06/disparaging-marriage-in-early-modern-england/> [accessed 7 Nov. 2020].

[26] TNA, STAC 8/30/12.

[27] TNA, STAC 8/154/1

[28] TNA, STAC 8/88/17.

[29] TNA, STAC 8/122/12 and STAC 8/63/22. See also STAC 8/271/16 and STAC 8/88/13.

[30] TNA, STAC 8/224/27.

described her as 'Frances the infant' in every reference to her in the bill of complaint, noting that the thirteen-year-old was 'small of stature' and 'but a child in her knowledge and understanding'.[31]

Whatever one might think of the nature of the consent given in these cases, some of the bills went further in alleging unambiguously violent abductions and coerced unions, with the willing agreement of neither the guardian nor the party to the marriage. In 1590, for example, Alice Elkin and her husband William accused John Skynner of forcefully abducting Margaret Robinson, Alice's twelve-year-old daughter from a previous marriage. They claimed Skynner and his associates seized Margaret from church, brandishing daggers and boathooks as they forced her into a boat and breaking 'both her face and her knee' in the melee. Skynner then married Margaret, in a ceremony to which she 'never yielded any free consent other than through force, fear, constraint or by compulsion'.[32] In 1605, the fourteen-year-old Mary Dyer was reportedly seized by Thomas Wade and his family and kept by force for four or five days against her will. Someone in Thomas's family faked a summons to appear before the Gloucester church court on a charge of fornication with Thomas; they said that Mary would be committed to prison for harlotry, whipped throughout the streets of the city, and forced to stand at the cross of reformation in a white sheet during market time unless she married Thomas. When she still refused, they threatened to kill her.[33] A bill from 1623 complained that the eleven-year-old Joan Cartwright had been taken by force from her guardians, given various intoxicants, locked away, carried to the banks of the Severn with threats of being drowned, and finally beaten, bruised and wounded before acquiescing to her marriage.[34]

We cannot know, of course, whether these individual stories of violence – or of drunkenness, simplicity, or deception – are accurate reflections of events even as the plaintiffs saw them. Lately, scholars have shown much interest in reading bills and depositions as narratives, in part because of the difficulties in determining 'what really happened' in any given case. The impulse to step aside from facts to studying fiction-telling is particularly strong with Star Chamber materials, partly because claims of violence helped get cases heard by the court and are thus automatically suspect, and partly because the court's records of judgements have disappeared. But for a

[31] TNA, STAC 8/88/15.

[32] TNA, STAC 5/E4/2; STAC 5/E15/39; STAC 5/E12/1; STAC 5/13/8; STAC 5/E10/12. This case came to light thanks to the in-progress cataloguing efforts of Helen Good. In this case, the court decided for the plaintiff, as indicated in the fines list, E 159/399, see <http://www.uh.edu/waalt/index.php/SCF_1590> [accessed 7 Nov. 2020].

[33] TNA, STAC 8/59/29.

[34] TNA, STAC 8/88/17.

few cases, we can at least learn the outcome, thanks to lists of fines kept by the Exchequer, collections of brief working notes abstracted from the now lost order and decree books, and sometimes from more discursive reports that summarized the judges' statements for future reference. Examining the narrativity and multivocality of the case files is worthwhile, to be sure, but looking at cases for which we have judicial decisions and indications of which stories the judges found compelling can help us trace shifting legal norms around consent, force and fraud in the construction of marriages in a system based on precedent as well as statute and equity.

To be sure, simply knowing the judges' decisions does not tell us everything we might want to know. An Elizabethan case illustrates the difficulties. In 1560, Agnes Croply complained that Edward Bardwell and a few fellow servants had forcibly abducted her twelve-year-old niece and ward, Mary Page. The deaths of Mary's parents had left her the heir to lands with the yearly value of '20 marks or thereabouts' and in the keeping of her mother's widowed sister, Agnes. On the Thursday of Easter week, Bardwell and his companions seized Mary from a field where she was sewing and tending cattle with one of Agnes's daughters. The men did so, Agnes said, 'not only against the will of your said supplicant but also against the will of the said Mary'. According to Agnes, the men dragged a crying young girl through a hedge then put her, shamefully, astride a horse. After Mary jumped off, one of the men sat astride behind her, holding her close. Another of the men went beside with sword drawn. One of the field labourers approached the scene and tried to speak with Mary, but Bardwell reportedly insisted that she was his wife and thus could not speak with anyone if he forbade it. Deponents called on Agnes's behalf emphasized the 'force and strong hands', the girl's crying and striving, and the presence of unsheathed weapons. In response, Bardwell did not dispute having seized Mary. In his version of events, Agnes had previously welcomed him as a suitor for Mary's hand, but then he heard that a rival was about to marry the girl, so he simply acted first. He tried suggesting that Mary was a bit older than Agnes claimed and that he had her goodwill. In the end, though, the court deemed Bardwell's offence well within the Marian statute. He was imprisoned for two years, and strikingly, the court effectively voided the marriage: Mary was restored to her aunt.[35]

In such a case, the judges' verdict siding with the guardian does not necessarily mean that the plaintiff's story was wholly accurate and that the girl was forcibly abducted and married against her will. Mary Page was of marriageable age and might well have been fully consenting by the

[35] TNA, STAC 5/C80/25; STAC 5/C8/37; British Library, Lansdowne MS. 639, fo. 71.

standards of the day; the judges may have passed their verdict based on the impropriety of Bardwell marrying a ward without her guardian's consent. But the stories of violent, non-consensual unions seem at least as probable as the tales of youthful love and women's agency that we often privilege in such cases. And when we attend to the decisions, not just the narratives crafted in the pleadings and proofs, we see not only instances of an age-old problem but also new judicial responses and signs that judges as much as plaintiffs were broadening their notions of the impediments to proper consent. A few other, better-reported Jacobean cases give us more detail, and let us see Star Chamber taking a more interventionist role, responding to statute and to plaintiffs' complaints to expand beyond force to fraud and beyond propertied maidens to girls and boys more generally.

In 1604, Edward Dawes of St Bride's parish, London, reported to the court that Charles Sherman had lured away Dawes's only child, Martha. Dawes described himself as a man with leases and chattels to the value of some £100. He described Martha as being 'in the custody and under the government of your said subject ... having accomplished twelve years of age and more, but under thirteen'. He said that Charles Sherman, a twenty-seven-year-old from Cambridge, was a gentleman by birth but otherwise a 'light and unthrifty person'. Charles's sister, Grace, had been a servant in the Dawes household on Fleet Street and had helped arrange meetings between Martha and Charles, including the fateful outing on 12 July when Charles took Martha to Cambridge to be married, without her parents' agreement and against their will. Edward Dawes implicitly acknowledged that Martha had gone freely and without force, but said she had been tricked by letters noting that the marriage would be conditional upon her parents' consent and soon after 'grievously repented herself'. The interrogatories posed by Dawes's counsel asked whether Charles had duped Martha with a forged letter and whether he had used any 'drug or enchantments [or] indirect means to cause the said Martha to love you or to yield unto you'? They asked Martha about Charles's courting, or grooming: did he not use 'light and toying behavior', praising her, singing 'bad songs', writing 'amorous flattering letters ... depicting himself as greatly inflamed with your love'? Did he not call her 'the mirror of his mind' and promise to spend his blood for her? Did he not brag of the great marriages he could have had with maidens worth thousands of pounds, but yet whisper that he would take her for much less, given his deep love for her? Did he not call her mistress and himself her servant? Did he not take her drinking and feasting to establishments throughout London? Martha said that she was 'after a sort married (as she thinketh) in Trinity church in Cambridge' but maintained that she had not lain with Charles and did not think him to be her lawful husband. Charles said simply that the person he continued to call his wife had shown him many signs of affection and that he had taken her away so abruptly merely because of an increase in sickness in London. In his petition to the court, Martha's father invoked both the Marian abduction act and a Henrician act against counterfeiting letters and tokens for fraudulent purposes. John Haywarde, a barrister who took notes on cases he observed in Star Chamber, devoted several pages to the hearing. He noted that ultimately, the court concluded that Sherman's deceits came within the terms of the Marian statute. They voided the marriage, returned Martha to her parents and sentenced Charles to a fine of £500 or five years' imprisonment.[36]

A set of cases a few years later had the privy councillors and judges once again examining the complexities of consent and coercion, but showing more concern for jurisdictional conflict with both the courts of common law and those of the church. Several reports address the cases, but the judges seem to have offered no clear resolution to the contending stories. William and Martha Hall of Rotherhithe, Surrey, complained in 1611 that Richard Baker had abducted from their care Martha's daughter, Jacomine Woodcock, a twenty-year-old widow who stood to inherit substantial properties upon her mother's death. Jacomine had entertained Richard Baker's suits for marriage, they said, but upon discovering how deeply in debt he was, she had cast him aside and made plans to marry a relative of her stepfather's, one John Hall. According to the Halls, Richard responded by having one of her household servants take Jacomine out on to the Thames one day, where he seized her and took her to East Tilbury and then on to Queensborough to be married. Richard Baker launched a countersuit, maintaining that the Halls had then kidnapped his wife from his lawful custody after the marriage and had conspired to take his life by having her file an indictment against him in the common-law courts under the Henrician abduction act. Baker also initiated a case before the ecclesiastical court of High Commission to assert the validity of the marriage. In this episode, it seems that whatever Jacomine's initial inclinations may have been, she eventually agreed to her marriage to Richard. The Star Chamber judges left the matter of the marriage's validity to the church courts. They debated whether the forcible taking away, or taking away by sleight, made the act a felony, whether or not the woman later consented – a discussion that allowed Lord Chancellor Egerton to attempt a thin joke about consent and women denying it after the fact. They commented, too, on the unusual nature of the Henrician

[36] TNA, STAC 8/114/14; J. Hawarde, *Les Reportes del Cases in Camera Stellata, 1593–1609*, ed. W. P. Baildon (London, 1894), pp. 259–61.

statute – the 'forceablist act ever made for felony' – in treating all accessories as principals, something otherwise only seen in treason cases. After two days of discussion, though, the judges finally refused to make a clear judgement on the matter, as doing so would effectively serve either to acquit or to condemn Baker for a hanging crime, something beyond their remit.[37]

While the privy councillors and judges in Star Chamber made no clear determination in the Woodcock case, a set of complaints in 1616 saw them more boldly establish new precedent, though still showing some care for jurisdictional limits.[38] John Brewton, a joiner living in St Olave's, Southwark, exhibited bills against Edward Morris, an embroiderer of London over forty years of age, charging him with having stolen away Brewton's twelve-year-old daughter Jane. Morris had taken her 'from the possession, custody or governance and against the will of the complainant', Brewton observed. According to his accusation, on 30 May, just days after Jane's twelfth birthday, Morris had one Joan Kippen, a former servant of the Brewtons, go to their home and ask Jane to walk with her to see a strange new ship from beyond the seas then at anchor in the Thames. Kippen and her husband then forced Jane to the Red Lion tavern in Ratcliffe, where Morris met them. The party travelled to Boxford, Purleigh and Kersey before finally finding a minister who would marry them, on 16 June. While Morris would claim that Jane married him willingly, several deponents affirmed that she had at one point dropped to her knees to implore her companions to let her go home, entreating them just to give her a horse to let her ride back to Southwark, and crying so hard that one worried she would harm herself. Some said that the Kippens threatened Jane that they would either ship her abroad or have her committed to prison unless she consented to the marriage. The consent, such as it was, seemed to come when Morris gave her gloves, a gold ring and a forged letter, purportedly from her parents, expressing their desire that she marry Morris. Deponents who spoke on Morris's behalf, in contrast, insisted that the twelve-year-old went 'merrily and freely' down the river and married Edward with her 'free consent and good liking'. Whether or not Jane had any such 'good liking', within weeks she turned to a justice of the peace who secured her return to her parents. Brewton took his complaint to Star Chamber, where Morris

[37] TNA, STAC 8/172/9 (*Hall* v *Baker*); STAC 8/67/8 (*Baker* v *Hall*); Brit. Libr., Lansdowne MS. 639, fos. 192r–193; Harvard Law School Library, MS. 149, fo. 103r; and the report of Sir Richard Hutton in 123 *English Reports* 1058. Egerton 'told a tale of a Welsh woman who complained that she was ravished and being asked whether it were by force and arms answered no force no harm'.

[38] For the Brewton cases, see TNA, STAC 8/68/17; STAC 8/68/16; Harvard Law School Library, MS. 149, fo. 117r; Folger Shakespeare Library, MS. X.d.337, fos. 17–24.

and his confederates offered as their chief defence the fact that Jane was neither heir nor ward, nor currently possessed of any wealth to speak of, and so was not covered by the statutes.

While Brewton awaited the hearing of this first complaint, Morris tried again. On Sunday, 1 December, Morris and his confederates waylaid Jane on her way to church. Purportedly with 'daggers drawn and pistols charged', they forced the girl into their waiting boat, threatened bystanders who tried to help and then rowed her away. Two watermen deposed that they had innocently been waiting at Queenhithe dock for a fare when Morris and his men leapt into their boat, having found their own to be taking on water. The watermen reported seeing one of the men carrying Jane under his arm, then throwing her into the boat. They affirmed that Jane did indeed 'cry out very pitifully' and insisted they had only participated as the men threatened to kill them, 'or worse'. Jane tried to leap out of the boat, they said, but her assailants held her down with such force that they almost suffocated her. Near St Towley's stairs, they saw Jane's mother, Joan, take a sculler and follow them, crying out the whole time for a faster boat, which she got at Tower Wharf. With the mother and others in hot pursuit, it seems that Morris gave up and abandoned Jane.

The case ultimately provoked much discussion in Star Chamber and beyond, and would later be cited as a precedent for the court's growing remit and for interventions that went beyond heiresses alone. First, the privy councillors and judges in Star Chamber wrestled with Morris's defence and demurrers: did Jane fit within the terms of the relevant statutes, not being an heiress? And if she did fit within the terms of the Henrician act, could Star Chamber pass a verdict that might later result in Morris's conviction in a common-law court on a capital felony charge? They referred the question to a full panel of the common-law judges who decided that as Jane was not an heiress and had no estates, the matter was not covered by the Henrician statute. But they all concurred that the matter might be tried in Star Chamber, either under the terms of the Marian act or as an evil in itself. They allowed that Star Chamber ought not to hear petty causes, but deemed this one '*magna in parvo*', a great matter within a small one. Henry Hobart, chief justice of the Common Pleas, insisted that 'every man hath power over his child, that whosoever taketh her away robs him'. The offence could be punished as a purposing to marry, for without the consent of the parents, it ought not to be considered a lawful marriage. The lord keeper maintained that 'children are the ends of men's labours and this is a growing offence, to be cut off in time'. The bishop of London agreed that marriage ought to be with the consent of the parents, and in this case, moreover, 'there could not be consensus, where there is not sense, she being but a month above twelve years old; therefore she wants her rudder'. The archbishop of Canterbury noted that the French had decided that marriages without parental consent were automatically void, and observed that if the English parliament moved to make such marriages felonious, 'he would agree to it and agree with the most'. The Anglican canons of 1604 had required parental consent for the marriage of anyone under age twenty-one, but the lack of such consent merely made the marriage irregular, not void; a bill to require parental consent for a valid union had appeared in the 1604 parliament, but failed to pass.[39] Archbishop Abbot, it seems, would have been happy with something more. Ultimately, the judges left the question of the validity of the marriage itself to the church courts, but decided to fine and imprison Morris and his confederates.

Star Chamber reached a little further still in attempting to regulate marriage formation in a 1625 case in which the victim was a sick young man.[40] Alice Woodrow, the widow of a wealthy London mercer, brought a case against Dorothy Crispe, a widow of Great Shefford, Berkshire, Dorothy's daughter Eleanor and several confederates, charging them with the unlawful marriage of Eleanor with Alice's son, Thomas. Thomas's mother said that he had claims to an estate worth some £15,000, but had also been incapacitated by the falling sickness, or epilepsy. Alice had sent him to Dorothy Crispe, as she had a reputation for being able to cure this disease. But through enchantments, spells and the help of Thomas's manservant, Dorothy had enticed a young man without his wits to marry Eleanor. According to Alice, Thomas had previously resolved never to marry, 'for it appeared that he was bursten greatly in his body and disabled', but Dorothy had preyed upon his weakness with arguments that 'marriage was a good help to cure his grief'. Dorothy's defence included efforts to prove her bona fides as a respected healer who did not rely on spells, evidence of her family's relatively high status to show that the marriage would not have disparaged Thomas, and

[39] *The Anglican Canons, 1529–1947*, ed. G. Bray (Woodbridge, 1998), p. 401; *Commons Journals*, I, 184, 206, 229–34. R. B. Outhwaite, *Clandestine Marriage in England, 1500–1850* (London, 1995), pp. 9, 65, 68. For the French situation, see esp. the 1579 Ordinance of Blois, which extended the earlier edict of 1557 and was in turn extended by additional decrees through to 1639, when all marriages came to require parental consent, regardless of the ages of the parties; see Hanley, 'Jurisprudence of the arrêts'.

[40] For the *Woodrow* v *Crispe* case, see TNA, STAC 8/295/13; Folger Shakespeare Library, MS. V.B.70, fo. 36d; Durham University Library, MS. 329, fo.191; J. Rushworth, *Historical Collections of Private Passages of State* (8 vols., London, 1721), iii. 13, 40. Upon hearing of the marriage, Alice had called Thomas back to London. Eleanor had then sued in the ecclesiastical courts for maintenance. A case was also launched in the court of Wards that decided he was an 'idiot'. Alice's suit to Star Chamber was presumably prompted by an effort from Eleanor and Dorothy to lay claim to Thomas's estate upon his death.

claims that Thomas had appeared happy about the match. Poor Thomas had died before the case went to trial and thus could not be heard directly. Instead, deponents spent much time presenting various proofs either for or against Thomas's mental capacity to offer consent. Could he read and write? Did he not frequently play at cards? Did he not attend divine service regularly? Could he not 'deliver his mind in sensible terms' between his fits? Some deponents told sad tales of delusions or behaviour from Thomas in the midst of his attacks (such as his talk of commanding an army of thousands in Mesopotamia, taking tobacco with the king or being elected mayor of London); others insisted that he was still of right mind once the seizures passed and had shown signs of delight with his bride. The dispute here focused not on his age but his illness as a bar to forming consent, and on Dorothy's deceits.

The judges decided quickly that Thomas had not been capable of consent. According to one, Thomas 'was not possessor of himself'. More bluntly, according to another, 'he was burst in body, cracked in mind'. Dorothy Crispe had abused her power over a vulnerable young man in her care to secure his estate for her daughter. But had she broken the law? The judges observed that the case fit neither the Henrician nor Marian statutes on abduction, the first of which applied only to women and the latter only to girls under sixteen years of age. But, they concluded, 'such contriving marriage, be it a male or female or of what age soever is evil in itself at the common law and punishable in this court'. They invoked the precedent of the Brewton case and the claim then that 'children are the special goods of their parents'. They fined both Dorothy and Eleanor £500 each, along with smaller fines for some of their confederates, and ordered a sizeable fine for the minister who performed the marriage, 'for thrusting his sickle into another man's business'. Strikingly, too, they declared that 'all benefit of the marriage is taken away by this decree'. In other disputed cases, they had become careful to leave the question of the marriage's validity to the church courts. Here, perhaps because Thomas was already dead, they simply wiped it away.

Star Chamber judges thus made some effort not to tread upon the felony jurisdiction of the common-law courts, with their ability to impose sentences of death upon abductors, or upon the jurisdiction of the church courts, with their ability to annul a marriage as invalid. But between these two limits they opened up new territory in regulating marriage formation and establishing norms for consent free of both force and fraud, offering plaintiffs an additional venue in which to press their complaints. And while the statute that authorized their interventions had focused on young heiresses, echoing the longstanding common-law concern for the property implications of marriage, the court leaned more towards the ecclesiastical courts in asserting a care for the marriages of all, including young men and women with no particular property of note. The evidence surveyed here should, at the least, make a case for turning to Star Chamber for our histories of marriage and for adding marriage to the list of Star Chamber's responsibilities. We see the privy councillors and justices who staffed the court wrestling with issues of consent and coercion, querying just whose consent, given in what circumstances, sufficed for a binding union and broadening coercion beyond force and fear alone to include fraud and deceit.

While these Star Chamber cases filled a gap between canon and common law, they also straddled the line between abductions by would-be spouses and parental force. Attending to them might thus let us bridge two historiographies on marriage. Some of the marriages at the core of these cases were not the coerced unions examined in histories of medieval abductions but clandestine matches of the sort historians of early modern marriage have long discussed. Some readers may have been asking if many of these cases might not be better seen in the frame of clandestine unions made without publicity and parental consent rather than that of child, early and forced marriage. (Some readers might also have recalled that shortly after Chief Justice Hobart spoke in support of a father's rights over his child to protect the twelve-year-old Jane Brewton from her abductor, the other chief justice consulted on that case, Sir Edward Coke, notoriously used the same argument to coerce his fifteen-year-old daughter Frances into a marriage she did not want.[41]) There is a long historiography, with highlights in work by Lawrence Stone and Alan Macfarlane, among others, that focused on the shifting balance between arranged versus free matches – parental control versus individual choice – with the latter valorized as a sign of liberal modernity, among other positive developments.[42] Force has not been absent from these discussions of marriage, but it is seen as coming from the parents, not the spouse. The Star Chamber evidence suggests that we need to allow that bridal abduction by husbands-to-be continued into

[41] See, e.g., J. Luthman, *Love, Madness, and Scandal: The Life of Frances Coke Villiers, Viscountess Purbeck* (Oxford, 2017), pp. 26–41.

[42] L. Stone, *The Family, Sex and Marriage in England, 1500–1800* (New York, 1977); A. Macfarlane, *The Origins of English Individualism: The Family, Property and Social Transition* (Oxford, 1978) and *Marriage and Love in England: Modes of Reproduction, 1300–1840* (Oxford, 1986). See also, e.g, Ingram, *Church Courts, Sex and Marriage*; R. B. Outhwaite, *Clandestine Marriage*; P. Rushton, 'Property, power, and family networks: the problem of disputed marriage in early modern England', *Journal of Family History*, xi (1986), 205–19; D. O'Hara, *Courtship and Constraint: Rethinking the Making of Marriage in Tudor England* (Manchester, 2002).

the early modern period.[43] And it also helps us see that unmarried women and unmarried men, and unmarried children and unmarried adults, had different interests – or sat at different fulcrums – in the balancing act between individual and family interests that has so dominated our discussions of consent and coercion in early modern marriage. If the individuals whose interests we centre are allowed sometimes to be women or children, that conflict sometimes looks different. We might pay more attention to how consent and coercion and the experiences of violence and freedom in marriage-making developed differentially according to age and to gender.

The post-Reformation remaking of marriage transpired very differently in England than elsewhere. England, notoriously, was the one place among all Protestant jurisdictions that did not come to allow divorce with remarriage. Its other distinction was the lack of change to the age of marriage and refusal to require parental consent to create binding marriages. Eventually, the short-lived marriage law of the Interregnum raised the ages to fourteen and sixteen for young women and men respectively and required parental consent for marriages by anyone under twenty-one years of age to be valid; the latter provision was only reenacted in 1753 with Lord Hardwicke's act.[44] The divergence around parental consent was even more striking than that in respect to divorce, given that even some Catholic countries made such changes. Eric Carlson looked at this 'dog that didn't bark' and concluded that no real calls were made for change in England; English marriage law worked, was well understood and accepted.[45] But we see in these Star Chamber cases evidence not just that some plaintiffs were unhappy with rules around consent as they stood, but some privy councillors and bishops, too. It is a history, then, that warrants revisiting, not least in being not yet past.

[43] On this point, see also Capern, 'Heiress'.

[44] *Acts and Ordinances of the Interregnum*, ed. C. H. Firth and R. S. Rait (London, 1911), pp. 715–18; 26 Geo. II, c. 33.

[45] E. Carlson, *Marriage and the English Reformation* (Oxford, 1994), pp. 96, 138, 141.

7. Labourers, legal aid and the limits of popular legalism in Star Chamber*

Hillary Taylor

In recent decades, historians have done much to enhance our understanding of the nature and extent of popular participation in the early modern English legal system. Common people contributed to the business of a range of courts, thereby helping to bring about a period of litigiousness from the second half of the sixteenth century that was – and remains – unique in English history.[1] While members of the labouring population were most likely to initiate suits outside of Westminster, they were not wholly absent from the central courts. Examinations of Exchequer have revealed customary tenants' recourse to litigation, while studies of Requests have demonstrated the degree to which less well-off litigants used the court in their efforts to resolve disputes about a variety of issues.[2] Taken in aggregate, this work suggests that the law was not the mystified preserve of the ruling gentry and professional groups; rather, it was harnessed by a broad swathe of the population for their own purposes.

* I am grateful to Krista Kesselring and Natalie Mears for organizing the conference that produced this volume and for their feedback on this chapter; to Richard Bell, Craig Muldrew and Keith Wrightson for reading an earlier draft; and to Amy Erickson, Paul Cavill and Laura Flannigan for discussing various points.

[1] For an inexhaustive discussion of these issues and the increase in litigation across various courts, see J. A. Sharpe, 'The people and the law', in *Popular Culture in Seventeenth-Century England*, ed. B. Reay (New York, 1985), pp. 244–70; C. W. Brooks, *Pettyfoggers and Vipers of the Commonwealth: the 'Lower Branch' of the Legal Profession in Early Modern England* (Cambridge, 1986); L. Gowing, *Domestic Dangers: Women, Words, and Sex in Early Modern London* (Oxford, 1996); C. Muldrew, *The Economy of Obligation: the Culture of Credit and Social Relations in Early Modern England* (New York, 1998); C. W. Brooks, 'Litigation, participation and agency in seventeenth- and eighteenth-century England', in *The British and Their Laws in the Eighteenth Century*, ed. D. Lemmings (2005), pp. 155–81.

[2] For Requests and the 'poverty' of its litigants, see T. Stretton, *Women Waging Law in Elizabethan England* (Cambridge, 1998); L. Flannigan, 'Litigants in the English "Court of Poor Men's Causes," or court of Requests, 1515–25', *Law and History Review,* xxxviii (2019), 1–35. For Exchequer suits regarding customary rights, see A. Wood, *The Memory of the People: Custom and Popular Senses of the Past in Early Modern England* (Cambridge, 2013).

H. Taylor, 'Labourers, legal aid and the limits of popular legalism in Star Chamber' in *Star Chamber Matters: An Early Modern Court and Its Records*, ed. K. Kesselring and N. Mears (London, 2021), pp. 115–133.

By contrast, Star Chamber presents fewer opportunities for exploring labouring people's participation in the legal system – at least as the instigators of suits. It lent itself, in Thomas Barnes's estimation, to 'gentlemen's business, first and foremost'.[3] While members of the labouring population did find themselves involved in Star Chamber litigation, it was more often as defendants. Nonetheless, historians have found ways around these issues. Where labouring defendants are concerned, they have made good use of suits related to one substantial portion of Star Chamber business: the prosecution of riot in general, and enclosure riot in particular. Among other things, they have used its records to analyse the politics surrounding access to and assaults on common rights; the ways in which those who were liable to prosecution sought to manipulate ambiguities in the law to their own advantage; and the social depth of 'law-mindedness' in the period.[4] Others have suggested that the court's significance should be assessed in relation to the opportunities that it provided for common people to participate in the legal process as witnesses. In their depositions, Steve Hindle has suggested that members of the labouring population evinced an 'almost compulsive tendency to think in terms of "rights"'.[5] Labouring people's involvement in Star Chamber litigation therefore not only facilitated the expression of popular – if not national – legal and political cultures, but also played a constitutive role in their formation over the course of the early modern period.

This chapter advances a more pessimistic vision of popular legalism and plebian experiences of the legal process by exploring another genre of suits that comprised a fair amount of Star Chamber's business: namely, those featuring allegations related to the perversion of justice.[6] It is something of a companion piece to a recent article of mine, which examined the forms

[3] T. G. Barnes, 'Star Chamber litigants and their counsel, 1596–1641', in *Legal Records and the Historian*, ed. J. H. Baker (1978), pp. 7–28, at p. 10. Barnes estimated that – where occupational statuses are known – husbandmen, artisans and labourers accounted for 6% of litigants in this period. For women's use of the court, see D. Youngs, '"A besy woman … and full of lawe": female litigants in the early Tudor Star Chamber', *Journal of British Studies*, lviii (2019), 735–50.

[4] For recent examples, see J. Walter, '"Law-mindedness": crowds, courts, and popular knowledge of the law in early modern England', in *Law, Lawyers, and Litigants in Early Modern England: Essays in Memory of Christopher W. Brooks*, ed. Lobban, et al. (2019), pp. 164–85; B. McDonagh, 'Making and breaking property: negotiating enclosure and common rights in sixteenth-century England', *History Workshop Journal*, lxxvi (2013), 32–56.

[5] S. Hindle, *The State and Social Change in Early Modern England, c.1550–1640* (New York, 2002), pp. 89–91. He estimates that 38% of Star Chamber deponents were husbandmen, artisans or labourers.

[6] This category of offences includes perjury, subornation, corruption, extortion, maintenance, etc.

of instrumentalization and coercion that could result in labouring people's testifying on behalf of their litigious superiors – typically, though not exclusively, in property disputes that were of no immediate concern to them – and the potential consequences of their doing so. Among other things, these included their being sued in Star Chamber for perjury as a result of giving 'false' evidence under oath in previous suits.[7] The volume of suits involving allegations of subornation and/or perjury is sizeable, particularly from the Elizabethan period, after the latter became a statutory offence in 1563 and as the overall volume of litigation increased. Contemporary observers of Star Chamber remarked on this phenomenon.[8] For the most part, these records do not lend themselves to quantitative analysis.[9] To be sure, recurring tropes do emerge from sustained engagement with this material. But it is not reduceable to such factors because individual suits varied considerably in their level of detail and complexity.[10] And while a portion of this litigation was almost certainly generated by 'vexatious' in-fighting between individuals of roughly comparable socio-economic position, it remains the case that labouring people not infrequently became ensnared in it.[11] Even where their involvement did not result in formal prosecution or punishment by the court, it could – at the minimum – occasion annoyance.[12]

At their best, Star Chamber subornation and perjury suits – as well as those involving allegations of legal corruption more broadly – shed light on

[7] H. Taylor, 'The price of the poor's words: social relations and the economics of deposing for one's "betters" in early modern England', *Economic History Review*, lxx (2019), 828–47.

[8] For the growth in perjury suits, see W. Hudson, *A Treatise of the Court of Star Chamber*, in *Collectanea juridica, vol. II*, ed. F. Hargrave (1792), p. 74

[9] This is primarily due to the way the records are catalogued (particularly STAC 5) and the often fragmentary nature of the surviving records.

[10] For some suits, the only surviving documentation is a rather perfunctory and formulaic bill of complaint. For others, bills are accompanied by answers, rejoinders, etc, and – in some cases – depositions ranging in number from a few to dozens. The quality of depositions varies from suit to suit. Some are laconic de-facto reproductions of the interrogatories that were put to deponents, while others are in-depth statements that deviate from the interrogatories.

[11] For an inexhaustive list of instances in which labourers were sued for perjury, see The National Archives of the UK, STAC 5/A12/16; STAC 5/S3/8; STAC 5/W/36; STAC 8/83/18; STAC 8/83/20; STAC 8/92/7; STAC 8/85/2; STAC 8/87/11; STAC 8/107/11; STAC 8/123/6; STAC 8/132/19; STAC 8/159/19; STAC 8/162/23; STAC 8/177/6; STAC 8/206/27. For vexatious litigation, see Brooks, *Pettyfoggers and Vipers*, pp. 107–11.

[12] Even where labouring people refused to testify in property disputes, they could still end up having to appear before the justices. For a 1630 case involving labourers who were (unsuccessfully) pressured to depose in a controversy about their deceased employer's will, but nonetheless examined at the quarter sessions, see Somerset Heritage Centre (SHC), Q/SR/62, fos. 44–47.

alternative aspects of labouring people's participation in both civil and criminal litigation prior to the court's abolition in 1641. They illuminate the multiple and sometimes contradictory ways in which members of the labouring population individually or collectively thought about the prospect of engaging in the legal process, as well as their knowledge of the technicalities of legal procedure. They also offer a salutary reminder that litigation did not occur in a vacuum. Rather, the processes that resulted in labouring people's participation – whether as witnesses or as defendants – were informed by socio-economic factors and relationships that preceded their appearance 'in court'. Upon arrival, common people's experiences could be further shaped by the actions of their relative peers and their superiors who comprised the ranks of the legal profession. Whatever the individual virtues of legal functionaries may have been, they were nonetheless products of a society that was inclined to view members of the labouring population in particular (and not entirely favourable) ways. As such, they had inherited attitudes and assumptions about their inferiors, which could colour their encounters with them during the legal process.[13]

This chapter explores these themes by analysing a convoluted and protracted set of Star Chamber suits and countersuits that were filed between 1602 and 1606.[14] The imbroglio was occasioned by a dispute about who should inherit the property of Richard Cockshott, an innholder from St Giles in the Fields, London, who had considerable assets at the time of his death in 1592. His testamentary arrangements – or, as it happened, alleged lack thereof – subsequently proved controversial.[15] On one side

[13] To my mind, these contentions hold even when confronted with the familiar counter-argument regarding the extent to which (partisan) legal records can be used to recover anything approximating 'reality'. Even if the comments and behaviours described in such documents were fabricated in the interests of advancing particular claims, they nonetheless had to be socially plausible in order to get traction.

[14] The relevant references are TNA, STAC 5/C70/39 (1602/3, *Cockshott* v *Parke, Codnor, et al.*); STAC 8/312/50 (Feb. 1604, *Cockshott* v *Parke, Codnor, et al.*); STAC 8/232/33 (July 1604, *Parke* v *Cockshott and Wilkinson*); STAC 8/103/10 (1606, *Cockshott* v *Parke, Codnor, et al.*). A total of 27 depositions were generated in these suits. Bills of complaint are in STAC 5/C70/39 and STAC 8/103/10. STAC 8/232/33 and STAC 8/312/50 consist of depositions and interrogatories. A search of The National Archives online catalogue also lists material in STAC 8/232/34 and STAC 8/233/12, but these documents appear to no longer exist as discrete references in their own right, having been combined with the previous 4 references.

[15] According to various estimates, when he died Richard Cockshott was worth somewhere in the range of £300–500 and was possessed of a lease for about 50 acres of land in Knightsbridge, 5 horses, almost a dozen cows, and either 16 or 18 featherbeds. See TNA, STAC 8/103/10, Thomas Cockshott (bill), Christopher Hill and John Wilkinson (depositions); STAC 8/312/50, John Codnor and Thomas Parke (depositions). Parke

Table 7.1: Parties involved in the disputes between Thomas Parke and Thomas Cockshott

Name	Occupational status	Role
Richard Cockshott	innholder (London)	Dies in 1592; will disputed. At time of his death, purportedly worth somewhere in the range of £300–500, also possessed of a lease for c. 50 acres in Knightsbridge, etc.
Thomas Parke	dyer (London)	Richard Cockshott's brother-in-law. In 1595, after the death of his sister Alice, enlists Codnor to depose about Richard Cockshott's nuncupative will and gets his property. Files Star Chamber counter suit against Thomas Cockshott and John Wilkinson for maintenance in 1604.
Thomas Cockshott	yeoman (Surrey)	Richard Cockshott's nephew. Attempts to get his uncle's property from Parke in various courts, and from 1602 launches multiple Star Chamber suits against Parke and Codnor for subornation of perjury and perjury, respectively.
John Codnor	labourer (London)	Worked for Richard Cockshott. Deposed about nuncupative will for Parke in 1595, and again in King's Bench. Sued in Star Chamber for perjury by Thomas Cockshott in 1602. His answer – containing a confession – is produced under dubious circumstances with the help of John Wilkinson.
Christopher Hill	labourer (London)	Labourer who worked for Richard Cockshott, alongside Codnor. Deposes for Thomas Cockshott against Codnor in Star Chamber.
John Wilkinson	baker (London)	Associate of Thomas Cockshott's who helped him prosecute various suits against Parke in Star Chamber and elsewhere. Involved in procuring Codnor's answer to Cockshott's 1602 suit. Sued by Parke in Star Chamber in 1604 for maintenance.

Source: Works cited in note 14

was Thomas Parke, a London dyer and Richard's brother-in-law, who had, after the death of Richard's wife Alice in 1594, successfully positioned himself as sole inheritor. On the other side was Thomas Cockshott, a Surrey yeoman who, as Richard's nephew, claimed that he was entitled

mentions an inventory, but I have been unable to locate records that could corroborate any of these accounts.

to the innholder's remaining assets. The dispute trundled through multiple courts before eventually making its way to Star Chamber. There, Cockshott embarked on a last-ditch effort to wrest his uncle's property from Parke by challenging the veracity of the evidence that Parke had marshalled to procure it. A pair of London labourers called John Codnor and Christopher Hill were at the centre of this suite of Star Chamber litigation in various capacities. The former appeared three times as a defendant who was accused of committing perjury for Parke, while the latter served as a key witness for Cockshott.

The material considered here enables an analysis on multiple and complementary scales. The first section explores the ways in which a general phenomenon played out in a particular instance: in this case, how and why the two labourers became involved in the dispute, as well as the legal and extra-legal consequences of their involvement. The following section reconstructs issues that are often obscured due to a lack of available documentation: namely, the nature and practical limits of an individual labouring defendant's legal knowledge, the ways in which these limitations shaped his room for manoeuvre and the forms of legal aid that were available for socio-economically disadvantaged defendants. The concluding section assesses the extent to which this Star Chamber case can enhance our understanding of labouring people's interconnected experiences of both civil litigation and the criminal law in early modern England.

***

To the extent that Star Chamber records were concerned with uncovering malfeasance that had purportedly occurred in earlier rounds of litigation, they are useful for reconstructing the factors that caused labouring people to testify in the first place. Such witnesses were typically drawn into property disputes as a result of knowledge they had accumulated – or could plausibly claim to have accumulated – over the course of their employment histories. In some instances, they were enlisted to depose about incidents that they had witnessed decades previously. In others, they were procured to comment on more recent events. By the time some disputes made it to court, labouring people were the only witnesses who were still alive or in a position to testify about the incidents in question; this presumably made their testimony all the more valuable. All of these factors were at play in the case considered here. By their own accounts, John Codnor and Christopher Hill had worked for Richard Cockshott for about fifteen years prior to his death. Along with two servants and Richard's wife Alice, both were present during his final illness.

The parties at variance – Thomas Parke and Thomas Cockshott – both sought to capitalize on the quartet's experience, albeit in different ways. Parke was first off the mark. In 1595, about a year after his sister Alice's death, he recruited Codnor and two of Richard's other servants to depose in London's commissary court about a nuncupative will that Richard had allegedly made.[16] As a result of their testimony, Parke secured his brother-in-law's property. Thomas Cockshott then sued Parke for trespass in King's Bench; once again, Parke relied on Codnor's testimony to thwart Cockshott's claims. Finally, in 1602, like other litigants whose ambitions had been frustrated, Cockshott turned to Star Chamber as a court of last resort.

Cockshott used Star Chamber to attack the credibility of Parke, his witnesses and their testimony by suing them for subornation of perjury and perjury, respectively, and by claiming that his uncle had in fact died intestate. Cockshott's bill of complaint, like others in this subgenre of suits, formulaically traded in commonplaces regarding the direct correlation between poverty and dishonesty. This link purportedly became more pronounced when prospective witnesses were offered rewards or were subjected to pressure by those who sought their testimony.[17] Such ideas continued to enjoy purchase well after Star Chamber's abolition. As one minister remarked in an assize sermon from 1682: 'the most usual occasions and common temptations to this sin [of perjury were] poverty and necessity; covetousness and hope of reward'.[18] Cockshott's bill of complaint alleged that Codnor 'did falsly and corruptly sweare and depose [as he had] because [he] was hyered and suborned thereunto by Parke' on multiple occasions: first in the commissary court, and then in King's Bench.[19] Yet the most detailed and damning information against Parke and his witnesses was presented not by Cockshott himself, but by Christopher Hill. Of the four labourers and servants who were ostensibly privy to their employer's final arrangements, Hill was unique not only in his willingness to present a

[16] These servants were called Katherine Jorden and Elizabeth Ewen. Jorden managed to avoid being charged with perjury because she died before Cockshott filed his first Star Chamber suit. Ewen was sued alongside Codnor for perjury, but – in comparison to Codnor – few details survive about her experience of the legal process.

[17] For examples of the scripts, see Taylor, 'Price'. Sometimes, litigants who believed that they would be inconvenienced by witnesses' testimony threatened to take them to Star Chamber in an effort to dissuade them deposing at all. E.g., see TNA, STAC 8/173/25.

[18] J. Allen, *Of Perjury: A Sermon Preach'd at the Assizes Held at Chester, April 1682* (1682), p. 19.

[19] TNA, STAC 5/C70/39, Thomas Cockshott (bill).

version of events that was amenable to Cockshott, but also in his readiness to testify against his former co-workers.

Lawsuits could create circumstances in which members of the labouring population were brought into conflict with one another. Where labouring individuals were recruited into temporary alliances with their litigious superiors, they were often expected to provide evidence against their relative peers. In his Star Chamber suits against Codnor, Cockshott relied heavily on both Hill's testimony and his willingness to denounce his former co-worker. To support the allegation that Codnor had been bribed by Parke to provide false evidence about Richard's nuncupative will, Hill made multiple points. He deposed that his fellow labourer was of 'small creditt or abilitie'. To buttress his own credibility, Hill claimed that although he and Codnor had both allowed Parke to buy them dinner, he left when they were offered 'some hosehold stuffe' if they would give 'false' evidence in support of the dyer's claims about the will. According to Hill, Codnor had no such scruples. Hill outlined the disbursements that had underwritten the other labourer's testimony, recalling – among other things – that Codnor had 'confesse[d]' in private conversation 'that he had coles & wood given him by [Parke] to say as he would have him'.[20] In making such points about Codnor's socio-economic position and his susceptibility to material encouragements, Hill employed tropes that were used to cast aspersions on and discredit labouring witnesses throughout the period.[21]

Indeed, for Hill, Codnor appears to have been little more than a means to an end, and he used the prospect of a post-depositional windfall as a kind of security to back mundane transactions. John Browne, a journeyman shoemaker, recalled that the labourer had come to his master's shop, demanding that they hurry to repair the shoes he had left because he wanted to wear them when he testified.[22] Browne said that he would be more inclined to do so if Hill would 'bestowe some drinke uppon' him

[20] TNA, STAC 8/103/10, Christopher Hill (deposition). Codnor previously admitted (STAC 8/312/50) that he received 'some coles' and 'other trifflinge thinges' from Parke, but denied that this had been a payment for testimony. Katherine Codnor (John's wife) admitted that Parke's wife had given her a 'busshell of coles', a 'necke of mutton' and an 'olde rugge' when the family found themselves 'in verie great want and extremitie'. See STAC 8/103/10, Katherine Codnor and Joan Castlyn (depositions).

[21] For these attitudes and their expression in the ecclesiastical courts, see A. Shepard, *Accounting for Oneself: Worth, Status, and the Social Order in Early Modern England* (Oxford, 2015).

[22] This is the only example I have come across featuring a labouring witness who appears to have been concerned about sartorial respectability when deposing. The allegation that witnesses were loaned less shabby clothing to wear when they testified is more common. See, e.g., TNA, STAC 5/W12/36.

and repay an outstanding debt to his master. Hill replied that although he was unable to do either at the time because he had 'but 6d.', he expected that a significant amount of money (indeed, an implausibly high sum of 'a hundred powndes or two'!) would be coming his way 'if all things [fell] owt right' and Cockshott won his case. He promised to use this to pay off his debts and buy Browne a drink.[23] It is unclear what came of Hill's offer or expected reward; presumably little.

As the case of Christopher Hill and others suggest, fleeting and mutually self-interested alliances between litigants and labouring witnesses may well have provided the latter with an opportunity to make a bit on the side.[24] But such gains – whether real or illusory – could come at the expense of their peers. We might note a degree of irony here. Where perjury accusations were levelled against members of the labouring population, other labouring witnesses were, as a result of the circles in which they moved, often uniquely placed to comment on the actions of the accused. One labourer's denunciation of another presumably carried a patina of legitimacy that was lacking in a labourer's denunciation of, say, a gentleman.[25] Furthermore, from the perspective of a labourer who did the denouncing, the stakes were lower; their testimony was presumably less likely to result in retribution in the form of extra-legal exactions related to employment and so forth. The momentary elevation of some labouring deponents 'in court' was thus predicated upon their willingness to cannibalize those of roughly comparable socio-economic position. If some categories of litigation occasioned the expression of solidarities among the ranks of the labouring population, others generated antagonisms within it that furthered the ambitions of their 'betters' in the final instance.

***

[23] TNA, STAC 8/232/33, John Browne (deposition).

[24] For witnesses admitting that they deposed for remuneration, see Taylor, 'Price'; A. Wood, 'Subordination, solidarity and the limits of popular agency in a Yorkshire valley, *c*.1596–1615', *Past and Present*, cxciii (2006), 41–72.

[25] Here, a theme to consider is scenarios in which labourers who had deposed on previous occasions discussed their testimony (and, in some instances, allegedly confessed to having committed perjury) while working with labourers, husbandmen, etc. I have not come across any examples in which supposedly perjured employers discussed their testimony with those who worked for them. This might be because they had few interactions with them or did not regard such topics as fit for conversation. If such conversations *did* happen, there are obvious reasons why labourers, etc would be reluctant to recount them in court.

Social bonds shaped labouring people's experiences of litigation in other ways. The degree to which defendants were able to mount a successful defence in Star Chamber depended partly on the nature of the social networks of which they were a part and the connections that they enjoyed. Historians have highlighted the degree to which labouring defendants might benefit from a combination of communal fellow-feeling and (in)formal legal advice when responding to the charges against them. In their depositions, some who were accused of riot demonstrated knowledge that enabled them to manipulate loopholes and ambiguities in the law to their own advantage.[26]

But where members of the labouring population found themselves in Star Chamber as relatively atomized defendants – as appears to have been the case with Codnor – matters were more complicated. It was one thing to have an abstract notion of what constituted law and justice, or a sense of one's rights (customary or otherwise).[27] It was another to have a detailed understanding of how one might assert oneself while navigating the vagaries of a relatively unfamiliar legal process. In such circumstances, there were educational, monetary and social barriers to overcome, and labouring defendants might find themselves reliant on the advice and assistance of their better-informed superiors. Where the motivations of particular superiors were ambiguous – if not baldly self-interested – this dependency could occasion difficulties for defendants.

Codnor's case offers an example of the sort of predicament in which solitary labouring defendants might find themselves. Around the time Cockshott first sued him in Star Chamber in 1602, the labourer was in Newgate. He claimed that a debt of '£5 or thereabouts' had landed him in prison. His detractors – presumably attempting to undermine his credibility further – heard that he had been arrested for 'stealing [a] silver cup or goblett' and had been in Newgate 'diverse tymes [for] theft and cosenage'.[28] Whatever the exact cause of his imprisonment, Codnor was still expected to put in an answer to Cockshott's bill of complaint against him. By analysing the well-documented processes that resulted in the

[26] E.g., see TNA, STAC 8/83/18.

[27] It should, however, be noted that poverty could prevent people contributing to the so-called common purses that tenants collected to litigate in defence of their common rights. For a labourer from Waterbeach (Cambridgeshire) who remarked that he would have 'give[n] monie if he had anie to spare which he hath not being a verie poore man', see TNA, STAC 8/311/3, Henry Redman (deposition).

[28] TNA, STAC 8/232/33, John Codnor (deposition). See also John Wilkinson in this reference and in STAC 8/103/50 (depositions). Codnor said this debt was to a John Winterskill, but I have been unable to locate additional information that could substantiate his account or relation to Winterskill.

production of Codnor's answer, we can better appreciate the factors that could shape the experience of a labouring defendant and circumscribe the options available to them.

The labourer was initially left to his own devices. Although he was being sued as a result of his involvement with his co-defendant Parke, the dyer apparently neglected to shepherd him through the relevant stages of Star Chamber litigation.[29] A saviour (of sorts) then appeared. Perhaps thinking that the labourer's current position would render him susceptible to an offer that would transform him from a legal obstacle into an asset, an associate of Cockshott's, a London baker called John Wilkinson, visited him in Newgate. (Wilkinson was assisting Cockshott in the prosecution of various suits and would eventually be countersued by Parke in Star Chamber for maintenance – that is, assisting and supporting another person's litigation; he was motivated to do so in part because he was trying to lease the disputed land in Knightsbridge from Cockshott.[30]) Wilkinson told Codnor that 'if [he] would unsaye that which he had previously saied' and would 'say as Christopher Hill had saied' (that is, deny that the evidence he had given for Parke in the testamentary dispute was true and admit that he had been bribed by Parke to depose as he had), he would 'helpe [him] owt of prison'.[31] Codnor refused, maintaining that he had told the truth and therefore wished to deny the charges against him. Wilkinson then reminded him that he was nonetheless obliged to make his answer to Star Chamber. The labourer asked how 'he might make his answere to the bill w[it]hout charge for that he had no monie'. At this point, Wilkinson generously stepped into the breach, offering to make a petition requesting he admitted *in forma pauperis*.[32] The labourer consented. Why might he have agreed to receive assistance from an ally of the person who was suing him?

To appreciate Codnor's situation, we should consider the likelihood of a labourer having a robust familiarity with the legal options that were available for socio-economically disadvantaged defendants in Star Chamber. Relevant

[29] Parke appears to have filed his own answer – in which he denied the charges of subornation – separately. See STAC 5/C70/39 for both answers.

[30] Maintenance remains under-studied in the early modern period, but see J. Rose, *Maintenance in Medieval England* (Cambridge, 2017). Wilkinson had allegedly spent £100 towards Cockshott's suits; because land was involved, it might be more accurate to call his behaviour champerty (a form of maintenance).

[31] TNA, STAC 8/232/33, John Codnor (deposition).

[32] TNA, STAC 8/232/33, John Wilkinson (deposition). Knowledge regarding legal aid presumably circulated in London's prisons, particularly where lawyers were imprisoned for debt. For an example of a 'veryе poore distressed prisoner' of unspecified occupation in King's Bench who successfully petitioned to exhibit a bill *in forma pauperis* in Requests, see TNA, SP 46/42, fo. 259.

here is the 1495 statute intended to ensure that poor individuals were not barred from taking legal action and receiving justice in the common-law courts.[33] Persons worth less than £5 (or who received less than 40*s* a year from land) could petition to be admitted *in forma pauperis*. If successful, they were assigned counsel and their legal costs were waived. By the sixteenth century, similar practices operated in the equity and conciliar courts, though the precise mechanisms by which they had developed remain obscure. Historians have noted the provision's role in enabling individuals to initiate litigation – particularly in Requests, where persons admitted *in forma pauperis* are estimated to have accounted for around 10% of plaintiffs.[34] (Though it must be noted that a sizeable portion of these individuals creatively defined their worth and should not be counted among the ranks of the chronically impoverished.) Comparatively little attention, however, has been paid to legal aid provisions for defendants. We know even less about how knowledgeable the legitimately poor were about the discretionary dispensations to which they could be entitled in such circumstances, or the routes whereby they may have acquired such knowledge.[35]

While *in forma pauperis* status was granted to defendants in the conciliar and equity courts, evidence suggests that it was rare in comparison to the provisions available for those seeking to initiate suits. A small sample of petitions requesting admission *in forma pauperis* in the late sixteenth and early seventeenth centuries indicates that 4% were made by defendants, the majority in Requests (and none in Star Chamber).[36] To explore Star Chamber's willingness to allocate legal aid, we therefore have to triangulate between various sources while engaging in a bit of conjecture. According to William Hudson, Star Chamber discouraged petitions requesting *in*

[33] For the statute, see 11 Henry VII, ch. 12, *Statutes of the Realm*, ii. 578.

[34] Stretton, *Women Waging Law*, p. 85.

[35] For a 1602 petition signed by 46 people requesting that William Thomas, a 'verie pore laborer' from Southampton, be 'admitted *in forma pauperis* for answering the malicious information' of a yeoman who had reported him for 'ingrossinge … graine to the quantitie of ffowe hundred quarters', see TNA, SP 46/163/2, fo. 217. That Thomas had such community backing might suggest that he was receiving informal legal advice or encouragement from some of the signatories. Guidance on how to obtain admission *in forma pauperis* was included in legal manuals. For a later example, see H. R., *Countrymans Counsellour: Or, Every Man Made His Own Lawyer* (1682), p. 10.

[36] Of 92 sampled petitions, 8 were from defendants (2 of whom were labourers; occupational statuses were unspecified for the others). These estimates are calculated from petitions listed in the appendix of A. Prossnitz, 'A comprehensive procedural mechanism for the poor: reconceptualizing the right to *in forma pauperis* in early modern England', *Northwestern University Law Review*, cxiv (2020), 1673–722. Petitions may be an imperfect guide to practice because some admissions *in forma pauperis* might have involved verbal transactions. See Flannigan, 'Litigants', p. 10.

forma pauperis status on the part of would-be litigants; this was done partly out of a desire to prevent the court becoming host to the 'clamorous and vexatious suits of poor people living in remote parts'. But he continued, hinting at the ways in which the less affluent could become the tools of their litigious superiors: 'poor people shall be made defendants in this court, for many times they are made instruments to do the greatest offences'. In such circumstances – where poor individuals were 'joined defendants' with 'able persons' – Hudson remarked that they '[ought] upon their oath … to be admitted [*in forma pauperis*], and have counsel assigned unto them'.[37] This logic was similar to points made in scripture and canon law, which maintained that socio-economically disadvantaged persons should be enabled to defend themselves from 'legal oppression and exploitation' at the hands of the more powerful.[38] Surviving – if fragmentary – evidence from the sixteenth century suggests that it was indeed possible for Star Chamber defendants (as well as plaintiffs) to receive counsel and have their fees waived. But it is difficult to gauge whether such isolated examples were representative of broader trends, or to assess the precise socio-economic positions of the defendants in question.[39]

For the present purposes, we might assume that Codnor was statistically unlikely to have been friendly with anyone who had appeared as a plaintiff *in forma pauperis* in Star Chamber (or even in Requests). He was presumably even less likely to have known someone who had done so as a defendant. If so, he was ill-equipped to gainsay the advice and assistance offered to him by an individual with knowledge of the relevant process. Codnor's assent to Wilkinson's proposal to petition on his behalf for legal aid might appear naïve, but it is unclear what he might have done otherwise.

Although Wilkinson's offer set in motion a chain of events that *technically* enabled the labourer to participate in the legal process, little suggests that Codnor was able to shape the proceedings in a meaningful way. Instead, he was pushed through the stages of procedure by various of his superiors who had little interest in directly engaging him. Codnor's answer was effectively

[37] Hudson, 'Treatise', pp. 128–9, 140.

[38] For these points, see J. A. Brundage, 'Legal aid for the poor and the professionalization of law in the middle ages', *Journal of Legal History*, ix (1988), 169–79, at p. 170. For *personae miserabili* in the European context, see G. Vermeesch, 'Access to justice: legal aid to the poor at civil law courts in the eighteenth-century Low Countries', *Law and History Review*, xxxii (2014), 683–714.

[39] For a suit in which both complainant and defendant were admitted *in forma pauperis*, see J. Hawarde, *Les Reports del Cases in Camera Stellata, 1593–1603*, ed. W. P. Baildon (London, 1894), pp. 83–4. For two examples of plaintiffs admitted *in forma pauperis* during Wolsey's tenure, see J. Guy, *The Court of Star Chamber and its Records to the Reign of Elizabeth I* (London, 1985), p. 62.

drawn up and submitted without his having any say in its production or precise knowledge of its contents. This was possible because legal functionaries at multiple stages of the process were apparently content to interact only with Wilkinson – the labourer's self-appointed intermediary – rather than the labourer himself. As we have seen, Wilkinson had a vested interest in securing an answer that contained a confession. After his attempts to pressure the imprisoned labourer into 'voluntarily' making such a statement failed, he appears to have accomplished the same result due to the carelessness of legal professionals. That such carelessness was exhibited suggests that we might do well to be sceptical about the quality of legal aid that the legitimately poor could expect to receive, even if – in theory – their poverty did not work to their disadvantage.

Negligence was initially displayed by the attorney who was appointed to assist the labourer's case. When Wilkinson successfully petitioned for Codnor to be admitted *in forma pauperis* to make his answer, a Mr Lancaster of Gray's Inn was assigned as his counsel. In a passing encounter, Lancaster was subsequently questioned by an acquaintance and fellow attorney about what, precisely, he had done for Codnor. The answer appears to have been rather little. Lancaster admitted that he 'never spake' with the labourer, 'nor ever saw him to his remembrance'.[40] He added that someone – an associate of Wilkinson's – had brought the answer to him 'ready ingrossed' and told him that it was Codnor's 'owne confession and answere [so] he did sett his hand to the same', apparently without further ado.[41] It is difficult to say whether Lancaster or someone else in his position would have been as willing to sign off on an answer in the absence of a more socio-economically advantaged defendant. The issue here is less to do with the ability of a particular defendant to pay the requisite legal fees and more to do with the regard, or lack thereof, accorded to labouring defendants. Lancaster may well have calculated that Codnor would be unable or unwilling to protest any perceived legal impropriety committed against him. Perhaps he did not bother to think much about it at all.

Having procured the answer, Wilkinson returned to Newgate to collect Codnor and proceed with the next step of the Star Chamber process. The labourer remembered that about a week after their first conversation, Wilkinson gave money – either '3*s* 3*d* or 3*s* 9*d*' – to one of the keepers to 'paie [his] ffees for his release owt of prison' for a day and took him to

[40] When questioned as to how Codnor's answer materialized, Wilkinson admitted that Codnor had never interacted with Lancaster, but claimed that he had simply helped the imprisoned labourer to formalize the confession he wanted to make but lacked the ability to do independently. STAC 8/232/33, John Wilkinson (deposition).

[41] TNA, STAC 8/232/33, Thomas Baldwin (deposition).

see William Mill, the clerk of Star Chamber. En route, Wilkinson told Codnor that he would be swearing on two issues that were enumerated in the document. First, that it represented his 'true answere' to Cockshott's bill of complaint against him. Second, that he 'was not worth above five pownd' (the relevant threshold to be admitted *in forma pauperis*). At the time, Codnor appears to have operated under the impression that the document's contents did in fact resemble what he had previously told Wilkinson in Newgate – namely, that he had told the truth when he deposed for Parke and, as such, wished to deny the charges against him. And because – as Codnor subsequently told others – he 'was not worth half [£5]', he had seen no problem in assenting under oath to that portion of his answer's alleged contents.[42]

As he told it, Codnor had been reduced to a passive actor in the brief time he spent before the clerk. In theory, when Star Chamber defendants exhibited their answers, they were meant to be sworn and (at the clerk's discretion) examined on the accuracy of their statement.[43] This procedure appears to have been followed laxly in the case under consideration. The labourer recalled that before and during his time in Mill's chambers, he was shown a 'writinge in parchment'. But none of the individuals involved, including the clerk, apparently bothered to read the document to him or ask him anything about his intended answer. Codnor offered no retrospective commentary on whether he might have had reservations about the document or felt too intimidated to request that it be read to him; neither seems entirely beyond the realm of possibility. In any case, when questioned, he assented under oath to the veracity of its contents. His answer was filed, and he was returned to Newgate.

It was not until months later – after Codnor's release from prison – that he realized he had, in fact, formally confessed to perjury in this answer.[44] Thomas Baldwin, a lawyer who either worked for or socialized with Parke, corroborated the labourer's (and aspects of Wilkinson's) version of the events leading up to his time before the Star Chamber clerk. He also provided details about how outraged Codnor had been when someone finally bothered to read 'his' answer to him. Baldwin recalled that he had been at Parke's house in Holborn with a handful of others, who, having

[42] TNA, STAC 8/232/33, John Codnor (deposition).

[43] For this process, see Guy, *Court of Star Chamber*, pp. 38–9. Codnor described going to see Mill in Charterhouse, which suggests that he may have been working out of his residence rather than the Star Chamber office in Gray's Inn that was established during his clerkship.

[44] This was the result of a conversation with Wilkinson, who found Codnor while he was working in the Strand.

received a copy of Codnor's answer, questioned the labourer about how it had materialized. Codnor said that was never 'given counsel or gave any counsel for directions to draw up his answer'. When questioned further, he became angry and described the degree to which he had been systematically deprived of knowledge about stages of the process that bore directly upon him. He 'swore a great othe that [he] neither heard [Cockshott's] bill, nor [his own] answeare ever reade before that tyme: but saith that by reason that he coulde not reade, he p[er]ceaved that he had bene abused [by Wilkinson]'.[45] Codnor might have been hoodwinked, but his answer had nonetheless been produced. The legal drama in which he was – in the estimation of its more significant players – little more than an extra could continue.

How much stock should we put in these accounts of Codnor's manipulation and mistreatment, particularly in light of Star Chamber litigants' penchant for melodrama? Of course, the labourer may well have been strategically emphasizing his illiteracy in an effort to present himself as a hapless victim of Wilkinson's – and by extension, Cockshott's – chicanery. Calling attention to his ignorance and weakness could serve a dual function: one immediate and the other more abstract. On the one hand, it enabled Codnor to distance himself from involvement in the construction of a document that could prove inconvenient for his co-defendant Parke (whose house he was in when this outburst occurred). On the other, plebeian narratives of powerlessness could play well in the equity courts.[46] Much of the information regarding the production of the labourer's answer was generated when Parke filed his countersuit against Cockshott and Wilkinson. As such, there could have been good reasons for Codnor to present the dyer's opponents in the worst possible light.

But equally, it remains the case that the labourer's illiteracy – like his poverty and relative lack of familiarity with the relevant technicalities of legal procedure – was a form of dependency. When expected to answer the Star Chamber charges against him in the absence of funds or disinterested legal advice, Codnor had been obliged to take the word of the more knowledgeable Wilkinson at face value. As a result, he had inadvertently placed himself in a position that made it difficult for him to dispute the dictated terms of his legal engagement. While the labourer could retrospectively attempt to save face by highlighting the ways in which he had been abused by various of his superiors, he could not erase the conditions that rendered him vulnerable in the first place.

[45] TNA, STAC 8/232/33, Thomas Baldwin (deposition).

[46] See A. Wood, 'Fear, hatred, and the hidden injuries of class in early modern England', *Journal of Social History*, xxxix (2006), 803–26, at p. 812.

***

In relation to the total number of labouring witnesses who deposed in sixteenth- and seventeenth-century litigation of various types, it is impossible to quantify the proportion that eventually landed in Star Chamber as a result of their testimony. To be sure, *all* members of the labouring population were susceptible to having their depositions called into question because of the subordinated and dependent socio-economic positions they occupied. Filing perjury charges against labouring witnesses in Star Chamber was akin to picking low-hanging fruit: the negative stereotypes were in place, and all that was required were inconvenienced litigants who had the inclination, time and disposable income to capitalize on them. Nonetheless, in the grand scheme of things, the experience of those who became defendants in Star Chamber was probably not comparable to that of the majority of their peers.

We might assume that John Codnor's experience was even less representative. It could be added to the pile of Star Chamber stories: a colourful incident of individual misfortune, perhaps, but an aberration in an otherwise well-intentioned and functional system. To gain a holistic appreciation of labouring people's experiences of litigation and the law, it would be more profitable to consider the extent to which his case might be illustrative of more widespread phenomena that were – for a variety of reasons – unlikely to generate much of an evidentiary record.

Codnor's case provides an opportunity to reflect on the nature of plebeian legal knowledge and the degree to which it enabled labouring people to assert themselves in various settings. To be sure, many were aware of their rights and knew how legal institutions could be employed in an effort to maintain them. Nor were they particularly squeamish about initiating proceedings against their 'betters', should the circumstances require. Copyhold tenants knew about the customs in their locality; labourers knew that they could take action against employers who failed to pay their wages; and so forth. While such context-specific knowledge was useful, it was not transferrable to every legal scenario in which labouring people might conceivably find themselves. A given labouring individual might be capable of navigating some situations with relative confidence but be hamstrung in others. Codnor's dilemma – occasioned in part by his lack of familiarity with the right that poor defendants had to petition for the discretionary dispensation of legal aid – illustrates one way in which members of the labouring population could operate at a structural disadvantage in court.[47]

[47] For useful, albeit later, commentaries on the obstacles faced by the poor in legal contexts,

Where labouring individuals were compelled to navigate their way through relatively unfamiliar legal situations, their ability to assert themselves was further shaped by legal functionaries that they encountered. Although legal aid had theoretically been obtained for Codnor, in practice it amounted to little; his engagement with members of the legal profession was perfunctory in some instances and virtually non-existent in others. While Codnor's experience offers an extreme example of the lack of regard that could be paid to a poor defendant, by consulting other sources we can appreciate the factors that had enabled it to occur in the first place. Various commentaries on the legal system and the duties of those who comprised its ranks observed that members of the labouring population could be tedious to interact with and suggested that functionaries might be tempted to treat individuals differently based on their socio-economic position. For example, one seventeenth-century treatise noted that 'a right jurisprudent … acts not *pro imperio*, arbitrarily, but humbly, honestly, and conscientiously converses with all sorts of clients, whether *in forma pauperis*, or *divitis*, rich or poor'.[48] In presenting an ideal standard and exhorting lawyers and justices to strive towards it, such commentaries implied that alternative modes of engagement existed. This is not to suggest that all of these people were wilfully negligent or dismissive in their interactions with the poor; rather, the point is that they had the capacity to become so on any given occasion without a great deal of effort.

Plebeians' ability to use the law for their own purposes or mount a successful defence when they found themselves on the wrong side of it was therefore predicated on a number of contingencies. Here, we might be tempted to reaffirm familiar points about the discrepancies between the criminal and the civil law in the period. If the operation of the former laid bare and reinforced the fundamental inequalities of early modern society, the workings of the latter enabled them to be temporarily suspended in court.[49] Where members of the labouring population are concerned, however, this distinction holds in some instances, but less so in others. The category of Star Chamber suits examined here reveals some of the ways in which their involvement in civil litigation – however well-intentioned – could sour. As Codnor's experience demonstrates, labourers could be

---

see J. Bentham, 'A protest against law taxes' in *The Collected Works of Jeremy Bentham: Writings on Political Economy, Vol. 1*, ed. M. Quinn (2016), pp. 271–93; W. Minchin, *An Essay to Illustrate the Rights of the Poor, By Law* (1815).

48 M. Hildesley, *Religio Jurisprudentis: or, the Lawyer's Advice to His Son* (1685), p. 91.

49 For the different emphases in the historiography of the criminal and civil law, see C. W. Brooks, 'Law, lawyers, and the social history of England', in his *Law, Litigation, and English Society Since 1450* (London, 1998), pp. 179–98.

penalized for participating in civil suits as witnesses in one court; then, in another, even the structures of aid that underwrote their participation in the criminal proceedings against them could be used to disenfranchise them of a voice. To the extent that the legal system generated circumstances that allowed plebeians to be shuffled through stages of procedure that they grasped imperfectly, it was scarcely conducive to their empowerment.

8. Jacobean Star Chamber records and the performance of provincial libel

Clare Egan

'This Court, the right institutions and ancient orders thereof being observed, doth keep all England in quiet.'[1]

In keeping with modern and contemporary divisions over how to interpret the court of Star Chamber, Edward Coke's statement on the court's role in keeping Jacobean England in quiet can be read as either reassuring or oppressive, depending on the reader's interpretation. Does it invoke the exemplary nature of the court as an expedient and innovative way to deliver justice aimed chiefly at preventing breaches of the common peace? Or does it carry a more sinister tone that might hint at the court's reputation for secretive and silencing practices? Although the myth that the Star Chamber was associated with tyrannical monarchical prerogative has been attributed to the work of Whig historians by modern scholarship, the court remains notorious and scholarship is still divided on its role and reputation.[2] This chapter focuses on private libels, an offence newly criminalized by the Star Chamber in the 1590s, the trial of which reached 'near-epidemic' proportions during the Jacobean period.[3] For the early seventeenth century, libels – both political (attacking public officials) and private (between everyday individuals) – were unanimously characterized as the 'pratling' and 'hurrying sound' of envious tongues.[4] It was particularly important for the

[1] E. Coke, *The Fourth Part of the Institutes of the Laws of England* (London, 1644; Wing / C4929), *Early English Books Online*, p. 65.

[2] T. G. Barnes, 'Star Chamber mythology', *The American Journal of Legal History*, v (1961), 1–11, at p. 4; H. Potter, *Law, Liberty and the Constitution: a Brief History of the Common Law* (Woodbridge, 2015), see 'Star Chamber: keeping England in quiet', pp. 103–8.

[3] D. Cressy, *Dangerous Talk: Scandalous, Seditious, and Treasonable Speech in Pre-Modern England* (Oxford, 2010), p. 35; S. W. May and A. Bryson, *Verse Libel in Renaissance England and Scotland* (Oxford, 2016), p. 6.

[4] From James I's 1623 poem criticizing verse libels: 'The Wiper of the Peoples Tears', ii. 56–7 (in 'Early Stuart libels: an edition of poetry from manuscript sources', ed. A. Bellany and A. McRae, *Early Modern Literary Studies*, i (2005) <http://www.earlystuartlibels.net/

C. Egan, 'Jacobean Star Chamber records and the performance of provincial libel' in *Star Chamber Matters: An Early Modern Court and Its Records*, ed. K. Kesselring and N. Mears (London, 2021), pp. 135–153.

Star Chamber itself, this chapter argues, that it practically and symbolically silenced, or 'ke[pt] … in quiet', the unruly noise of libelling.

This chapter advances three major suggestions to substantiate the claim above. The first of these is that we pay more attention to Star Chamber libel records as evidence of an overlooked genre of provincial performance. It was frequently observed at the 'Star Chamber and its Records' conference in July 2019 that Star Chamber cases cannot always be trusted to tell us what actually happened. This statement tended to be triggered by the vexatious nature of much of the court's litigation; the elaborately constructed, often contrasting narratives found in the records; and the kinds of 'dramaturgy' seen in show-cases choreographed by the elite.[5] However, taking up the performance-orientated terminology in this last observation, this chapter argues that instead of looking at the court's records for the truth or falsity of the matters contained there (after all, it is a quirk of the court's records that most of the case outcomes are lost), we analyse libel records as documenting *possible interpretations* by a varied body of spectators for performed and performative communal events.[6] The court was worried about libelling precisely because it was a form of publication shown by a variety of spectator interpretations to cause real damage to reputations regardless of the truth or falsity of events.

While acknowledging and analysing the fictions of the archives, the second suggestion this chapter makes, however, is that we should look again at the veracity of some elements of Star Chamber libel suits. For libel cases, 'the cause was considered invalid unless a copy of the text or a verbatim recitation of the offending words could be produced by the plaintiff'.[7] This legal requirement that the words or 'matter' of the libel be contained in the bill of complaint and, where possible, that a copy of the original libel be appended to the bill means that the records can contain concrete evidence of libellous content.[8] The material features of such libel

htdocs/spanish_match_section/Nvii.html> [accessed 28 Aug. 2020]. See also A. Bellany, 'The embarrassment of libels: perceptions and representations of verse libelling in early Stuart England', in *The Politics of the Public Sphere in Early Modern England*, ed. P. Lake and S. Pincus (Manchester, 2007), pp. 144–67, at p. 150.

[5] S. Hindle, 'Self-image and public image in the career of a Jacobean magistrate: Sir John Newdigate in the court of Star Chamber', in *Popular Culture and Political Agency in Early Modern England and Ireland: Essays in Honour of John Walter*, ed. M. Braddick and P. Withington (Woodbridge, 2017), pp. 123–43, at p. 135.

[6] Such an approach is indebted to N. Z. Davis, *Fiction in the Archives: Pardon Tales and their Tellers in 16th Century France* (Cambridge, 1988).

[7] A. Fox, 'Ballads, libels and popular ridicule in Jacobean England', *Past & Present*, cxlv (1994), 47–83, at p. 57.

[8] W. Hudson, 'Treatise of the court of Star Chamber', in *Collectanea Juridica*, ed.

texts speak for themselves now as they did then – they still bear the marks of careful composition, folding and placement, which testify to the veracity of information about their communal circulation found in bills of complaint. Libel texts therefore introduce a tangible counterpoint to the court's reputation for fictitious or vexatious cases and secretive, corrupt practices, demonstrating that the Star Chamber was meticulously concerned with the specific circumstances of material that threatened to throw England into disquiet.

This chapter finally analyses how the court framed libellous words that were copied into bills of complaint when cases were called up at Star Chamber. It shows that the court carefully reframed such libellous content by taking away its verse lineation and making sure the material contained was not laughed at in the court itself. By removing the communal performance circumstances of the libel, the court symbolically quietened this form of unruly noise. Metaphors of poison and disease were used to characterize libellous communications as the epitome of deceitful speech, and the court saw this as directly opposed to its own style of plain and authoritative speaking. Libels were therefore an important symbolic antithesis to the court's publicly performed style of being seen to deliver justice. Coke's claim that the Star Chamber kept all England in quiet demonstrates how important it was for the court's own reputation as upholder of the king's justice to suppress the period's 'sea of mischiefs … which daily doe flow from euill tongues': libels.[9]

Star Chamber libel cases as records of performance

As early as 1275, the Statute of Westminster forbade the publication of 'false News or Tales whereby discord … or slander may grow between the King and his People or the Great Men of the Realm'.[10] From its thirteenth-century origins, the medieval offence of defamation consisted of two distinct forms: either as a moral transgression against private individuals tried in church courts or as a criminal offence targeting the monarch or magnates, outlined above in the Statute of Westminster and referred to as *scandalum magnatum*.[11]

F. Hargrave (2 vols., London, 1791–2), ii. 1–240, at p. 154.

[9] F. Pulton, *De Pace Regis et Regni, viz. A Treatise Declaring which be the Great and Generall Offences of the Realme* (London, 1610; STC (2nd ed.)/20496), fo. 1.

[10] D. Ibbetson, 'Edward Coke, Roman law, and the law of libel', in *The Oxford Handbook of English Law and Literature, 1500–1700*, ed. L. Hutson (Oxford, 2017), pp. 487–506, at p. 490.

[11] Ibbetson, 'Coke and the law of libel', pp. 488–90. For accounts of early defamation law see: *Select Cases on Defamation to 1600*, ed. R. H. Helmholz (London, 1985); W. S. Holdsworth, *A History of English Law* (17 vols., London, 1903–24), v. 205–12; L. Kaplan,

However, libelling a private individual was redefined as a criminal offence due to a series of high-profile precedential cases in the 1590s and Edward Coke's report in 'The Case *de Libellis Famosis*' in 1605.[12] Thereafter, private libel was tried at the court of Star Chamber, alongside cases relating to the slander of monarchy and government. Star Chamber newly held that for private libel the truth was no defence and the offence did not die with the person because libel fell under the court's jurisdiction over breaches of the common peace.[13]

William Hudson, the author of a 'Treatise of the Court of Star Chamber' based on his twenty-five years' practice as a barrister there, categorized the most common forms of libel, including humorously insulting verses, plays or visual symbols made from horns, books or even playing cards.[14] Libellers read verses aloud, impersonated others or displayed images to public, communal audiences. While scholarship has recognized the novelty of Star Chamber's redefinition of private libel, significantly more attention has been paid to political libels against public figures.[15] Historians such as Adam Fox have done invaluable work on private disputes, but as Fox points out they should now 'enable us to move the history of popular literature beyond the study of form and content and towards the analysis of performance and reception'.[16]

Following the 'spectatorial turn' in performance studies, the audience has become an increased focus for critical attention: 'where one sits or stands, and how one sees and hears a production, profoundly influence what a play means in performance and how one responds to that performance as a thinking, feeling witness', not to mention the part played by 'issues such as class, occupation, wealth, age, religious affinity, and gender'.[17] Just as

The Culture of Slander in Early Modern England (Cambridge, 1997); D. Shuger, *Censorship and Cultural Sensibility: The Regulation of Language in Tudor-Stuart England* (Philadelphia, 2006).

[12] A. Fox, *Oral and Literate Culture in England 1500–1700* (Oxford, 2000), pp. 299–334; A. Bellany, 'A poem on the archbishop's hearse: puritanism, libel and sedition after the Hampton Court conference', *Journal of British Studies*, xxxiv (1995), 137–64. For Coke's report see: *The Selected Writings and Speeches of Sir Edward Coke*, ed. S. Sheppard, (3 vols., Indiana, 2003), i. 146–8.

[13] Hudson, 'Treatise', pp. 102–3; Bellany, 'Poem on the archbishop's hearse', p. 156.

[14] Hudson, 'Treatise', p. 100.

[15] A. Bellany, 'Embarrassment of libels', p. 146. On political libel see A. Bellany, *The Politics of Court Scandal: News Culture and the Overbury Affair, 1603–1660* (Cambridge, 2002); A. McRae, *Literature, Satire and the Early Stuart State* (Cambridge, 2004); M. O'Callaghan, 'Performing politics: the circulation of the "parliament fart"', *Huntington Library Quarterly*, lxix (2006), 121–38.

[16] Fox, *Oral and Literate Culture*, p. 302.

[17] J. J. McGavin and G. Walker, *Imagining Spectatorship: From Mysteries to the Shakespearean*

such factors influenced how each individual spectator interpreted a play on a stage, communal witnesses to the public reading of a libel each made an individual interpretation of its content based on their material and social conditions. Accounts of witnessing such libellous communications contained in the records of Star Chamber give us glimpses of the wide range of spectatorial interpretations possible in early modern communities. Crucially, the legal context of such accounts adds a layer of self-reflexivity to these interpretations because it means that the witness recounts the version that they think will be acceptable and plausible to the authorities.

In the case of *King* v *Lawrence* from Compton Abbas, Dorset (1608), a libellous verse was allegedly composed, written and published by the defendants Elizeus Lawrence, the parson of Compton Abbas; his wife, Margaret; Christopher Horder, a yeoman; and John King, a husbandman. The verse, which according to the bill of complaint called itself 'a litle verse of Stephen Kinge', mocks 'King Steeven' for having married a woman who was already pregnant, having lost a previous marriage arrangement through his lust and clumsiness, and finally having mismanaged his income so that 'his hundred pound is come to tenn'.[18] Stephen King, a yeoman, and his wife, Edith, complained to the Star Chamber that the defendants had composed and written the verse on 16 October 1607, and on Sunday 18 October, being St Luke's Day, they 'did … vnlawfullye fixe & nayle vpp the said infamous libell vppon the church doore in Compton … against the tyme that the people shold resorte to their morninge prayer'.[19] Later that day, the defendants allegedly spread copies of the verse and did 'themselues reade & cause the same to be read to diuers p*er*sons att seu*er*all tymes both in the howse of the said [Elizeus] Lawrence & elswhere'.[20] This account contains elements of performance: the verse was pre-planned and written out, like a script; its location on the church door and the timing, St Luke's Day at morning prayer, made meaning in staging the libel; a large communal audience was engineered; and when it was read at Lawrence's house, the identity of the speaker was important. Whether it is true or not, this narrative tells us that libel was perceived as a form of public communication to local spectators in significant communal locations on important occasions.

Stage (Oxford, 2016), p. 6.

[18] The National Archives of the UK, STAC 8/190/7, m. 22 and m. 16. See also: C. E. McGee, 'Pocky queans and hornèd knaves: gender stereotypes in libelous poems', in *Oral Traditions and Gender in Early Modern Literary Texts*, ed. M. E. Lamb and K. Bamford (London, 2008), pp. 139–51, at p. 146.

[19] TNA, STAC 8/190/7, m. 22.

[20] TNA, STAC 8/190/7, m. 22.

This libel dispute, as many do, had a backstory in the social relations of early modern Compton Abbas.[21] The complainants said that they knew Elizeus and Margaret Lawrence were responsible for the verse because it contained information on private matters known only to them and the complainants. These 'private matters' related to King's previous, unsuccessful marriage arrangement mentioned in the verse: 'In Glostersheire this Grasier good/ He would appease his lustfull strife/ … W*hi*ch was the cause he lost his wieffe'.[22] King claims that the arranged marriage in Gloucestershire was set up by Elizeus and Margaret Lawrence, whereas Margaret says that King overtook her and her husband on the way to Gloucestershire and that he was refused by his suitor because of his drunkenness.[23] Both sides concur that there was a previous arrangement; what King finds offensive is the sharing of this private information publicly, and the shame that the alleged reasons for its failure cast on his masculinity and therefore his public reputation.[24] Such records demonstrate that the formation of reputation in early modern provincial communities was publicly performative, fluid and fragile, as well as being tied up in systems of litigation.

While we might question the veracity of Stephen King's account, one of the defendants' depositions appears to corroborate it. John King, a husbandman aged twenty-four, admits that he saw the libel 'on the church doore and tooke it downe as he passed by about his fathers busines not knoweing then what it was' because he 'could not himself read'.[25] King said he delivered the libel to Elizeus Lawrence, the parson, a little before evening prayer, having 'forgotten' about it being in his pocket all day. John King deposed that his father, Walter King, along with Walter Combe and Nicholas Davy alias Apprichard, arranged this delivery by sending for

[21] The defendant Christopher Horder (the complainant's uncle) and Margaret Lawrence deposed that Horder and Elizeus Lawrence had previously taken Stephen King to Blandford's spiritual court over King having called Lawrence a 'Rascall Knave' (TNA, STAC 8/190/7, m. 2).

[22] TNA, STAC 8/190/7, m. 16.

[23] TNA, STAC 8/190/7, m. 2 and m. 15.

[24] For work on court records and gender see: B. Capp, *When Gossips Meet: Women, Family and Neighbourhood in Early Modern England* (Oxford, 2003); L. Gowing, *Domestic Dangers: Women, Words and Sex in Early Modern London* (Oxford, 1996); L. Gowing, 'Language, power and the law: women's slander litigation in early modern London', in *Women, Crime and the Courts in Early Modern England*, ed. J. Kermode, G. Walker (London, 1994), pp. 25–46; M. Ingram, *Church Courts, Sex and Marriage in England, 1570–1640* (Cambridge, 1990); A. Shepard, *Meanings of Manhood in Early Modern England* (Oxford, 2003); G. Walker, *Crime, Gender and Social Order in Early Modern England* (Cambridge, 2003).

[25] TNA, STAC 8/190/7, m. 3.

Lawrence to read the libel at Walter King's house.[26] John King deposed that the libel

> was begone to be reade in the hall of his fathers howse where his mother in lawe wife to the said walter Kinge … at that time lay in child bedd and soe she also hearinge the same beginninge to be reade, as she lay in her bedd, wished mr Lawrenc eyther to burne the said paper or to carry it away w*i*th him or gett out of her company.[27]

These details further reveal a carefully staged performance in the hall of Walter King's house where his wife lay in childbed with gathered spectators. In John King's account, the most prominent spectator, Walter King's wife, interpreted what she heard as insulting, or at least not fit to be rehearsed in her childbed chamber, and dismissed the party. The verse ridicules Stephen King by claiming that his wife had wept on their wedding day: 'I knowe not where twas for greif or Joye/ But twas reported twas breeding of a Boye.'[28] This hint of scandal over an unwanted pregnancy matched with the location of reading, the childbed chamber, and the occasion, St Luke's Day and the christening of Walter King's child.[29] Libellous meaning derives not only from the identity of the orator Lawrence, but also the location and timing of the performance, all of which were designed to be actively interpreted by communal spectators.

In John King's deposition we are given the perspective of a purportedly unwitting spectator who reports the reactions of other witnesses, but his account does not stop there. Although he claimed to be ignorant of the content upon discovering and first hearing the verse, his interest had clearly been piqued. After leaving the childbed chamber, John King reported that Lawrence

> went forthe into a new howse adioyninge togeather w*i*th Combe, this deponent*es* father and Apprichard where this deponent thinketh mr Lawrence read [the libel] quite over to them aforesaid, for this deponent beinge in the court fast by heard a readinge, but could not vnderstand what it was because he read it not loud enoughe for this deponent to heare it and this deponent heard not the said mr Lawrence to laughe but thincketh that he heard his owne father King and Combe, and Apprichard that were at the hearinge thereof to laughe.[30]

[26] The nature of the relationship between Walter and John King (defendants) and the complainant, Stephen King, is unknown. However, there may be familial connections given that Christopher Horder, another defendant, was Stephen King's uncle.

[27] TNA, STAC 8/190/7, m. 3.

[28] TNA, STAC 8/190/7, m. 16.

[29] Stephen King's replication specifies it was the christening (TNA, STAC 8/190/7, m. 19).

[30] TNA, STAC 8/190/7, m. 3.

This account tells us that when it was met with a disapproving reaction in the space of the childbed chamber, the core group who remained intent on reading the libel had to move to a semi-private location – one which could still be overheard from the courtyard outside, but not clearly. More importantly, this report establishes that ridiculing laughter was also one of the responses to hearing the libel, alongside the offence taken by Mrs King, and John King's own curiosity roused sufficiently for him to follow the group and listen in.[31] The examination process sought to establish precisely *the range of audience interpretations* of the libel upon its being read aloud.

These varied narratives might seem unhelpful if what we were trying to ascertain was the truth or falsity of what happened. However, if we are looking for the range of potential spectator interpretations to the reading of a libel verse, they tell us a great deal. They reveal the communal dynamics: first, between the parson, Lawrence, and the group of men who summon him to read the libel; second, of a woman in childbed with the authority to control occurrences in her populated chamber; and third, the operation of factions dividing the libellers and their targets. These accounts also demonstrate the plurality of communal audience reception, from offence to intrigue to laughter, and interaction with a piece of verse, from finding it to delivering it to reading it aloud to rejecting and burning it, in early modern provincial communities. In terms of spectatorship studies, this reveals how individuals reacted actively and in a variety of different ways to hearing a verse libel read aloud. With a libel these varied reactions, of offence, intrigue and laughter, and the communal dynamics they brought about, were what made the libel publicly notorious and therefore damaging to the target's reputation. Such accounts of reading and reaction also demonstrate that the court was not only trying to establish that the verse existed, but where it travelled, when and where it was read, and what the interpretations or reactions of audiences were.

Among the multiple interpretations possible, the records also include negative confirmation of where the offence lay; the defendants' depositions present different ways of excusing the perceived offence. We have already heard John King's defence that he 'could not himself read' the verse.[32] In another line of defence, Margaret Lawrence deposed that

> her husband did read parte of the writing … to Edward Brookeman and Joane Morres … because this deponent*es* said husband called [them] … to be wittnesses of the burninge of the said writinge, and they requested to heare it

[31] The complainants incorporated John King's account into their replication (TNA, STAC 8/190/7, m. 19).

[32] TNA, STAC 8/190/7, m. 3.

> first bycause they would knowe whato they were wittnesses … the said readinge was at her husband*es* howse where it was burnt.[33]

Elizeus's burning of the verse would be seen as an appropriate suppression of the libel in the eyes of the law, so seeking witnesses would be legitimate. Margaret also specifies that no more than the two witnesses were present as audience and suggests that Lawrence only read a part of the text. These defences remove the performance circumstance of having a large audience present and deny any attempt by the orator to convey the full effect of the verse. Whether they are real or fictious defences, Margaret's claims demonstrate that the removal of performance circumstances could be perceived as removing the offence.

The defendant Christopher Horder, a husbandman aged sixty and uncle to Stephen King, gave this account in his defence:

> Elizeus Lawrenc tolde this deponent that ther was a letter on the church doore where in this deponent*es* name was, w*hi*ch made this deponent desirous to heare it and the said Elizeus Lawrence read the same in his owne hall in the p*re*senc of the wyves of this deponent and m^r Lawrenc after evening prayer on the sabboath day soe farr as this deponent*es* name was therein w*hi*ch was twise and farder this deponent neither heard nor cared to heare nor esteemed the same.[34]

Like Margaret Lawrence, Christopher Horder used in his defence the fact that the libel was not read in full and that his reaction to this reading was not to care or esteem the reading aloud of the verse. As it named him, Horder had a legitimate motivation to hear the libel, which would change a reading from a mocking humiliation of those named into a neighbourly reporting of offensive content to someone who might be harmed by it.

Those composing, dispersing, reading, spectating, reacting to, targeted by and accused of libel were precisely aware of the effectiveness of performance for ruining reputation and knew how to use the denial of performance circumstances in their own defence. From the narratives found in Star Chamber records, we can see that reading a libel verse in public could be interpreted variously as humiliating, offensive, inappropriate, humorous or a reporting mechanism. Even though they are biased reconstructions of (sometimes fictitious) events, they reveal people's perceptions of the law, of what constituted offence or threatened to cause damage to individual reputation, and of how information was interpreted and circulated in the public spheres of the provinces.

33 TNA, STAC 8/190/7, m. 2.
34 TNA, STAC 8/190/7, m. 2.

Libel texts as evidence in Star Chamber

In libel cases presented to the Star Chamber, the court required that the content of the libel be repeated verbatim in the bill of complaint or that a copy of the text be appended. In this sense, libel cases did attempt to establish facts based on evidence, and the records include texts which circulated in the provincial communities of early modern England, rather than just the words of the libel copied into bills by legal clerks. In *King* v *Lawrence* (1608), the complainants Stephen and Edith King encountered problems getting hold of the libel for use in their case. Christopher Horder's deposition claims his name was mentioned twice in the libel, but the text appended to the bill of complaint makes no mention of him. The bill claims that despite having 'gotten into their handes' 'p*ar*t of … [the] libell & wrytinge', which is indeed filed in the case records separate to the bill, 'the rest thereof is by the cunninge & subtiltye of the said Elizeus Lawrence & the rest of his said confederat*es* kept from your said sub*jectes*'.[35] One interrogatory enquired:

> Did not … Stephan King in yo*ur* hearing demaund and intreate of the said Elizeus Lawrence to see or to haue the said lybell, yf yea, what day was yt, whether was yt not the same saboth day that yt was taken from the said church dore, and about what tyme of the said daye was yt that he so required the same … & what answeare did he then make vnto the said compl*ainan*t, whether did he answeare him that he could not haue yt, because he had burnt yt … & whether did he then tell the said compl*ainan*t, Stephan that he thought the compl*ainan*t should haue some coppyes therof, but the originall was burnt, what coppyes did he meane by these words.[36]

The circumstances of King requiring the copy appear to be a crucial part of the libel's circulation and directly connected with the libel being fixed on the church door, discovered on St Luke's Day and read aloud in the community.

The distinction made in this question between the 'originall' and 'coppyes' of the libel is telling. Stephen and Edith King's replication suggests a crucial difference between the original and the copies: the handwriting. The replication alleges that Elizeus Lawrence 'hath deliu*er*ed out in speeches that he would not shewe the compl*ainan*t the said lybell for feare he would then espye out the handwritting therof', which the case alleges was either Elizeus's or his brother Israel's handwriting.[37] The replication does stress, however, that 'the def*endan*t Margaret deliu*er*ed out in speeches in

[35] TNA, STAC 8/190/7, m. 22.
[36] TNA, STAC 8/190/7, m. 15.
[37] TNA, STAC 8/190/7, m. 19.

the p*re*sence of divers that ther was a coppye of the said lybell w*hi*ch the compl*ainan*t might p*er*adventure see'.[38] These details suggest that both the complainants and defendants saw the 'original' as incriminating evidence because it could identify the person who had produced it. Margaret Lawrence's examination claimed that although she had seen Stephen King come to talk to her husband that day, she did not hear King 'require the coppye of the said writinge of her husbande'.[39] Margaret appears to be very careful to suggest that if he had required it, then he had required a *copy* rather than the original of the libel.

It seems probable, then, that the libel text appended to the bill of complaint was part of one of the copies made by the libellers after they had read aloud and burnt the 'original' text, and the fact that the defendants would let King have a copy suggests it was less likely to incriminate them. One of the interrogatories asks:

> Is this note of p*ar*te of the said lybell fixed to the byll in this honorable court a true note of p*ar*te of the matter of the said lybell, yf not, then shewe wherin yt doth differ, & how many more verses were there in the said lybell as you knowe or can*n* nowe remember?[40]

This question demonstrates that different versions of the libel text functioned in different ways in both communal and court settings. In the community, the handwriting of the 'original' could be deciphered, whereas the copy could not. That the court felt the need to question whether this was a 'true note' of 'parte of the matter' of the libel shows that to them this copy was also, in some senses, a less incriminating form of evidence, being a step removed from the original libel and only part of the total verse. Margaret Lawrence answered this question as follows:

> now she remembreth not the p*ar*t of the libell annexed to the bill, because it is a good while since this deponent sawe the said parte at her putting in her aunswere to the said bill, but this deponent thinketh it was no true coppy of the writinge that was burnt.[41]

Margaret's deposition uses the court's own processes as a reason to deny the value of the libel copy: she claims not to know the answer to this interrogatory because it had been so long since she was presented with the text. Her answer shows that although libel texts were referred to in examinations to establish the details of production and circulation, in this

[38] TNA, STAC 8/190/7, m. 19.
[39] TNA, STAC 8/190/7, m. 2.
[40] TNA, STAC 8/190/7, m. 15.
[41] TNA, STAC 8/190/7, m. 2.

case they were only shown to defendants in the initial phase of the court process.[42] Complainants, defendants and court officials demonstrate a detailed awareness of the various ways that 'original' libel texts and written copies functioned, as well as being concerned to establish their value as evidence and their relation to processes of production, publication and circulation.[43]

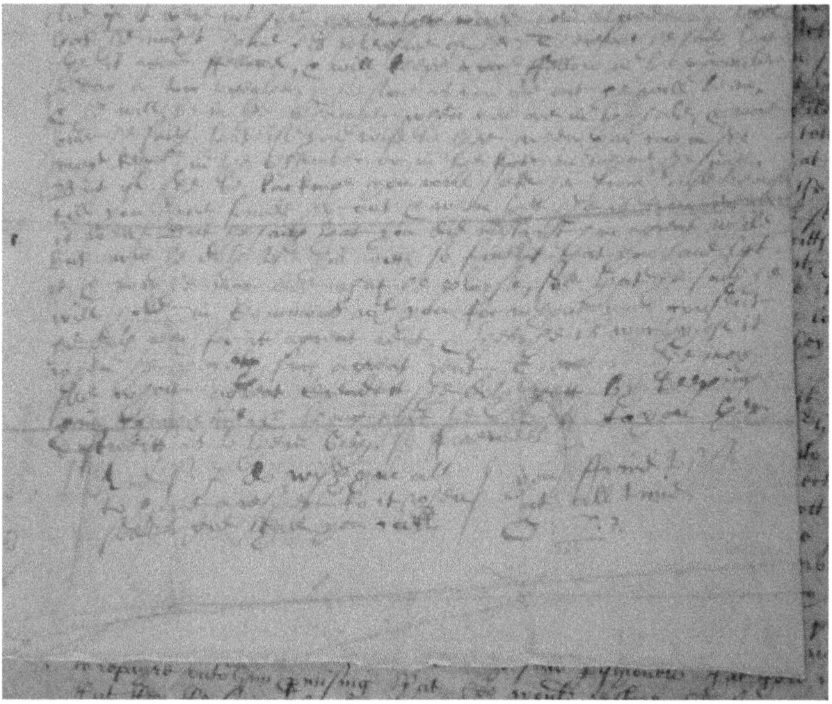

Figure 8.1. Libel letter from the case of *Robynns v Cornishe* (TNA, STAC 8/254/29, m. 1)

On closer inspection, these libel texts also still communicate as material objects designed to facilitate widespread circulation in their communal circumstances. In the case of *Robbyns* v *Cornishe* (1610), from Whitstone,

[42] E. P. Cheyney, 'The court of Star Chamber', *The American Historical Review*, xviii (1913), 727–50, at p. 738; H. Taylor, 'The price of the poor's words: social relations and the economics of deposing for one's "betters" in early modern England', *The Economic History Review*, lxxii (2019), 828–47.

[43] See, e.g., A. Cambers, 'Reading libels in early 17th century Northamptonshire', in *Getting Along?: Religious Identities and Confessional Relations in Early Modern England – Essays in Honour of Professor W. J. Sheils*, ed. A. Morton, N. Lewycky (Abingdon, 2016), pp. 115–32, especially at pp. 127–8; and Hindle, 'Self-image and public image', pp. 133 and 137.

Cornwall, the text appended to the bill of complaint was the 'original' libel and its material features provide evidence as to its communal circulation.[44] In this case, Walter Robbyns, a yeoman, accused John Cornishe, a clerk, and others of writing a libellous letter to him. The libellous letter purported to be a friendly warning that Robbyns's wife and mother-in-law had been having illicit relations with another man in their house. The bill of complaint repeated the contents of the letter verbatim, but the records of the case also contain the letter itself. (See figure 8.1 above.)

The top section of the document has been torn away along a fold, but on the section that remains intact the creases where the letter has been folded are clearly visible. The fold along the bottom section shows the letter direction, designed to be public-facing when the letter is sent. The superscription reads:

> And so I do wish you all | your ffrind to vse
> to have a respect to it when | at all times
> soever god shall you call | O: D:[45]

However, where the fold has been made at the upper edge of this superscription the last line of the letter content would also be left visible when the letter was sent. The ostensibly private line reads: 'dyscreditt is to them bothe. so ffarewell'.[46] In other words, the line is clearly suggestive of the scandalous contents of the letter and has been left visible to identify the content to anyone discovering the folded letter. Letters and other literary forms with exterior directions suggestive of libellous contents are frequently described in other bills of complaint where they are reported to have been left lying in the streets to be found and taken up by passers-by.[47] The material features of the text appended to the bill in *Robbyns* v *Cornishe* indicate how this content could circulate in the community; this suggests that we should pay more attention to the materiality of such 'original' libel texts as evidence that can speak for itself.

We can also compare appended texts to the content of libels copied into bills of complaint. In the case of *King* v *Lawrence*, there is a small difference between the two versions: the bill gives the first lines of the libel verse as 'Gentlemen all I will begin a litle verse of Stephen Kinge', whereas

44 TNA, STAC 8/254/29.

45 TNA, STAC 8/254/29, m. 1.

46 TNA, STAC 8/254/29, m. 1.

47 C. Egan, '"Now fearing neither friend nor foe, to the worldes viewe these verses goe": mapping libel performance in early-modern Devon', *Medieval English Theatre*, xxxvi (2014), 70–103, at pp. 83–7; Cambers, 'Reading libels', p. 120; G. Schneider, 'Libelous letters in Elizabethan and early Stuart England', *Modern Philology*, cv (2008), 475–509.

the appended text has 'A litle verse by Steeven Kinge'.[48] Although the difference between a verse 'of' or a verse 'by' may seem negligible, the fact that 'personating' or impersonation of targets was one of the major forms for private libel makes it more significant.[49] Other cases feature the target caricatured and impersonated with a speaking part in libellous verses.[50] Perhaps the first two lines of the verse in *King* v *Lawrence* set up the rest of the poem as delivered *by* an impersonation of King. The little verse by Stephen King in performance could include an orator impersonating King delivering a humiliating story about himself, which opens 'I tell you a thing of Kings Steeven/ Who married a wiffe that had noe livinge'.[51] Whether or not this difference between 'of' and 'by' was meaningful for communal performance, it highlights the potential for differences between an appended text and the copying of libellous content into bills of complaint. If an appended text was evidence of libel, what did the copying of libellous words into the bill of complaint add to the case?

Styles of speech at Star Chamber

While a copy of the libel is appended to the bill of complaint in the case of *King* v *Lawrence*, the bill itself only repeats the first two lines of the libel verse because, it says, the 'vnlawfull and filthie libell [is] not fytt to be rehearsed in this honerable courte'.[52] The phrase 'rehearsed in … courte' directs us to the hearing of the case in the courtroom and its theatrical potential; to copy a libel text into a bill of complaint verbatim was to ensure its being read out in court.[53] The majority of bills do contain the words of the libel in full, but in some cases the content was judged too rude to be permissible. This shows us that it was important to have the libel copied into the bill of complaint, but also that the court was sensitive to what rereading a libel in the courtroom did in terms of perpetuating and reperforming its contents. The Star Chamber's controlled repetition of libellous noise seems to exploit the slippage between the two meanings of

[48] TNA, STAC 8/190/7, m. 22 and m. 16.

[49] Hudson, 'Treatise', p. 100.

[50] E.g., *Hole* v *White*, Wells, 1607–8 (TNA, STAC 8/161/1; *Records of Early English Drama: Somerset*, ed. J. Stokes, R. J. Alexander (2 vols., Toronto, 1996), i. 261–367), or *Painter* v *Yeo*, Launcells, 1612 (TNA, STAC 8/236/29; *Records of Early English Drama: Dorset and Cornwall*, ed. R. C. Hays, et al. (Toronto, 1999) pp. 486–9).

[51] TNA, STAC 8/190/7, m. 16.

[52] TNA, STAC 8/190/7, m. 22.

[53] Coke, *Selected Writings*, i. 146; Cheyney, 'Star Chamber', p. 739. See also: H. S. Syme, *Theatre and Testimony in Shakespeare's England: A Culture of Mediation* (Cambridge, 2011); L. Hutson, *The Invention of Suspicion: Law and Mimesis in Shakespeare and Renaissance Drama* (Oxford, 2007).

the term 'rehearse', both to report, recite, narrate at length and to practice something for public performance; by reciting them the court wants to acknowledge the performance potential of such words while rebranding them as criminal.[54] The court exploited the difference between performing libels in communal public spaces with a multiplicity of audience reactions and repeating those same words in an honourable courtroom to the silent reception of authority figures.

Visually and formally, the court changed libels when they copied them into bills of complaint: they very rarely preserved the verse lineation of libels when they were given in bills, whereas when they were appended to the bill they almost always retained their original format or lineation.[55] This might be for reasons of economy; bills of complaint are usually long and densely packed on to one large piece of vellum, so retaining verse lineation wastes a lot of space. However, it does impact how verse libels appear and how they are read aloud – an unlineated poem makes it harder for the orator to know where to place emphasis, such as on rhymed words at the end of lines. The most common practice was to copy the text into the bill in full. However, some bills just gave a few lines, like in *King* v *Lawrence*, and others gave a tactful summary of content if the libel was deemed too rude. Alastair Bellany reports that in the case of the Staines fiddlers, 'Attorney General Sir Robert Heath circulated written copies of the offending songs to the assembled lords of the council, thus avoiding the awkwardness of reading the libels aloud in open court'.[56] When cases were heard at court, it mattered how the libellous words were presented to those assembled, both visually and aurally.

Whether the libellous words were read out or circulated, one thing was certain: the court of Star Chamber was 'a formal and orderly assemblage' where 'all speeches made were in restrained and sober language and in the midst of the profound silence of all present except the speaker'.[57] Cheyney points out that this sobriety and silence was in stark contrast to other courts of the period in which judges were 'often noisy, hectoring, coarse-grained and foul-mouthed'.[58] The silence of those listening meant, in particular, no laughter – a crucial stipulation in libel cases where laughter at libellous content repeated at

[54] 'rehearse, v.', *Oxford English Dictionary Online* <www.oed.com> [accessed 3 Nov. 2020].

[55] Of *c.*40 cases consulted from Dorset, Devon, Cornwall and Somerset only one bill preserved verse lineation (see *Robbins* v *Vosse*, Whitstone, 1620 (TNA, STAC 8/246/13; *REED: Dorset and Cornwall*, p. 525)).

[56] A. Bellany, 'Singing libel in early Stuart England: the case of the Staines fiddlers, 1627', *Huntington Library Quarterly*, lxix (2006), 177–94, at p. 177.

[57] Cheyney, 'Star Chamber', p. 730.

[58] Cheyney, 'Star Chamber', p. 731.

court would undermine the case. Cheyney gives multiple examples of the Star Chamber's attempts to deny mirth and merriment, including an example of a case heard in June 1602 where the rules were broken:

> Certain ridiculous matter inserted by the plaintiff in his appeal moved the court to momentary laughter. The lord keeper said, "Although it be goode to be merrye some time, and this be St. Barnabas' daye, the longest daye in the year, yet let us not spende the whole day in this place with wordes to no purpose", and so they returned to work.[59]

The Star Chamber's insistence on a silent audience that did not laugh and court proceedings that used words in a restrained and purposeful manner deliberately contrasts to libellous words and spectatorial reactions in their communal contexts. For the person libelled the court hearing reperformed the libel as a criminal utterance and thus restored their reputation. However, libel cases can also be seen as part of the court's wider sense of its own role and reputation – its style of administering justice.

The court of Star Chamber conducted its hearings with pride for the dignity and authority of the court in its own right.[60] As administrators of justice, court officials were to conduct their proceedings not only without laughter but also without grand rhetoric or elaborate speeches. William Hudson stated that it

> cannot be denied that there is no bar of pleading which yieldeth so large a scope to exercise a good orator, as th[is] court; the usual subject being the defence of honour and honesty. But the grave *chancellor Ellesmere*, affecting matter rather than affectation of words, tied the same to laconical brevity; an honour to the court of justice, to be swayed rather by ponderous reasons than fluent and deceitful speeches.[61]

Hudson specifies that, because the court was hearing cases that defended and restored honour by honest means, the style in which it did so should be the opposite of those words that damaged honourable reputations in the first place.

Adopting this fashion of conducting court procedure, Hudson claimed, should be the responsibility of any 'grave lawyer' and all those involved in the court, but the lord chancellor placed above all in the court in

[59] Cheyney, 'Star Chamber', p. 730.

[60] Potter, *Law*, p. 106; M. Stuckey, 'A consideration of the emergence and exercise of judicial authority in the Star Chamber', *Monash University Law Review*, xix (1993), 117–64, at pp. 117–18.

[61] Hudson, 'Treatise', p. 18.

authority was also crucially to act as the regulating 'mouth of the court'.[62] As such, the lord chancellor must appoint and call counsel to speak at the bar and keep general rule and order when they did so. Speaking of Lord Chancellor Ellesmere, whom Hudson championed as the model of Star Chamber's unique brand of justice, Hudson recalled that if the counsel were to 'wander into vain circumlocutions or iterations, that grave judge w[ould] tie them to a point which maketh the resolution not difficult'.[63] The lord chancellor regulated the speech of the court and its officials just as the court itself regulated the language of the nation; conduct at Star Chamber was the model of appropriately regulated speech. According to Hudson, the very selection by the chancellor of those that spoke at the bar was deliberately tailored to cultivate this plain-speaking style:

> For that the lord chancellor being careful that the court should not be troubled either with silly or ignorant barristers, or such as were idle and full of words, and not careful of the truth of their informations … [would] appoint … men of sincerity and experience.[64]

Even the barristers of the court were chosen for their language and style at the bar, and this especially privileged those who succinctly and lucidly expressed the truth of the matter. In his own practice at the court, Hudson was known to be concise, 'avoiding grandiloquence, which he clearly detested and for which he tacitly condemned Francis Bacon'.[65] The words of the bills and proceedings that surrounded libels in the Star Chamber, then, were vital in counteracting the offence of libel. The court's words must specifically highlight the 'fluent and deceitful' nature of libellous constructions by being in stark contrast to them.

At the heart of the matter of the style of speech was the Star Chamber's role in delivering justice. Hudson, among others, drew particular attention to the court's star-spangled ceiling as a metaphor for how its representative authority functioned:

> *Camera Stellata* … is most aptly named … because the stars have no light but what is cast upon them from the sun by reflection, [the court] being his [Majesty's] representative body, and as his Majesty himself was pleased to say … representation must needs cease when the person is present. So in the presence of his great majesty, the which is the sun of honour and glory, the shining of those stars is put out.[66]

[62] Hudson, 'Treatise', p. 27.
[63] Hudson, 'Treatise', p. 27.
[64] Hudson, 'Treatise', p. 26.
[65] T. G. Barnes, 'Hudson, William (*c.*1577–1635)', *Oxford Dictionary of National Biography* (2008), doi: 10.1093/ref:odnb/14042.
[66] Hudson, 'Treatise', p. 8.

This court's day-to-day 'shining' was thus borrowed from a higher source, the king, but Hudson's statement reminds us that monarchical power was being represented, or performed, whenever the court was in session.

James I resolved to appear at the Star Chamber in person for the first time in 1616, fourteen years into his reign, to make a point about monarchical power, the court system and its judges.[67] To the judges, James's messages were particularly pointed.[68] First, do justice 'vprightly' because you will have to answer to both God and the king. Second, do justice 'indifferently', acting 'without delay, partialitie, feare or bribery, with stout and vpright hearts, with cleane and vncorrupt hands'.[69] Third, remember that courts have judges, not one judge, so that they can give considered, collective sentences. On the second point, James elaborated that judges should do justice indifferently because their role was not as 'makers of Law', but as 'Interpretours of Law'.[70] This distinction was crucial for James:

> As Kings borrow their power from God, so Iudges from Kings … And as no King can discharge his accompt to God, vnlesse he make conscience not to alter, but to declare and establish the will of God: So Iudges cannot discharge their accompts to Kings, vnlesse they take the like care, not to take vpon them to make Law, but … to declare what the Law is.[71]

James's emphasis on the manner in which royal courts and their judges should *deliver* justice is significant; judges were the orators, the mouthpieces that represented the monarch's power. They were, as James further specified, 'iudges, to declare, and not to make Law'; 'for when you make a Decree neuer heard of before, you are Law-giuers, and not Law-tellers'.[72] This speech was James's attempt to curb the power of his judges, but it stresses the symbolic importance of speech, performance and representation, by both kings and judges, in the royal prerogative courts. The style of speech at the court of Star Chamber, as the representative of monarchical prerogative, was crucially important to the symbolic perception of law and justice in Jacobean England.

***

[67] *The Political Works of James I*, ed. C. H. McIlwain (New York, 1965), p. 328.

[68] On the disputes between Coke, Ellesmere and James I behind the 1616 speech: M. Fortier, 'Equity and ideas: Coke, Ellesmere, and James I', *Renaissance Quarterly*, li (1998), 1255–81.

[69] *Political Works of James I*, p. 332.

[70] *Political Works of James I*, p. 332.

[71] *Political Works of James I*, p. 327.

[72] *Political Works of James I*, p. 336.

Closer examination of Star Chamber libel cases reveals narratives of spectatorship which suggest the danger of this new form of libelling was as a performed and performative genre. Whether fictional or factual, the narratives we find in Star Chamber libel records tell us about the perceived nature of offensive material, the way reputation was formed and damaged in the provinces and the way that those involved in libel cases, on both sides, understood and tried to manipulate the law. The records, moreover, do contain evidential documents when it comes to libels. Paying attention to these libel texts as material objects, as well as how complainants, defendants and court officials discussed them, counters the court's reputation for fictional and vexatious litigation. 'Original' libel texts appended to bills of complaint speak for themselves now as they did then through their folds, creases and textual variants compared to libellous words copied into bills of complaint. Additionally, libels copied into bills tell us a great deal about how the court stage-managed the hearing of libel cases when they were called up. The careful framing of libellous words and the removal of audience laughter in reaction were crucial for punishing libels, but also for the court's own reputation for delivering justice in a concise, plain-speaking, and therefore honourable, style. The court was the representative of monarchical authority, of justice and mercy, and therefore it must declare the law in the right manner.

Ferdinando Pulton's 1609 treatise *De Pace Regis et Regni* describes libellers pouring out their 'venim in writing … [and] by son[g]s, scofs, iests, or taunts: & diuers times by hanging of pictures of reproach'; the libeller is a 'secret canker' that 'priuily stingeth' his targets and libellous words are a 'foule puddle that ouzeth fro[m] the … corrupt gogmire, & distelleth out of a heart … infected with malice & enuie'.[73] Edward Coke likewise characterized the libeller as someone who poisoned his adversary and wrote that one could spot a libeller by 'shipwreck of conscience'.[74] Such metaphors for libel demonstrate the perception of it as the lowest and most deceitful form of speech. In order to be the open, honourable mechanism for justice in the stead of a divine-right monarch such as James I, it was particularly pressing for the Star Chamber not only to uphold high standards of speech and conduct, but also directly and symbolically to oppose itself to such foul, corrupt and venomous utterances as libels.

[73] Pulton, *De Pace Regis et Regni*, fo. 2.
[74] Coke, *Selected Writings*, pp. 147–8.

9. A marine insurance fraud in the Star Chamber*

Emily Kadens

The Star Chamber dealt frequently with accusations of fraud. A slippery topic with which the common law struggled, fraud was more comfortably adjudicated before judges sitting in equity who could weigh the particular facts and look the parties in the eye.[1] Fraud consequently became an important part of the Star Chamber docket, and alleging fraud was a reliable means for plaintiffs to obtain jurisdiction in that court.[2]

Equity bills of complaint being notoriously untrustworthy,[3] however, it is quite clear that many accusations of fraud brought in the Star Chamber were false, with parties making the charge merely to obtain jurisdiction and block a suit brought elsewhere.[4] And yet dishonest though they may be, the Star Chamber records provide evidence, often very detailed, of many different frauds, the existence of which may be known to historians but not necessarily well documented.[5]

* The author would like to thank Verde D'Aquino for her remarkable research in the Italian archives and translations, Gijs Drijer for checking the Dutch archives and notarial records, Oliver Finnegan for enthusiastically sending photographs of documents from The National Archives of the UK, and Sarah Whale at Hatfield House for also supplying photographs. Given the coronavirus restrictions, this chapter could not have been completed without their assistance, for which the author is very grateful. The author would also like to thank Amanda Bevan, Sabine Go, Bruce Markell and Francesca Trivellato.

1 D. Ibbetson, 'Fraud: English common law', in *The Oxford International Encyclopedia of Legal History*, ed. S. N. Katz (6 vols., 2009), iii. 101; M. Lobban, 'Contractual fraud in law and equity, *c.*1750–*c.*1850', *Oxford Journal of Legal Studies*, xvii (1997), 441–76, at pp. 446–8.

2 H. Mares, 'Fraud and dishonesty in King's Bench and Star Chamber', *American Journal of Legal History*, lix (2019), 210–31, at pp. 217–18.

3 C. Churches, 'Business at law: retrieving commercial disputes from eighteenth-century Chancery', *Historical Journal*, xliii (2000), 937–54, at pp. 940, 944.

4 T. G. Barnes, 'Star Chamber litigants and their counsel, 1596–1641', in *Legal Records and the Historian*, ed. J. H. Baker (1978), pp. 7–28, at p. 15.

5 One example is the fraud now known in US law as a bustout. For Star Chamber examples see E. Kadens, 'The dark side of commerce', *Cardozo Law Review*, xl (2019), 1995–2027, at pp. 2004–18.

Deliberately sinking a ship to defraud the shipowners or insurers provides an excellent example. Fraud on bottomry loans – loans made to a shipowner repayable if the ship arrived safely at its destination but forgiven if it did not – was already attested in the fourth century BCE, when an Athenian court heard the case of an attempted fraudulent scuttling,[6] and it remained common in the middle ages.[7] But the spread of marine insurance in the sixteenth and seventeenth centuries made the scam even more attractive,[8] as the isolation of early modern insurance markets in different cities permitted shipowners and merchants to overinsure without much risk of discovery.[9] By 1717, deliberate shipwreck had become such a serious problem that the British parliament made it a capital crime.[10] Despite this threatened punishment, in the eighteenth century, deliberate shipwreck was frequent enough that intentionally sunk ships acquired the name of 'coffin ships' and became the subject of plays and novels.[11] The scam continues to be 'prevalent and persistent' today.[12]

The mechanics of the fraud are clear and did not seem to change much over time.[13] The fraudster had to find an old ship worth more sunk for the insurance money than in active service; buy the cooperation of a captain; load the ship with scrap packed to look like real wares; use false bills of lading to overinsure the ship and cargo; sink the ship at a convenient location; purchase the silence of complicit or suspicious sailors; obtain a certificate of shipwreck; and collect on the insurance policy.

The fraud may have been relatively easy to accomplish, but the loss of most of the early English insurance records in the 1666 Great Fire of London means that accounts of particular cases prior to the eighteenth century are

[6] Demosthenes, 'Plea of Demo against Zenothemis', *Orations Volume IV: Orations 27–40: Private Cases*, trans. A. T. Murray (Cambridge, 1936), pp. 178–97.

[7] G. Rossi, *Insurance in Elizabethan England: The London Code* (Cambridge, 2016), p. 190 n. 131.

[8] Rossi, *Insurance*, p. 280; G. Jackson, 'Marine insurance frauds in Scotland, 1751–1821', *The Mariner's Mirror*, lvii (1971), 307–22, at pp. 307–8 (assuming that deliberate shipwreck to defraud insurers was an eighteenth-century development).

[9] Jackson, 'Marine insurance', p. 316.

[10] 4 Geo, I, c. 12, § 3. See also, 11 Geo. I, c. 29 (1724); 43 Geo. III, c. 113 (1803).

[11] A. C. Campbell, *Insurance and Crime* (London, 1902), pp. 39–45; A. J. Wilson, *The Business of Insurance* (London, 1904), pp. 113–14; C. Reade, *Foul Play* (London, 1869); H. Heijermans, *Op hoop van zegen* (1900); B. Traven, *Das Totenschiff* (Frankfurt am Main, 1926).

[12] R. G. Bauer, 'A short history of maritime fraud', *Tulane Maritime Law Journal*, xii (1987), 11–8, at p. 12; D. M. Collins, 'Marine insurance fraud: sinking ships in a falling market', *Malabu: Maritime Law Bulletin*, ii (2011), 11–5, at p. 12.

[13] Jackson, 'Marine insurance', p. 314 (describing a fraudulent shipwreck in nearly the same terms as occurred in the cases discussed here).

scarce. Furthermore, maritime transport was inherently dangerous, and, the evidence having gone down with the ship, insurers had difficulty proving duplicity, suggesting that suits may not have been commonly brought.[14]

A pair of duelling Star Chamber cases from 1613 and 1614, however, illustrate this marine insurance fraud in great detail.[15] At the same time, the cases also provide an example of the complex challenges inherent in trusting court archives as evidence.[16] The 1613 suit alleged the scam, but the 1614 responding suit claimed that the facts in the earlier case had been fabricated. Obviously, someone was lying, but the evidence does not permit us to be certain whether the account of the shipwreck was a story *about* a fraud or was *itself* the fraud.

Nonetheless the possibility that the story of the insurance swindle was false does not render it unfit to be evidence that this type of fraud did occur and did so in the manner asserted in the suit. Presumably, the litigation fraudster who wanted a court to take his case seriously needed to make credible claims. Alleging frauds that sounded too improbable or that the judges and lawyers would not believe took place risked getting the suit dismissed as frivolous. Consequently, the story of this 1613 case – as it can be reconstructed from the Star Chamber files and related lawsuits in the courts of Chancery and Admiralty, together with facts gleaned from archives in Italy and the Netherlands – can usefully add another chapter to the study of the Star Chamber's docket and the long history of maritime fraud.

***

The original lawsuit, *Attorney General* v *Goodlake*, began with an information filed in June 1613 by Attorney General Henry Hobart at the relation of Dominic Bowen.[17] In relator suits, private parties purchased the services of the attorney general in exchange for paying the costs of suit. If the attorney general won, the relator shared in the judgement fine.[18] Bowen was a Dutch merchant who had lived in London for many years.[19] He often served as the

[14] Jackson, 'Marine insurance', pp. 308, 316; Campbell, *Insurance and Crime*, p. 39.

[15] TNA, STAC 8/12/6, *Attorney General ex rel. Bowen* v *Goodlake, Povey & Webb*, 1613; STAC 8/20/20, *Attorney General ex rel. Goodlake* v *Bowen, Povey & Bollen*, 1614.

[16] R. Starn, 'Truths in the archives', *Common Knowledge*, viii (2002), 387–401, at p. 388 ('One fundamental truth of the archives, surely, is that they are not to be trusted').

[17] TNA, STAC 8/12/6, bill of complaint, 19 June 1613.

[18] E. Kadens, 'New light on *Twyne's Case*', *American Bankruptcy Law Journal*, xciv (2020), 1–84, at p. 53.

[19] O. P. Grell, *Dutch Calvinists in Early Stuart London: The Dutch Church in Austin Friars, 1603–1642* (Leiden, 1989), p. 294. Bowen was already in London by 1601. See TNA,

London agent for Dutch traders abroad, especially those in Amsterdam, whose interests he claimed to be defending by bringing this suit.[20]

According to the information, in December 1608, Roger Goodlake, a young English merchant resident in Florence, assisted Antonio and Diego Texera – who were pointedly described as being 'of the Nation of the Jewes' and 'men well knowne to be forward in plotting of anie villony that might torne to the preiudice of Christians' – in committing insurance fraud.[21] Diego Texera intended to load a ship with bales and chests packed to look as if they contained rich and expensive cloth. He would then obtain insurance on the freight based on a bill of lading, identifying the goods as 'Cloth of Gould, velvettes, Chambelettes, [and] Silks' to be shipped from Livorno to Cadiz and Alicante in Spain. In reality, the containers held nothing but old paper and soap, so that when the ship sank, as Texera intended for it to do, his payout from the insurers would be pure profit.[22]

To put his plan into action, Texera needed a ship and a shipmaster willing to sacrifice it. This was where Roger Goodlake came in. Goodlake convinced an English (or possibly Irish) captain named John Povey to carry the wares on his old and leaky – and thus sacrificeable – ship,[23] the *Hope* or *Hopewell* of London. Goodlake then served as an interpreter between Povey and Texera to work out the details of the deception. For a payment of 400 crowns (£100), plus £80 for his share of the ship, Povey agreed to sink the *Hopewell* with all its freight and return to Livorno with a certificate that Texera could send to his insurers as proof of the shipwreck.[24] For his services in helping to organize the scheme, Goodlake would share in the insurance proceeds.

Working through Jeronimo Henriques, their factor in Livorno, the Texeras had their wares loaded on to the ship. Eighteen chests and thirty bales went aboard, marked in the manner in which the Texeras 'allwaies used to marke the Bailes of their best and richest Comodities'.[25] But while

E 115/21/96, 17 May 1601 (certificate of residency).

[20] TNA, STAC 8/20/20, answer of Dominic Bowen, 6 June 1614 (wrongly dated as 11 Jac. I, which would be 1613; Francis Bacon brought the information in the suit as attorney general, and he did not assume that office until Oct. 1613).

[21] TNA, STAC 8/12/6, bill of complaint, 19 June 1613.

[22] TNA, STAC 8/12/6, 19 June 1613.

[23] TNA, STAC 8/12/6, answer of Roger Goodlake, 28 June 1613 (referring to the *Hopewell*, Roger Goodlake stated in his answer that, 'he well knewe, for the same was sometymes this def*endan*tes vessell but finding her to be full of flawes, decayes, & Leakes, this def*endan*t solde her away').

[24] TNA, STAC 8/12/6, 19 June 1613.

[25] TNA, STAC 8/12/6, 19 June 1613.

they laded forty-eight bales and chests, the bill of lading recorded a cargo nearly double that.[26]

Shortly before departing, Povey hired a crew. He intentionally sought out mariners of different nations – Italians, Portuguese, English and Dutch – so that they could not communicate effectively among themselves and discover the plot. To further the charade, Goodlake took the English boatsman, John Newton, aboard the ship and pointed out to him two cases, admonishing him to take special care to keep them safe because they contained cloth of gold. In fact, they contained trash.[27]

Diego Texera sent the bill of lading to his agent in Amsterdam, Duarte Fernandes, with instructions that he should obtain insurance worth £8,000 for the cargo. In Fernandes, Texera had the perfect representative. 'One of the most important Portuguese Jewish merchants' in Amsterdam at the time,[28] he both frequently acted as a factor for foreign traders[29] and did extensive business with Dutch merchants.[30] Fernandes obtained underwriting from twenty-four prominent local merchants for insurance worth 3,700 Flemish pounds, equivalent to 2,220 English pounds sterling.[31] The remainder of the insurance – or rather the over-insurance – came from merchants in other cities, including Genoa and Florence.[32]

Povey set sail on 25 December 'purposelie to disgrace the Christian faith'.[33] In addition, the *Hopewell* was accompanied by a 'gundelo'[34] that Diego

[26] TNA, STAC 8/12/6, 19 June 1613.

[27] TNA, STAC 8/12/6, 19 June 1613.

[28] E. M. Koen, 'Duarte Fernandes, koopman van de portugese natie te Amsterdam', *Studia Rosenthaliana*, ii (1968), 178–93, at p. 178 ('Duarte Fernandes, een van de belangrijkste kooplieden der sefardische Joden die zich aan het einde der zestiende eeuw te Amsterdam vestigden').

[29] Koen, 'Duarte Fernandes', p. 186. Fernandes may have been known to Texera through Fernandes's son Simão Henriques, who lived in Italy and knew Diego's father and brother-in-law. Koen, 'Duarte Fernandes', p. 185; J. N. Novoa, 'The many lives of two Portuguese conversos: Miguel Fernandes and Rui Teixeira in the Tribunal of the Holy Office in Rome', *Hispania Judaica Bulletin*, xii (2016), 127–84, at p. 135 (both discussing Simão Enriques).

[30] Koen, 'Duarte Fernandes', p. 187; J. V. Roitman, *The Same But Different? Inter-cultural Trade and the Sephardim, 1595–1640* (Leiden, 2011), pp. 294–6.

[31] TNA, STAC 8/12/6, bill of complaint, 19 June 1613. The merchants mentioned in the pleading were Dirck van Os, Barent Sweerts, Claes Andriesz, Jacques van Hanswijck and Jacques Merchijs. All of them were prominent insurers of Jewish shipments in Amsterdam. See Roitman, *The Same But Different?*, pp. 128, 132, 137–9, 163–4, 174–5, 203–4, 209.

[32] TNA, STAC 8/12/6, answer of Roger Goodlake, 28 June 1613.

[33] TNA, STAC 8/12/6, bill of complaint, 19 June 1613.

[34] A gondola was at this time a small boat with a sail, used for fishing and for carrying people and cargo over short distances. See S. Bellabarba and E. Guerreri, *Vele italiane della costa occidentale dal medioevo al Novecento* (Milan, 2002), pp. 108, 111.

bought to rescue the sailors when Povey sank the ship.[35] Despite having a fair wind to take him to Alicante, Povey put into port on the Îles de Hyères off the coast of southeast France.[36] He mumbled to his crew about needing victuals, but ended up taking on only 'one quarter of Mutton and some duckes' during the several days the ship remained in port.[37] On the last day of the stay, Povey sent the crew ashore on some invented errands. While they were gone, he used an augur to bore a hole in the stern hull, which he stopped with a plug. That night, the *Hopewell* set sail once more.[38]

When the ship was three or four leagues (about twelve or fifteen miles) from shore, Povey secretly pulled the plug. At 2:00 am, he woke the crew with the announcement that the hull had filled with water and the ship was sinking and had to be abandoned. The crew, however, saw not even a foot of water in the ballast, the freight was still dry, and they argued they could save the ship by pumping and bring it back to shore. Povey would have none of this. He ordered the crew off the ship and on to the gondola. The boatsman John Newton's attempts to save the wares to which Roger Goodlake had so insistently alerted him forced Povey to admit that the goods were valueless and not worth saving.[39]

The gondola carried the sailors to the town of Hyères on the French mainland. There Povey obtained a certificate of shipwreck, which he brought back to Diego Texera in Livorno.[40] In return, he received a bill from Roger Goodlake for the £80 reimbursement for his share in the ship,[41] and, in lieu of the 400 crowns owed him in payment, he was given four pieces of expensive cloth.[42]

Texera sent Povey's certificate to Duarte Fernandes in Amsterdam, asking him to obtain payment on the insurance policy. The Amsterdam merchants, having heard rumours of Texera's duplicity, refused to pay.[43] Fernandes brought suit against them in the Amsterdam Chamber of Insurance in May

35 TNA, STAC 8/12/6, bill of complaint, 19 June 1613.

36 TNA, STAC 8/12/6, 19 June 1613.

37 TNA, STAC 8/12/6, 19 June 1613.

38 TNA, STAC 8/12/6, 19 June 1613.

39 TNA, STAC 8/12/6, 19 June 1613.

40 TNA, STAC 8/12/6, 19 June 1613.

41 TNA, STAC 8/12/6, 19 June 1613.

42 TNA, STAC 8/20/20, bill of complaint, 6 June 1614.

43 Their reluctance may also have been related to the sudden drop in Dutch insurance rates after the signing of the Twelve Years' Truce between the Spanish and Dutch in Apr. 1609. J. Israel, *Empires and Entrepots: Dutch, the Spanish Monarchy and the Jews, 1585–1713* (London, 1990), p. 201.

1610. Lacking evidence of the fraud, the merchants lost and were forced to pay out 3,700 Flemish pounds on the policy.[44]

The plotters, 'haveing so closelie and cunningly behaved themselves in the managing of the said wicked and divilishe plott and practise aforesaid as that they escaped unpunished …, were so imboldned and incouraged in their said practises' that they decided to try their scam again.[45] In November 1609, they hired Christopher Webb, a mariner from Bristol who was master of the ship the *Patience*, another old and leaky ship,[46] to carry goods from Livorno to Lisbon. Once again, they gave out that they had freighted the ship with rich goods, when in fact the packs were mostly full of trash. And once again they obtained insurance from Amsterdam, Antwerp and this time also from London. When Webb made a stop en route in Malaga, his ship was searched on suspicion of being a pirate vessel, and the Spanish searchers discovered the false-packed freight.[47]

What the complaint strategically neglected to mention was that Bowen obtained his information about the *Patience* from four members of Webb's crew,[48] who were on trial in Admiralty in 1611–12 for piracy.[49] This evidence, untrustworthy though it may be since it came from men on trial for their lives, fills in many of the gaps left by the complaint's much briefer treatment of the *Patience* fraud.

The most detailed testimony came from the brothers Nicholas and Thomas Dirdo, Dorsetshire gentlemen.[50] The brothers, both in their early twenties at the time, explained that they had found themselves virtually penniless in Livorno after travelling over the Alps from the Netherlands. Seeking a way home, they became passengers on Webb's ship.[51] After boarding the ship a few days before it was to depart, they saw it laden with fifteen packs or chests, three of which belonged to Webb and one to Richardson, and the rest, as Webb told them, to a Portuguese merchant

44 TNA, STAC 8/12/6, bill of complaint, 19 June 1613.

45 TNA, STAC 8/12/6, 19 June 1613.

46 TNA, HCA 1/47, fo. 269v, deposition of Nicholas Dirdo, 19 March 1612.

47 TNA, STAC 8/12/6, 19 June 1613.

48 TNA, STAC 8/20/20, bill of complaint, 6 June 1614.

49 TNA, HCA 1/47, fos. 174v–176v, 179v–181v, 218v–220v, 259v–260v, 267r–273v. One suit in Admiralty against Webb's men was brought by two merchants of Antwerp and Amsterdam, Guilliam van Aalst and Jacques de Letter, and the other apparently by the crown. C. M. Senior, 'An investigation of the activities and importance of English pirates, 1603–40' (unpublished University of Bristol PhD thesis, 1972), p. 228.

50 A. Aurejac-Davis, 'The Dirdoe family of Gillingham, Dorset, and their capture by pirates', *Somerset and Dorset Family History Society* (2016) <https://sdfhs.org/blog/the-dirdoe-family-of-gillingham-dorset-and-their-capture-by-pirates> [accessed 28 Oct. 2020].

51 TNA, HCA 1/47, fo. 267r, deposition of Thomas Dirdo, 12 March 1612.

and a Jew.[52] Thomas Dirdo testified that three of the merchant's packs were later transferred to a Flemish ship.[53] While the Dirdos never named the merchant, another witness says Webb called him 'Trecera'.[54] Only the fourth time the brothers related the story, this time in a deposition taken on behalf of the crown, did they also mention seeing a certain Goodlake come aboard to talk to Webb.[55]

Thomas Dirdo related that Webb said he had been in great trouble and imprisoned in Livorno. To get himself released, he made a deal with a Jew or a Portuguese.[56] Their contract specified Webb would sink his ship or let it be taken by pirates in order to defraud the freight insurers.[57] In return, Webb could keep the goods, which he was told were rich merchandise of great value.[58]

Tempting pirates was, of course, dangerous, as Thomas Dirdo would find out in later life when he and his son were captured by Turkish pirates and sold into slavery.[59] But 'feigning the capture of the ship by pirates' was a known form of insurance fraud,[60] and Webb may have planned to sell his ship and goods to a friendly English pirate in order to obtain a certificate of capture.[61]

After setting sail, Webb stopped for several weeks in Malaga, Spain, where his boasting about his expensive freight led the Spanish authorities to suspect he sailed a pirate ship.[62] They briefly imprisoned Webb and his men while they searched the *Patience*. Opening four of the packs, they found brickbats, rope ends, old rugs, turbans, glass beads and four pieces of cloth of gold or silver. And yet, on these slim pickings, the Governor of Malaga supposedly decided Webb was a merchant and let him go.[63] Realizing

52 TNA, HCA 1/47, fo. 180r, deposition of Thomas Dirdo, 17 Apr. 1611.

53 TNA, HCA 1/47, fo. 180r, deposition of Thomas Dirdo, 17 Apr. 1611.

54 TNA, HCA 1/47, fo. 198v, deposition of William Stephens, 18 June 1611.

55 TNA, HCA 1/47, fo. 268v, deposition of Nicholas Dirdo, 19 March 1612; fo. 271v, deposition of Thomas Dirdo, 19 March 1612.

56 TNA, HCA 1/47, fos. 179v–180r, deposition of Thomas Dirdo, 17 Apr. 1611.

57 TNA, HCA 1/47, fo. 180v, deposition of Thomas Dirdo, 17 Apr. 1611; fo. 198v, deposition of William Stephens, 18 June 1611; fos. 219r–220r, deposition of Matthew Hutchinson, 31 July 1611.

58 TNA, HCA 1/47, fos. 175v, deposition of Nicholas Dirdo, 23 March 1611; fo. 221r, deposition of Matthew Hutchinson, 31 July 1611.

59 TNA, SP 16/348, fo. 128, petition of Thomas Dirdo, Feb. 1637.

60 Rossi, *Insurance*, p. 280.

61 TNA, HCA 1/47, fo. 267v, deposition of Thomas Dirdo, 12 March 1612.

62 TNA, HCA 1/47, fo. 220r, deposition of Matthew Hutchinson, 31 July 1611.

63 TNA, HCA 1/47, fo. 175r, deposition of Nicholas Dirdo, 23 March 1611; fos. 269r–v, 19 March 1612; fos. 180v–181r, deposition of Thomas Dirdo, 17 Apr. 1611; fo. 272v, 19 March 1612; fo. 195r, deposition of Matthew Kevel, 3 June 1611.

his freight was worthless and believing that if he returned to Livorno the freighters would not keep their promises,[64] Webb sailed to Mamora in Barbary (now Mehdya, Morocco). Upon his arrival there, he opened the remaining packs only to find nothing of value.[65] He then decided to become a pirate and spent the year 1610 hunting down Portuguese ships carrying sugar.[66]

In Amsterdam, the insurers got word of the 'foul play in loading the ship', and they again brought suit in the Amsterdam Chamber of Insurance.[67] Meanwhile in London, Christopher Goodlake, a merchant and brother of Roger, had also purchased insurance worth £1,025 underwritten by twenty-two London merchants on three chests of 'Tabines,[68] Cloth of Gould, Silke stockinges, and other goodes and merchaundizes of verye greate value' that he claimed Roger had freighted for him in the *Patience*.[69] Advised of the discovery of the false cargo, Christopher sought payment on the policy. But the insurers refused to pay, claiming fraud by Texera and Roger Goodlake. As a consequence, in June 1610, Christopher sued the insurers in the London Assurance Chamber, the court with jurisdiction over insurance disputes.[70] The commissioners of the court had resolved to give judgement in his favour, so Christopher claimed, when Dominic Bowen got involved and changed their minds.[71]

Bowen laid the responsibility for his intervention on his foreign principals. He explained that the Amsterdam merchants who had written Texera's insurance policies wrote to him 'acquaynting him w*i*th the unlawfull practizes … and advised him to take some Course of Justice here in England for the better discoveringe and punishinge of the said practizers'.[72] The merchants also obtained letters from the Amsterdam town magistrates addressed to Noel de Caron, the Dutch ambassador to the English court, asking him to assist Bowen in furthering the matter and providing evidence of the fraud. And, said Bowen, when King James 'did Cast his eye upon the

[64] TNA, HCA 1/47, fo. 199r, deposition of William Stephens, 18 June 1611.

[65] TNA, HCA 1/47, fo. 180r, deposition of Thomas Dirdo, 17 Apr. 1611.

[66] Senior, 'An investigation', pp. 87–8.

[67] E. M. Koen, 'Notarial records relating to the Portuguese Jews in Amsterdam up to 1639', *Studia Rosenthaliana*, v (1971), 106–24, at pp. 114 n. 376, 219–45, 221 n. 434.

[68] E. Kerridge, *Textile Manufactures in Early Modern England* (Manchester, 1985), pp. 71–2 (tabines or tobines were silk cloths 'embellished with lines and diamonds or rectangles formed by warp threads alternately floating over and dipping under two or more weft shoots').

[69] TNA, C 2/JasI/G7/37, *Goodlake* v *Bennett, et al.*, bill of complaint, 12 Aug. 1614.

[70] Rossi, *Insurance*, p. 86; TNA, STAC 8/20/20, bill of complaint, 6 June 1614.

[71] TNA, STAC 8/20/20, bill of complaint, 6 June 1614.

[72] TNA, STAC 8/20/20, answer of Dominic Bowen, 15 June 1614.

said examynacions and testimonyes', he 'advise[d] that a Course of Justice should be helde against the said practizers for the due punishing of them'.[73] This naturally led Bowen to bring the information 'in the name of' the attorney general in the Star Chamber.[74]

Both Roger Goodlake and John Povey submitted responses to Bowen's information. Povey demurred, arguing only that the court had no jurisdiction over him because all the wrongs he stood accused of were committed outside of England and no Englishmen were harmed. Furthermore, even if the court did have jurisdiction, the events occurred before the general pardon granted in the parliament of 1610, the benefit of which he requested.[75]

Goodlake gave a more detailed response. While he admitted to knowing Diego Texera and doing business with him, he denied the rest of the allegations. He asserted that Texera was a Christian, not a Jew. He claimed not to know the other co-conspirators or Duarte Fernandes. He said he had nothing to do with the lading or insuring of the *Hopewell*, or any other part of the alleged scam. While he did not deny freighting wares on the *Patience*, he stated that at least four others did as well:[76] Don Antonio de' Medici, the illegitimate son and erstwhile heir of Francesco I de' Medici, the deceased grand duke of Tuscany; the Tuscan merchant Fabio Orlandini;[77] Duarte Dias, a leading merchant and Diego Texera's brother-in-law;[78] and Dinis Fernandes, who may have been Texera's teenage nephew.[79] If these were mere phantom shippers, then the scam was even larger than Bowen knew, because Dinis Fernandes obtained insurance on freight in the *Patience* in Amsterdam. This policy generated its own litigation in Holland.[80]

As sensational as the accusations were, the case apparently did not proceed beyond the pleadings. Instead, the court dismissed the lawsuit on

[73] TNA, STAC 8/20/20, 15 June 1614.

[74] TNA, STAC 8/20/20, 15 June 1614.

[75] TNA, STAC 8/12/6, demurrer of John Povey, 2 Dec. 1613.

[76] TNA, STAC 8/12/6, answer of Roger Goodlake, 28 June 1613.

[77] M. Berti, 'La pesca ed il commercio del corallo nel Mediterraneo e le prime "Compagnie dei coralli" di Pisa tra XVI e XVII secolo', in *La Pesca in Italia tra Età Moderna e Contemporanea. Produzione, Mercato, Consumo*, ed. G. Doneddu, A. Fiori (2003), pp. 77–170, at p. 106 (naming Orlandini among the 'attori importanti degli affari pisani e livornesi').

[78] Berti, 'Le pesca', at p. 125 n. 111 (calling Diego Texera and Duarta Dias merchants 'più importanti'); Novoa, 'The many lives', p. 133 (identifying Dias as Diego's brother-in-law).

[79] J. N. Novoa, 'A family of the Nação from the Atlantic to the Mediterranean and beyond (1497–1640)', in *Religious Changes and Cultural Transformations in the Early Modern Western Sephardic Communities*, ed. Y. Kaplan (2019), pp. 22–42, at p. 34 (identifying Dinis as the son of Miguel Fernandes); Novoa, 'The many lives', p. 131 (mentioning baptism of Miguel's son in 1594).

[80] Koen, 'Notarial records', v. 114 n. 377.

two grounds. First, it observed that it had no jurisdiction over the claims concerning the *Hopewell* because all the events occurred overseas and no Englishmen suffered damages. Second, it found the complaint defective with regard to the accusations about the *Patience* because it did not name the specific English insurers aggrieved by the alleged scam but spoke only in general terms. The court, however, gave leave for Bowen to refile the information correctly.[81]

Before Bowen did so, the alleged conspirators fought back, probably with the same intention Bowen had, namely to influence the deliberations of the London Assurance Chamber. In June 1614, the new attorney general, Francis Bacon, brought suit against Bowen in the Star Chamber at the relation of Christopher Goodlake.[82] In Goodlake's version of the story, Diego Texera (acting alone) negotiated with John Povey to carry genuinely valuable freight to Spain. Diego insured the goods, Povey sailed, and the ship sank due to misfortune. The complaint pointed out that Povey and the other mariners swore to this point upon their 'Corporall oathes uppon the holy Evangelist in dewe forme of the Lawes there used' before the duly authorized magistrates of Hyères.[83] Roger Goodlake, meanwhile, never talked to Povey about sinking the ship, and he never served as interpreter for Diego about any such matter.[84]

With regard to Webb and the *Patience*, Christopher repeated the point that Roger and Diego were only minor shippers – Roger freighting three chests and Diego five – among a larger group of other merchants 'of greate and speciall account in Italie'.[85] Christopher detailed how he had sought payment of the insurance policy after Webb made off with the goods. When the insurers denied him, he sued them in the insurance court.

Then the bill took an unexpected turn and accused Bowen of convincing Povey to lie about the *Hopewell* scam. In other words, the fraud was not Texera's cheating of his insurers but rather Bowen's fabrication of the evidence about the shipper's alleged duplicity.

According to Goodlake, Bowen had an incentive to invent a swindle. He realized that if he could get testimony that the *Hopewell* was sunk by fraud, he would be rewarded by the Dutch insurers, who would not only get their money back from Diego Texera but also a premium the latter had promised if they proved his deceit.[86] Bowen also saw that if he could associate Roger

[81] TNA, STAC 8/20/20, answer of Dominic Bowen, 15 June 1614.
[82] TNA, STAC 8/20/20, bill of complaint, 6 June 1614.
[83] TNA, STAC 8/20/20, 6 June 1614.
[84] TNA, STAC 8/20/20, 6 June 1614.
[85] TNA, STAC 8/20/20, 6 June 1614.
[86] TNA, STAC 8/20/20, 6 June 1614. For another example of this sort of promise from

Goodlake with Diego in both the *Hopewell* and the *Patience* affairs, he could discredit Christopher's suit in the London Assurance Chamber and get yet another reward from the insurers.[87]

In Goodlake's version of the affair, Bowen learned that Povey was in Ireland in 'Brace about fortie miles from Gallowaye'.[88] He conspired with another Dutch merchant living in London, Walter Bollen,[89] to obtain a letter from the Privy Council to the lord deputy of Ireland to apprehend Povey and depose him concerning the sinking of the ship. Armed with a warrant from the lord deputy, Bollen pretended to arrest Povey, who was in on the conspiracy, and took him to Galway, where the current and a former mayor of the town administered interrogatories to him under oath.[90]

A letter from the Privy Council to the lord deputy of Ireland in January 1611 confirms part of this story. The councillors wrote the lord deputy telling him they had received a 'strange complaint' from merchants of Amsterdam and elsewhere that Povey and 'divers Portingales and Jews' of Livorno or Florence had engaged in insurance fraud. Povey, 'fearing a discovery of the fraud', had fled England and gone to Ireland 'in the province of Connaught, at a place called Barane [Burren] or Breaschalle [Burrishoole]'. The lords, 'desiring to punish so notorious a fraud forged by ungodly Jews', ordered Povey to be arrested and deposed.[91]

Bowen allegedly took great care in preparing his story. After ensuring Povey's deposition was properly filed 'under the Seale of the Lord Maior of London' and convincing Henry Montague, the recorder of London, to arrest Roger Goodlake and keep him prisoner while the commissioners of insurance in London (of which Montague was one)[92] decided the *Patience* affair, he also persuaded four of Webb's men, on trial in Admiralty, to depose about the false freighting of the *Patience*.[93]

1615, see E. M. Koen, 'Notarial records relating to the Portuguese Jews in Amsterdam up to 1639', *Studia Rosenthaliana*, viii (1974), pp. 300–7, at p. 300 n. 841.

87 TNA, STAC 8/20/20, 6 June 1614.

88 TNA, STAC 8/20/20, 6 June 1614.

89 This is probably Wouter Bolle, who had worked with Bowen previously on insurance matters on behalf of one of the same Amsterdam merchants who had insured the *Hopewell*. Koen, 'Notarial records', v. 233 n. 485.

90 TNA, STAC 8/20/20, 6 June 1614. The information named Sir Thomas Rotheram, governor of St Augustine's fort and mayor in 1612, and Richard Martin, who was mayor in 1607. See J. Hardiman, *The History of the Town and County of the Town of Galway* (Dublin, 1820), p. 212.

91 *Calendar of the State Papers Relating to Ireland, of the Reign of James I, 1611–1614*, ed. C. W. Russell and J. P. Prendergast (5 vols., 1872–80), iv. 236–7.

92 TNA, C 2/JasI/G7/37, bill of complaint, 12 Aug. 1614; G. Rossi, *Insurance*, p. 86.

93 TNA, STAC 8/20/20, bill of complaint, 6 June 1614.

According to Goodlake's complaint, by filing his Star Chamber information, Bowen raised questions in the minds of the commissioners of insurance. Where they had been tending towards supporting him, Goodlake said, after the commencement of Bowen's suit, they put off giving judgement. Then in September 1613, they ordered the insurers to deposit their payment with the Assurance Chamber to be held until the Star Chamber decided the matter. In light of this, Goodlake was forced to bring his own relator suit in 1614 to obtain the intervention of the Star Chamber.[94]

This time Povey did not make a reply, but Bowen's answer reaffirmed his original allegations, asserted the truth of Povey's depositions and added a final bombshell. After the dismissal of his 1613 information, he claimed to have 'receave[d] from the p*ar*tes of Italye a Sentence Awthenticall' showing that Diego Texera had been condemned to die for a 'like Fact as is menc*i*oned and Conteyned in the said Informac*i*on exhibited into this honorable Courte Concerning the shipp called the Hopewell' and that the captain of the same ship had been sentenced and hanged.[95]

As with the 1613 suit, the 1614 file lacks depositions, and no record exists of its resolution.[96] But a Chancery suit brought by Christopher Goodlake in August 1614 provides a bit more information about what happened next.[97] The bill rehearsed the history of the voyage of the *Patience*, Goodlake's initial suit before the Assurance Chamber, and that court's September 1613 order that if the Star Chamber dismissed Bowen's suit, the insurers would have to pay on the policy.[98] Goodlake pointed out that the Star Chamber did dismiss the suit, and yet the insurers continued to refuse to pay. Furthermore, he complained, in light of Bowen's accusations, the insurers had pressured the commissioners, causing the latter to revoke their 1613 order and replace it with a new one in June 1614 – which probably provides the real explanation for Goodlake's Star Chamber relator suit filed in the same month.[99] The new order required the insurers to repay Goodlake only

94 TNA, STAC 8/20/20, 6 June 1614; C 2/JasI/G7/37, bill of complaint, 12 Aug. 1614.

95 TNA, STAC 8/20/20, answer of Dominic Bowen, 15 June 1614.

96 The Exchequer records contain no indication that Bowen, Goodlake or Povey were fined. See T. G. Barnes, 'Fines in the court of Star Chamber, 1596–1641', manuscript available at The National Archives of the UK.

97 TNA, C 2/JasI/G7/37, *Goodlake* v *Bennett*, *et al.*, 1614.

98 TNA, C 2/JasI/G7/37, bill of complaint, 12 Aug. 1614. The bill also asserted that the policy was for £1,025 and not £1,700, as stated in the Star Chamber bill.

99 TNA, C 2/JasI/G7/37, bill of complaint, 12 Aug. 1614; C 2/JasI/G7/37, plea of defendants, [1614]; C 33/127, fo. 73r, 24 Oct. 1614 (Chancery order).

the 10% premium he had paid to them. Upon repayment, their names were to be crossed off the policy, meaning they had no further liability.[100]

Because Goodlake sued in Chancery before asking the insurers to repay their proportional part of the premium and be struck from the policy, they demurred. They argued that the clause of the Assurance Act of 1601 mandating that any person aggrieved by a decision of the commissioners of insurance might sue in Chancery only after he should 'execute and satisfie the saide Sentence soe awarded' meant that Goodlake had to accept the premium repayment and remove the names of those repaying from the policy before he could sue.[101] Goodlake's counsel, Francis Moore, pointed out the absurdity of this argument because Goodlake had not been ordered to pay anything but rather to receive payment.[102] But the lord chancellor, upon reviewing the act and the parties' pleadings, disagreed. In April 1615, he found in favour of the insurers, dismissing Goodlake's complaint until he had abided by the requirements of the statute.[103] And so the litigation apparently ended.

***

While combating fraud was an important part of the Star Chamber's jurisdiction, the concurrent suits before the London Assurance Chamber and Chancery suggest that Bowen and Goodlake were mainly using the Star Chamber in another of its principal capacities: 'to mount a collateral attack, either to shore up or to cross' the other proceedings.[104] Perhaps because the parties did not intend for the Star Chamber suit to progress very far, their pleadings left out key information about the eventful backgrounds of Diego Texera and Roger Goodlake; information that everyone involved probably knew about.

Goodlake came from a Berkshire gentry family.[105] He was apprenticed in 1597 to Richard Cockayne,[106] brother of the famous London merchant,

[100] TNA, C 2/JasI/G7/37, bill of complaint, 12 Aug. 1614.

[101] 'An Act Concerning Matters of Assurances Amongst Merchants', 43 Eliz. c. 12, § 3 (1601); TNA, C 2/JasI/G7/37, plea of the defendants, [1614].

[102] TNA, C 33/127, fo. 73r, 24 Oct. 1614 (Chancery order).

[103] TNA, C 33/127, fo. 861v, 4 Apr. 1615 (Chancery order).

[104] T. G. Barnes, 'Star Chamber litigants and their counsel, 1596–1641', in *Legal Records and the Historian*, ed. J. H. Baker (1978), pp. 7–28, at p. 15.

[105] *A History of the County of Berkshire*, ed. P. H. Ditchfield (4 vols., 1906–24), iv. 226; *Miscellanea Genealogica et Heraldica*, ed. J. J. Howard (4 vols., new ser., 1874–84), iv. 267; *Miscellanea Genealogica et Heraldica*, ed. J. J. Howard (5 vols., 3rd ser., 1896–1904), i. 150.

[106] *Miscellanea Genealogica et Heraldica*, i. 150.

William Cockayne.[107] In November 1604, Richard sent Roger as his factor on a trading voyage to Genoa in Richard's ship the *Royal Merchant*, but the ship never made it to its destination. Instead, Roger and the ship's captain, Richard Thornton, took it to Livorno, where they agreed (or were forced)[108] to put the ship to the use of Grand Duke Ferdinando I of Tuscany in his war against the Turks. In late 1605, the *Royal Merchant* seized a great Turkish galleon and brought her back to Livorno, causing an international incident.[109] The English merchants trading in Constantinople as part of the Levant Company reacted with 'great alarm' and expected reprisals.[110]

According to Richard Cockayne, the grand duke allegedly gave Goodlake the shipowner's portion of the prize, amounting to over £16,666 (which Goodlake never passed along to Richard), and also tried to commandeer the ship and its artillery.[111] By September 1607, Roger was imprisoned in Florence, perhaps because of a dispute with the duke over reoccupying the ship.[112] While in prison, Roger sent a carefully worded missive to George Rook – a man useful to Henry Wotton, King James's ambassador in Venice[113] – hinting at secret dealings.[114] But by the spring of 1608, Roger was back in Livorno, and the records of the Galli bank of Florence show him actively engaged in commerce.[115]

To complicate matters further, Roger may have been a Catholic. His mother was a recusant.[116] Many of the English merchants and Irish ship captains operating in Livorno in the early seventeenth century were Catholics, as was Richard Thornton, the captain of the *Royal Merchant* with

[107] TNA, C 78/204/6, *Richard Cockayne* v *William Cockayne*, 11 Feb. 1618 (identifying Roger Goodlake as Richard's apprentice and William Cockayne as his brother).

[108] British Library, Cotton Nero B/VII, fo. 237r, complaint of Richard Cockayne.

[109] TNA, REQ 2/424/31, *Cockayne* v *Goodlake, et al.*, bill of complaint, [1609]; Brit. Libr., Cotton Nero B.VII, fo. 237r; *Calendar of State Papers and Manuscripts Existing in the Archives and Collections of Venice, 1603–1607*, ed. H. F. Brown (38 vols., 1864–1947), x. lviii.

[110] *Calendar of State Papers and Manuscripts: Venice*, x. 320 n. 483 (10 Feb. 1606).

[111] TNA, REQ 2/424/31, *Cockayne* v *Goodlake, et al.*, bill of complaint, [1609]; Brit. Libr., Cotton Nero B.VII, fo. 237r–v; Archivio di Stato di Firenze, Mediceo del Principato 2082, unfoliated, letter from Ugolino Barisoni, 31 Dec. 1606.

[112] Hatfield House Archives, Marquess of Salisbury, CP 122, fo. 58r–v, 2 Sept. 1607; Brit. Libr., Cotton Nero B.VII, fo. 238r; Archivio di Stato di Firenze, Mediceo del Principato 2082, unfoliated, letter from Ugolino Barisoni, 31 Dec. 1606.

[113] J. W. Stoye, *English Travellers Abroad, 1604–1667* (London, 1952), p. 103; L. P. Smith, *The Life and Letters of Sir Henry Wotton* (2 vols., 1907), ii. 478.

[114] Hatfield House Archives, Marquess of Salisbury, CP 122, fos. 58r–v, 2 Sept. 1607.

[115] Archivio di Stato di Firenze, Fondo Galli Tassi 2100, fos. 161–162; R. de Roover, 'Thomas Mun in Italy', *Historical Research*, xxx (1957), 80–5, at p. 84 (the Galli bank 'was patronized by the entire English colony of Pisa and Leghorn').

[116] *Recusants in the Exchequer Pipe Rolls, 1581–1592*, ed. T. I. McCann (Southampton, 1986), p. 69 (recording recusancy of Alice Goodlake, 'wife of Edward Goodlake, esq., of Letcombe Regis, Berks.' in 1586).

whom Roger had thrown in his lot.[117] And most intriguingly, Roger may have been the Englishman Ruggiero Guidalao, who served as an emissary for the grand duke of Tuscany to the king of Spain during 1610 and 1611 to discuss the printing of books reforming Spanish liturgical music.[118]

Cockayne depicted Roger's brother Christopher as the mastermind of the scheme to steal Cockayne's ship, deny him a share of the prize money and ruin his good name and credit. Cockayne sued Christopher (although not Roger, probably because he was out of reach in Italy and protected by the grand duke[119]) and a number of other prominent London merchants in 1609 for harms caused him by the *Royal Merchant* affair.[120] His various lawsuits trying to straighten out his credit continued until 1618.[121] As some of the men who had paid into Christopher Goodlake's insurance policy in 1609 were members of the Levant Company in 1605 and had been kept abreast of the events surrounding the *Royal Merchant* by their Italian agent, Thomas Mun,[122] it is unlikely they were unaware of the Goodlake brothers' questionable history when the accusations of insurance fraud later arose.

As for the other alleged co-conspirators, Antonio and Diego Texera were brothers.[123] The Texera family were Portuguese New Christians who had come to Pisa from Portugal in 1594 at the behest of the grand duke of Tuscany.[124] The brothers' father Rui and brother-in-law Miguel Fernandes were prominent merchants of sugar and coral with knowledge useful to the duke about Brazil and the Atlantic trade.[125] In 1595, Rui Texera and Fernandes

[117] L. M. Lillie, 'Empire, community, nation: the English merchants of Livorno, Italy and the sociability of commerce in early modernity' (unpublished Washington University PhD thesis, 2017), pp. 9, 55, 105–6.

[118] Archivio di Stato di Firenze, Mediceo del Principato 4941, fo. 702, 26 Oct. 1610 and fo. 788, 20 Jan. 1611.

[119] Brit. Libr., Cotton Nero B.VII, fo. 237r.

[120] TNA, REQ 2/424/31, *Cockayne* v *Goodlake, et al.*, bill of complaint, [1609].

[121] TNA, C 78/204/6, 11 Feb. 1618.

[122] TNA, REQ 2/424/31, *Cockayne* v *Goodlake, et al.*, bill of complaint, [1609]; C 2/JASI/G7/37, *Goodlake* v *Bennett, et al.*, bill of complaint (12 Aug. 1614). The twenty-two insurers were Edward Beale, George Bennett, Thomas Bennett, Richard Champion (1605), Christopher Clitheroe, John Coghill, Henry Garraway (1600), William Gore, Lawrence Green (1605), Hugh Hamersley (1600), Thomas Havers (1605), William Haynes (1605), John Hodges, John Holloway (1605), Jeffrey Kirlie, Edward Lutterford, Giles Parslowe (1605), Thomas Simonds (1592), George Southerton, Gabriel Towerson, Edward Towerson, Robert Towerson. The dates in brackets indicate the year they joined the Levant Company, if this occurred by 1605. Spelling and Levant Company membership based on the lists at the end of volume 3 of T. K. Rabb, *Enterprise and Empire* (3 vols., 1967).

[123] Novoa, 'The many lives', p. 142.

[124] Novoa, 'A family of the Nação', p. 31.

[125] Novoa, 'The many lives', pp. 133, 136; Novoa, 'A family of the Nação', pp. 31–2.

fell afoul of the Inquisition and were imprisoned for several months in Rome on accusations of Judaizing.[126] The men were of such importance to the grand duke, however, that he used his money and influence to get them released.[127]

Rui apparently died a Catholic,[128] but Diego, around whom Bowen's narrative centred, had uncertain ties to Judaism. Documents refer to him as Portuguese rather than as a Jew, though Webb described him as both.[129] Diego's sister was brought before the Inquisition in 1618 and 1625 for Judaizing,[130] and his agent in Amsterdam, Duarte Fernandes, was a prominent Jew.[131] Diego did business with Jews in Italy[132] but also with Florentine bankers and English merchants.[133] And like his father, he had close ties to the grand duke. In his mid-twenties, he served the duke on a sensitive diplomatic matter in Morocco involving the revolt of Mohammad esh Sheikh el Mamun of Fez.[134] In return, the duke favoured Diego, using his influence to get him a larger house in Livorno[135] and encouraging granducal officials to pressure the Venetian Senate to find in Diego's favour in the latter's lawsuit there against a Jew for debt.[136]

Diego also displayed an untrustworthy side. He falsely accused a fellow Portuguese of relaying sensitive information about Tuscan interests in Barbary to the Spanish crown.[137] He made what a Florentine court found

[126] Novoa, 'The many lives', pp. 132, 137.

[127] Novoa, 'The many lives', pp. 133–4, 136.

[128] Novoa, 'A family of the Nação', p. 33.

[129] Archivio di Stato di Firenze, Mediceo del Principato 2999, fo. 52r, 25 Feb. 1605 ('Tescera pur Portughese'); Mediceo del Principato 1353, unfoliated, letter to Andrea Cioli, 8 Nov. 1613 ('signor Dioguo Teixeira Portughese'); TNA, HCA 1/47, fo. 271v, deposition of Thomas Dirdo, 19 March 1612 (testifying Webb described the person who freighted the *Patience* as a Portuguese and a Jew).

[130] Novoa, 'The many lives', p. 137.

[131] Koen, 'Duarte Fernandes', p. 180.

[132] Archivio di Stato di Firenze, Mediceo del Principato 3001, fo. 59r, 4 Apr. 1609 (debt owed to Texera by a Jew); E. Goldberg, *Jews and Magic in Medici Florence* (Toronto 2011), pp. 111–12 (trade with Jews).

[133] Archivio di Stato di Firenze, Fondo Galli Tassi 2100, fo. 106, March 1607 (paying Galli bank on behalf of the English merchant Edward Turner).

[134] Archivio di Stato di Firenze, Mediceo del Principato 4274, fos. 94r, 96r (undated *c.*1605–6); Mediceo del Principato 298, fo. 175r, 30 Oct. 1606; *Les Sources Inédites de l'Histoire du Maroc. 1. série: Dynastie Saadienne. Archives et Bibliothèques d'Angleterre*, ed. H. de Castries (3 vols., 1918–35), ii. 361 n.1 (concerning the 1605–6 voyage of Captain Pompilio Peretti, with whom Diego communicated, to Morocco).

[135] Archivio di Stato di Firenze, Mediceo del Principato 298, fo. 22v, 21 Apr. 1603.

[136] Archivio di Stato di Firenze, Mediceo del Principato 6038, fo. 30v, 6 March 1609; Mediceo del Principato 3001, fo. 59r, 4 Apr. 1609.

[137] Archivio di Stato di Firenze, Mediceo del Principato 2999, fo. 52r, 25 Feb. 1605.

were untrue claims about the non-payment of a commission by certain Jews in a sale of goods plundered from a captured ship.[138] In a letter about this case sent by the grand duke's attorney general to the granducal first secretary, Diego was described as an 'huomo molto sagace, et accorto',[139] which could be translated as a sagacious and shrewd man,[140] but also, given the context, as a shrewd and cunning one. He failed to repay money he owed to his relatives, who believed he was cheating them.[141] And during the litigation over the *Patience* in London, the unnamed agent whom Diego had sent to collect the insurance money wrote to the grand duke's secretary to complain that for over a year he had been unable to get any payment from Diego and was consequently stuck penniless in London.[142] He also made this suggestive comment, presumably referring to a trip Diego had made to England about 1605:[143]

> Dioguo Teixeira escaped from here because of fear of certain criminal complaints against him, and it seems strange to me that a man so rich as he was and with such a high reputation and so highly respected by the great memory of the Most Serene Grand Duke Ferdinando, has been involved in things against his honor.[144]

And yet, while Duarte Fernandes, Diego Texera's agent, was suspicious enough about the *Patience* voyage to send Ferdinando de Mercado, a

[138] Archivio di Stato di Firenze, Otto di Guardia e di Balìa del Principato 228, fo. 160r, 15 Feb. 1608; Mediceo del Principato 939, fo. 652r, 16 Feb. 1608.

[139] Archivio di Stato di Firenze, Mediceo del Principato 939, fo. 652r, 16 Feb. 1608.

[140] Goldberg, *Jews and Magic*, p. 112. Goldberg confused the Diego Texera of Livorno with Diego Teixeiro Sampayo, a well-known merchant in Antwerp and later Hamburg.

[141] *Processi del S. Uffizio di Venezia Contro Ebrei e Giudaizzanti (1633–1637)*, ed. P. C. Ioly Zorattini (19 vols., 1980–99), i. 219, 231.

[142] Archivio di Stato di Firenze, Mediceo del Principato 1353, unfoliated, unsigned letter to Andrea Cioli, 8 Nov. 1613.

[143] Archivio di Stato di Firenze, Mediceo del Principato 4274, fo. 94r (undated *c.*1605–6) (referencing trip to England).

[144] Archivio di Stato di Firenze, Mediceo del Principato 1353, unfoliated, unsigned letter to Andrea Cioli, 8 Nov. 1613 ('Dioguo Teixeira s'è fuggito di costà per temenza di certe querele criminali datogli, et mi pare strano che un huomo tanto ricco che era, et di tanta reputazione, et tanto stimato dalla felic.ma memoria del ser.mo GranDuca Ferdinando deva essere incorso in cose contro l'honor suo').

Portuguese Jew from Amsterdam who lived in London, to interview one of Webb's men in prison,[145] he was still doing business with Diego in 1613.[146]

Diego died in Spain, sometime between 1618 and 1625.[147] Thus, even if Bowen were telling the truth about the sentence of execution against Diego in 1613 or 1614, it was not carried out, possibly because Diego fled Tuscany and moved to Milan.[148]

This additional evidence demonstrates that Bowen had plausible conspirators with religious vulnerabilities to offer up to the court. While some of Bowen's accusations do look questionable under scrutiny – the trailing gondola whose existence no one questioned, the lack of evidence about how the *Hopewell* sailors' silence was bought, the implausibility that Webb believed his ship had been freighted with expensive wares, the fact that the Amsterdam merchants insured the second ship after the first had sunk mysteriously – many people wanted to believe Bowen's story. By forcing the issue in the Star Chamber, Bowen ensured the English insurers had success with the London Assurance Chamber. The Dutch insurers who lost their claims in the Amsterdam Court of Insurance appealed to the High Court of Holland (the Hof van Holland) on both policies,[149] and ultimately in 1620 obtained a judgement requiring Duarte Fernandes to hand over the proceeds of a judicial sale of goods belonging to Diego Texera in repayment for the insurance on the *Hopewell*.[150]

Of course, the courts and litigants may also have been willing to accept the claims for reasons other than their truth value. The English plaintiffs, for instance, were powerful merchants who were older, richer and better connected than the Goodlake brothers. In using Star Chamber case

[145] TNA, HCA 1/47, fo. 220v, deposition of Matthew Hutchinson, 31 July 1611. Mercado was forced to flee London after being identified as Jewish. He is attested in London as late as Jan. 1611, which might raise questions about whether it was in fact he who interviewed Matthew Hutchinson in prison, or rather someone posing as Mercado. Webb's men did not return to England until Jan. 1611 at the earliest. E. R. Samuel, 'Portuguese Jews in Jacobean London', *Transactions Jewish Historical Society of England*, xviii (1953–5), 171–230, at pp. 181–4; M. Woolf, 'Foreign trade of London Jews in the seventeenth century', *Transactions & Miscellanies Jewish Historical Society of England*, xxiv (1970–3), 38–58, at p. 39.

[146] Koen, 'Duarte Fernandes', p. 184.

[147] *Processi del S. Uffizio di Venezia*, i. 209, 282, 324 (indicating Diego was still alive in 1618 but had died by 1625, and that he died in Spain).

[148] *Processi del S. Uffizio di Venezia*, i. 209, 231.

[149] Koen, 'Notarial records', v. 238 no. 513 (*Patience*); Stadsarchief Amsterdam, Not. Arch. 156, fo. 60v, 17 Dec. 1618 (indicating Fernandes had lost his suit in the Hof van Holland in 1616); E. M. Koen, 'Notarial records', relating to the Portuguese Jews in Amsterdam up to 1639', *Studia Rosenthaliana*, xvi (1982), 61–84, at p. 82, no. 1999 (*Hopewell*).

[150] Koen, 'Notarial records', xvi. 81–2, nos. 1997, 1999; Stadsarchief Amsterdam, Not. Arch. 156, fo. 60v, 17 Dec. 1618.

files to study fraud, we are often hampered by lack of knowledge of the background that the pleadings leave out and of the other evidence available at the time. Consequently, we quite frequently cannot be certain whether the allegations in any given suit were true or were themselves a fraud on the court designed to do no more than obtain jurisdiction over the defendant. Yet even a fabricated story may offer valid evidence about the history of fraud. A good lie, after all, falls within the boundaries of the believable and the plausible. *Attorney General* v *Goodlake* was a good lie that told what was by then already a well-worn tale of phantom wares insured and holes drilled in hulls. Such a story was unlikely to be completely unfamiliar to the members of the court, and continues to be told to the present day.

10. Star Chamber and the bullion trade, 1618–20

Simon Healy

The records of the common-law courts of early modern England are notoriously difficult to use because of the paucity of evidence: the legal record offers no more than a bare summary of a case, occasionally illuminated by law reports. However, the surviving papers of Star Chamber present a different problem: lengthy bills and answers; bundles of depositions (carefully coached via leading interrogatories); but little evidence of orders or decrees, apart from the records of fines levied. This archive offers a wealth of detail, but beyond the cause papers themselves, there is often very little information about the broader context of a case.

Table 10.1: Bullion cases brought in Star Chamber by Attorney General Yelverton

Date of bill	**Defendants**	**Nature of case**	**Sources (at TNA)**
20 May 1618	Goldsmiths	Melting of coin; smuggling	STAC 8/25/20
11 June 1618	Merchant strangers and goldsmiths	Purchase and smuggling of coin	STAC 8/25/19; STAC 8/25/24; STAC 10/1/95
22 June 1618	Goldsmiths	Adulteration of gold; sale of coin for smuggling	STAC 8/25/22
27 Oct. 1619	Goldsmiths	Paying more than the Mint price for coin	STAC 8/25/21
4 Feb. 1620	Merchant strangers	Smuggling	STAC 8/25/23

The case under consideration here is a fortunate exception to this rule, a *cause célèbre* of its day with ramifications far beyond the immediate charges, which yielded a great deal of information about a clandestine trade spanning two continents. Probably the largest English fraud trial of the early seventeenth century, it involved a number of London goldsmiths and 160 merchant strangers, chiefly from the United Provinces and the Spanish Netherlands, all of whom had resided in London for many years. The

S. Healy, 'Star Chamber and the bullion trade, 1618–20' in *Star Chamber Matters: An Early Modern Court and Its Records*, ed. K. Kesselring and N. Mears (London, 2021), pp. 175–194.

charges brought by Attorney General Sir Henry Yelverton in the suits he initiated in 1618–20 (see table 10.1) stated that, since the accession of King James in 1603, numerous goldsmiths had privately supplied vast quantities of gold and silver coin and bullion to the merchant strangers. The latter then smuggled them to the Low Countries, where differences in the ratio between the precious metal content of the imported specie and the local coinage allowed the merchants to make a modest profit by arbitrage.

What was the wider significance of these cases? In the first instance, they shed light on the international bullion trade of early modern Europe, which many of its beneficiaries would rather not have seen exposed to public scrutiny. Second, they illuminated the political tensions of the age: the prosecution seems to have originated with a minor courtier who aspired to a share of any fines levied, but it became a vehicle for the political ambitions of more important figures; and it is possible the crown hoped to use the case as leverage in Anglo-Dutch trade talks then taking place in London (although nothing appears to have come of this).[1] Third, the proceedings highlighted the difficulties the English legal system had in dealing with a particular type of fraud, the smuggling of goods across international borders:[2] the law provided for the seizure of smuggled coin and the imprisonment of offenders for up to one year, but as the coin and bullion at issue in this case had long since departed the realm, there was nothing to seize. Finally, this case illuminates the courtroom tactics of each side in this dispute, which largely remain obscure in other cases due to the loss of the procedural records: Yelverton was uncertain whether to focus his efforts against the goldsmiths or the merchant strangers until the eve of the trial in Michaelmas 1619; while the defendants managed to cast some doubts on the credibility of a number of key witnesses, and temporarily persuaded one to retract his testimony.

***

Control of the coinage was one of the most ancient prerogative rights of the English crown. Two early items of legislation – the greater and lesser statutes of money – were enacted by the parliaments of Edward I, which stipulated that any smuggled coin was to be forfeit, with one-quarter of the seizure going to the informer, the rest to the crown. Foreign merchants

[1] *Court and Times of James the First,* ed. T. Birch (2 vols., London, 1848), ii. 110, 113, 132, 153, 168–70.

[2] I owe this point to David C. Smith of Wilfrid Laurier University, who also observed that this kind of fraud remains difficult to prosecute today.

who smuggled clipped and counterfeit coin into England were to lose their coin for a first offence, to forfeit all the goods they imported for a second offence, and for a third infraction they lost their goods and faced imprisonment. Another statute of 9 Edward III asserted that smuggling continued to be a problem, stipulating that unlicensed exports of English coin were to suffer forfeiture, while goldsmiths who melted English coin were to be imprisoned until they had paid a fine of half the value of the coin involved.[3] Over the following century and a half, exchange rates became a point of international contention, particularly in relations between England and the Duchy of Burgundy.[4] These tensions provoked a series of English statutes reiterating the ban on unlicensed export of coin: 2 Henry IV, cap. 5 ordered that merchant strangers who imported goods to England were to invest half their capital in the export of English goods, following which the crown would grant licence to export the other half in coin; while 2 Henry IV, cap. 6 barred all foreign currency from circulating in England; and 2 Henry VI, cap. 6 called for companies of foreign merchants to stand surety in Chancery that individual members would not export English coin without licence.[5]

English gold coins, the most convenient medium of exchange for international trade, attracted the attention of smugglers because of their fineness. With the exception of two notorious periods of debasement (under Edward III, and again in the 1540s), English gold contained a higher proportion of precious metal than most of its continental counterparts. This meant that if merchant strangers took payment in coin rather than bills of exchange, the proceeds would command a premium in many foreign countries. Moreover, in a country undergoing rapid debasement (such as Poland in the late 1610s), 'Gresham's law'[6] – that bad money drives out the good – meant English gold was likely to attract a premium well above the

[3] *Statutes of the Realm,* ed. T. E. Tomlins, et al. (12 vols., London, 1810–28), i. 219–20, 273–4.

[4] The geopolitics and economics of late medieval monetary policy are detailed in J. H. A. Munro, *Wool, Cloth and Gold: the Struggle for Bullion in Anglo-Burgundian Trade, 1340–1478* (Brussels and Toronto, 1972); C. Desan, *Making Money: Coin, Currency and the Coming of Capitalism* (Oxford, 2014), pp. 70–230.

[5] *Statutes of the Realm*, ii. 122, 219–20.

[6] J. Guy, *Gresham's Law: the Life and World of Queen Elizabeth I's Banker* (London, 2019), pp. 2–3, 102–3 suggests that the term 'Gresham's law' arises from a misinterpretation of his views by a Victorian economist. However, J. Blanc and L. Desmedt, 'Debating sound money in early modern Europe: from dualist to metallic monetary systems', in *Mining, Money and Markets in the Early Modern Atlantic: Digital Approaches and New Perspectives*, ed. R. Pieper, C. de Lozanne Jefferies, M. Denzel (Cham, 2019), pp. 40–1 observe that Gresham was merely summarizing views widely held at the time.

value of its bullion content.[7] For the same reason, Spanish silver was also popular with London bullion dealers.[8]

Bullion smuggling was commonplace in Elizabethan London; Exchequer records show that coin was regularly seized by customs officials, albeit usually in small quantities.[9] A proclamation of 1587 forbade the clipping or counterfeiting of English coin, publishing a table of official weights for each denomination and arranging for the mint to supply certified balances to enable local officials to identify 'light' or forged coin. The wording of this proclamation implied that much of the adulteration was carried out abroad – a situation which had apparently changed little two decades later, when the judges resolved that the unlicensed export of coin and bullion was forbidden by Edward I's statutes of money and the statutes of 9 Edward III, and 2 Henry VI, cap. 6 (discussed above); this ruling was broadcast in a fresh proclamation in 1607.[10] In the following year, Robert Cecil, earl of Salisbury, newly appointed lord treasurer, received a memorandum about bullion export. This accused the merchant strangers of paying above the mint price for Spanish silver and English gold, which they then shipped to Amsterdam and Middelburg where it was clipped or counterfeited with lower bullion content, before being returned to English merchants lying offshore at the Downs.[11] No immediate effort seems to have been made to tackle this problem, and the crown waived proceedings against the export of coin and bullion in the statutory pardon of 1610. This concession was

[7] The profits to be made in Poland are outlined by the depositions of Ralph Davidson in The National Archives of the UK, STAC 8/25/19, part 3, fos. 31v–32, which corroborate the arguments deployed in B. E. Supple, *Commercial Crisis and Change in England, 1600–1642* (Cambridge, 1970), pp. 75–80.

[8] The merchants' interest in Spanish silver is repeatedly stated by witnesses in TNA, STAC 8/25/19, part 1, fos. 19r–v (Henry Rowland, answers to questions 3–4, 8); fo. 52 (Derrick Hoste, answers to questions 1–2, 4); fo. 54v (Thomas Coteels, answers to questions 1, 4); fo. 68 (John Hill, answer to question 5); fo. 69v (Isaac Woodcock, answers to questions 2, 5); TNA, STAC 8/25/19, part 3, fo. 52v (Francis Samborne, answers to questions 3–4). The profits to be made in this trade are noted in the bill of complaint in TNA, STAC 8/25/21, fo. 2.

[9] Common informations in TNA, E159 include numerous bullion seizures, while TNA, E401 gives details of sums received by the Exchequer. See also D. R. Lidington, 'The enforcement of penal statutes at the court of Exchequer, *c.*1558–*c.*1576' (unpublished University of Cambridge PhD thesis, 1988), pp. 83–4, 247, 291–2.

[10] *Tudor Royal Proclamations,* ed. P. L. Hughes, J. F. Larkin (3 vols., London, 1964–9), ii. 539–41; *Stuart Royal Proclamations,* ed. J. F. Larkin, P. L. Hughes (2 vols., Oxford, 1973 and 1983), i. 158–61.

[11] British Library, Harley MS. 4087, fo. 65. The voluminous depositions in TNA, STAC 8/25/19 say nothing about English merchants collecting counterfeit coin from Dutch ships on the Downs.

short-lived, as a proclamation of 18 May 1611 renewed the prohibition of the melting and export of coin, while another of 14 May 1612 forbade the import of clipped or counterfeit coin and imposed a penalty of twice the value of the coin involved on goldsmiths who paid over the mint price for bullion or coin. The crown finally took effective action to undercut the smugglers' profits in a proclamation of 23 November 1611, which 'cried up' the value of gold coinage by 10% above face value – thereafter, the mint struck the enhanced values on the face of new coin. The same proclamation also revived a clause of the 1587 proclamation allowing sellers to refuse clipped coin, and exhorted the enforcement of medieval statutes against smuggling (namely Edward I's statutes of money, 9 Edward III and 2 Henry IV, cap. 5).[12] However, this enhancement of the gold coinage had little effect, merely inflating the sale price on the Dutch exchanges from 22*s* to between 24*s* and 24*s* 8*d* – a premium of 9% to 13.66%.[13] A fresh proclamation against the export of coin and bullion was issued on 23 March 1615, and in May 1616 several London goldsmiths, a Dutch merchant and a Dutch ship captain, Giles Tyse, were prosecuted in Star Chamber by Attorney General Sir Francis Bacon. The case was grounded on breaches of the proclamation of 18 May 1611, forbidding the melting or export of coin, but the defendants had clearly revealed nothing, as the bill of complaint gave no details of the infringements alleged to have taken place.[14]

***

The crown's attack on bullion smuggling began in earnest in May and June 1618, when Attorney General Yelverton launched three separate prosecutions in Star Chamber (table 10.1), two against the London goldsmiths and a third against various Londoners and a specimen group of fifteen merchant strangers. This latter bill reserved the right to add 'others unknown' to the list of defendants, and in October, Yelverton asked Francis Bacon (by then Lord Verulam and lord chancellor), to issue writs of *ne exeat regnum* to prevent the merchant strangers from fleeing abroad. Verulam not only

[12] *Statutes of the Realm*, iv. 1205; *Stuart Royal Proclamations*, i. 262–3, 272–6, 279–81.

[13] TNA, STAC 8/25/19, part 1, fo. 35v (deposition of Agmondesham Pickhayes); part 3, fos. 53 (deposition of Thomas Robinson), 59v (deposition of Robert Harrison). The European background to the crying up of English gold was the incremental enhancement of the main Dutch large-denomination coin, the silver riksdollar, in 1606, 1608, 1610 and 1619, for which see W. G. Wolters, 'Heavy and light money in the Netherlands Indies and the Dutch Republic: dilemmas of monetary management with unit of account systems', *Financial History Review*, xv (2008), 37–53, at pp. 38–43.

[14] *Stuart Royal Proclamations*, i. 336–8; TNA, STAC 8/25/17, fo. 3.

perceived the potential benefits of a successful prosecution, but saw that 'it will demonstrate also that Scotland is not the leech (as some discoursers say), but the Netherlanders that suck the realm of treasure', an outcome sure to please his royal master.[15] The king immediately approved the issue of writs of *ne exeat regnum*; and in November, Yelverton approached the judges of Star Chamber to authorize this grant, claiming that £7 million worth of gold had been exported since James's accession. The court issued 160 of these writs to merchant strangers under investigation, although the complaints which ensued apparently prompted their revocation in January 1619.[16]

How was the prosecution framed? The three bills of complaint filed in May and June 1618 were couched as informations, alleging that enormous (but entirely speculative) quantities of coin and bullion had been exchanged and smuggled abroad by the defendants – this form of indictment was standard practice among common informers, as it allowed the court to subpoena the defendants' accounts. The bill of 20 May 1618 (against the goldsmiths) was the only one which cited specific transactions, but the four instances described did not include enough detail to have been accepted in a common-law court and were almost certainly based on hearsay. Even more curiously, while all three of the bills of complaint mentioned the existence of statutes against the adulteration and smuggling of coin, none cited a specific law that had been infringed; instead, Yelverton opted to rest his case on breaches of the proclamation of 18 May 1611. This was almost certainly because the penalties imposed by the medieval statutes applied only to seizures of coin and bullion, whereas Star Chamber, operating under different rules, could fine upon reasonable suspicion that the defendants had defied a royal proclamation.[17]

Who instigated this case? In October 1618, Lord Chancellor Verulam identified 'Sir John Britton' as the projector; but having garbled the name of Sir Henry Britton, a Catholic who already held an interest in two patents, Verulam was clearly not the promoter of this prosecution.[18] Britton

[15] TNA, STAC 8/25/19, part 2, fo. 172; TNA, SP14/104/4; Brit. Lib., Add. MS. 72303, fo. 172; *Life and Letters of Francis Bacon,* ed. J. A. Spedding (7 vols., London, 1861–74), vi. 374.

[16] *Life and Letters of Francis Bacon*, vi. 375; TNA, SP14/104/4, SP14/105/64; Brit. Lib., Add. MS. 12497, fo. 33. One newsletter writer reported the slightly lower figure of 142 merchants under investigation: *Letters of John Chamberlain,* ed. N. E. McClure (2 vols., Philadelphia, 1939), ii. 245.

[17] TNA, STAC 8/25/19 (part 2), fo. 172; STAC 8/25/20, fo. 2; STAC 8/25/22, fo. 3.

[18] *Letters and Life of Francis Bacon*, vi. 374–5; History of Parliament Trust, *The House of Commons, 1604–1629,* ed. A. D. Thrush and J. P. Ferris (6 vols., Cambridge, 2010), iii. 309–10. Britton's patents were for the issue of licences to establish warrens and parks, and to compound for enclosure fines; he subsequently acquired interests in two more patents.

apparently compiled a list of those involved in the smuggling ring, which he presented to the king. This swiftly caught the eye of Sir Thomas Vavasour, knight marshal of the king's household, then trying to sell his office, who secured a royal promise that he should be awarded the fines or forfeitures levied on ten of the defendants as a reward for his services; his presumption in securing a grant in anticipation of conviction irritated Verulam.[19]

Britton's lack of experience in trade or customs administration suggests he had sought advice about how to proceed against the bullion smuggling cartel. The individual best placed to compile a list of the merchant strangers to be investigated was Lionel Cranfield, who held (among many other offices) the post of surveyor general of the customs. His clerks would have been able to cross-reference trade data to identify those who exported far less than they imported; and in the absence of proof that the profits had been invested in England, it was a reasonable assumption that the money had been sent abroad, either by bills of exchange or as specie. Cranfield's voluminous archive contains nothing about this case, but in November 1618 he wrote to the royal favourite, George Villiers, marquess of Buckingham, complaining that, while he had attended the lords (probably meaning the treasury commission) twice about 'the strangers' employment and alteration of the monies', Verulam had been dismissive of his efforts. It is worth noting that Cranfield had recently had extensive discussions with Vavasour in one of his minor roles, as a commissioner for reform of the royal household (1617–18) – so the knight marshal's early interest in the bullion case may not have been a coincidence.[20]

While the prosecution case against the smuggling cartel appealed to grasping courtiers, swingeing fines promised the crown a temporary respite from its financial problems. In December 1618, rumours circulated that the strangers had offered James £100,000 composition to dismiss the case, while a year later, with £143,000 of fines to spend, Verulam sent Buckingham a plan for fiscal retrenchment.[21] Since 1610, King James's finances had been hamstrung by his reluctance to summon parliament, and the level of ministerial corruption exposed after the fall of Lord Treasurer Suffolk in July 1618 – whose Star Chamber trial proceeded alongside that of the Dutch merchants – served to compound the king's embarrassment.[22]

[19] *Letters and Life of Francis Bacon*, vi. 374; TNA, SP14/104/4; *Court and Times of James the First*, ii. 114.

[20] *The Fortescue Papers*, ed. S. R. Gardiner (Camden Society, new series i, London, 1871), p. 62; Bodleian Library, MS Add.d.110, fo. 30; Kent History and Library Centre, U269/1/OW150. Lord Chancellor Verulam was one of the Treasury commissioners.

[21] *Court and Times of James the First*, ii. 113; *Letters and Life of Francis Bacon*, vii. 69.

[22] A. D. Thrush, 'The Personal Rule of James I, 1611–1620', in *Politics, Religion and*

Meanwhile, clouds of war were gathering in the Holy Roman Empire, and from September 1619, when James's son-in-law, the Elector Palatine, accepted election as King of Bohemia at the hands of rebels against the Habsburg claimant, Emperor Ferdinand II, England faced the prospect of becoming embroiled in a German war. Finally, with the Twelve Years' Truce between the Dutch and the Spanish due to expire in April 1621, James can hardly have wished to provoke a serious rift with the Dutch over the merchant strangers.[23]

***

The vague phraseology Yelverton had employed in his bills of complaint against the goldsmiths and the merchant strangers suggests that he had little idea where to begin his investigation. At the start of Hilary term 1619 he began by examining several of the defendants and other merchant strangers who would later be added to the charge sheet. Naturally, none could recall having exported any significant quantity of coin or bullion without licence, but some attempted to explain where they had invested their profits in England: James Desmaistres (or Demetrius) pointed out that he was a London brewer, not a merchant;[24] Robert de la Barr claimed to spend £1,000 a year purchasing fish at Great Yarmouth and in the West Country, for export to the Netherlands; Abraham Beck ran a silkweaving business in London; Philip Burlamachi reminded the court that his banking business included among its customers the crown and the Spanish and Dutch ambassadors; Samuel de Vissher indignantly protested that he had delivered almost £100,000 of imported foreign coin and bullion to the London mint for recoining; while Giles de Butt claimed the only Spanish silver he had handled was a consignment from a wreck in Sussex, which he took to London at the behest of the local admiralty officials, whence it was forwarded to its owners, the Dutch East India Company.[25]

Popularity in early Stuart England, ed. T. Cogswell, R. Cust, P. Lake (Cambridge, 2002), pp. 84–102.

[23] P. H. Wilson, *Europe's Tragedy: A History of the Thirty Years' War* (London, 2009), pp. 281–9, 314–20. For the English diplomatic perspective, see R. E. Schreiber, *The First Carlisle: Sir James Hay, first Earl of Carlisle as courtier, diplomat and entrepreneur, 1580–1630* (Transactions of the American Philosophical Society, lxxiv, part 7, Philadelphia, 1984), pp. 22–34.

[24] In his verdict, one of the judges argued (probably mistakenly) that Desmaistres the brewer had been charged in place of a namesake who was a silversmith: Brit. Lib., Add. MS. 12497, fo. 42v.

[25] TNA, STAC 8/25/19, part 1, fos. 7–10v. Question 5 on Yelverton's list asked about investments in England; question 7 about smuggling of coin and bullion.

On 2 and 3 March 1619 the prosecution made a breakthrough with the examination of William Noke and Henry Rowland, who had been apprenticed to the goldsmith, John Harris, at the start of James's reign.

Table 10.2: Prosecution witnesses against the London goldsmiths

Witness (and apprenticeship dates)	**Master goldsmith**	**Dates of depositions (all 1619)**	**Sources in TNA, STAC 8/25/19**
Henry Rowland (1598–1606)	John Harris	3 Mar., 30 Oct., 4 Nov.	Part 1, fos. 19–20v; Part 2, fo. 103; Part 3, fos. 9–12
William Earwood (1604–11)	John Harris	18 May, 28 Oct.	Part 1, fos. 24v–5, 61v
William Noke (1604–7)	John Harris	2 Mar., 27 Sept.	Part 1, fos. 17, 36 (same examination); Part 3, fo. 28
Peter Wright (c.1602–10)	Thomas Some	12 Apr., 31 May	Part 1, fos. 20v–22, 86v.
Thomas Phelps (1609–16)	Thomas Some	21 Apr.	Part 1, fos. 29–30
Henry Walley (1610–14)	James Feake	12 Apr., 4 Oct.	Part 1, fos. 22–3; Part 3, fo. 47
William Lasher (with Feake 1601–4, with Wood 1604–9)	James Feake, William Wood	20 May	Part 1, fos. 25v–6
Isaac Woodcock (1603–11)	William Wood	7 May, 1 June, 13 Oct., 28 Oct., 3 Nov.	Part 1, fos. 23v-4, 62, 69v, 89; Part 3, fo. 55v–7

Given a list of the merchant strangers suspected of smuggling, Noke acknowledged dealings with twenty-four of them during his service with Harris; Rowland thirty-six. Clearly citing figures from their account books, they offered a detailed breakdown of their deliveries to each merchant. Noke (having spent only three years with Harris) recorded £239,000 of coin and bullion, which he claimed was, at most, half the sum he had delivered during that time; Rowland reported the staggering sum of £1,584,000-worth of deliveries over eight years, which he claimed (most improbably) was no more than a quarter of the sums he had handled. Rowland provided separate figures for transactions during Queen Elizabeth's reign (exempted from prosecution by James's coronation pardon), but this still left £612,000 of transfers after

March 1603, which were admissible as evidence. Both men (coached by the interrogatories) explained that they had often transacted business with their master's clients at night or in the merchants' own homes. They also revealed that when (as often happened) their master could not satisfy demand for gold coin from his own reserves, he had resorted to four other goldsmiths: James Feake, William Wood, Thomas Some and William Haynes. Rowland further testified that he had been present when customs officials had seized £700 in Portuguese gold hidden under the galley of a Dutch ship.[26]

Armed with this list of goldsmiths who specialized in the bullion trade, Yelverton began tracing their other former apprentices. Several of the latter, having been excluded from this lucrative trade since they acquired their freedom, proved happy to testify against their erstwhile masters (table 10.2).

Rowland, Earwood and Walley proved the most cooperative witnesses interviewed by the prosecution, providing names, dates and figures, while Noke, having moved to Northamptonshire some years earlier, was initially unable to give figures. By contrast, Peter Wright, having been warned that talking about his former master's business affairs would breach his oath as a freeman of the Goldsmiths' Company, was studiously vague about the specifics of his former master's trade. Yelverton advised him to seek legal advice on this point, and to consult a bishop or other minister to settle his conscience. Thomas Phelps told Sir Henry Britton it would be better for the crown to interview his former master, who could consult his own accounts; while William Lasher and Isaac Woodcock carefully avoided citing any figures in their depositions.[27]

The detailed depositions offered by four of the witnesses furnished ample evidence that John Harris and James Feake had supplied their customers at above the mint price, and allowed the merchants to winnow out the best (i.e. least clipped) coins to purchase; activities which breached the proclamations of 18 May 1611 and 14 May 1612. However, they also explained that the goldsmiths operated on the narrowest of profit margins: while the merchant strangers, often requiring bullion to be provided quickly for a ship that was about to sail, were prepared to pay 4*d* to 14*d* in the £ (1.66% to 6%) over the odds for English gold, the goldsmiths could not afford to carry hundreds of pounds'-worth of stock on hand for long periods.[28] When the goldsmiths sought coin from their rivals, who knew the state of

[26] TNA, STAC 8/25/19, part 1, fos. 19–20v; C66/1625/1. The statutory pardon of 1610 did not extend to tampering with the coinage, see *Statutes of the Realm*, iv. 1201–6.

[27] TNA, STAC 8/25/19, fos. 20v–22, 25v–26, 30.

[28] With English coin trading at around 10% over par in the Low Countries, an offer to pay 5% above par indicates that the merchants offered to split their profits evenly with the goldsmiths.

the market as well as they did, they were commonly forced to settle for a brokerage fee of 1*d* to 1.5*d* per £ (0.42% to 0.63%). On an annual turnover of bullion well into six figures, the income from brokerage alone guaranteed well over £1,000, but as margins were tight, it is clear why this clique of five goldsmiths defended its interests so vigorously.[29]

While a partial breakthrough in the case against the goldsmiths must have pleased Yelverton, there was no prospect that Harris and Feake could have paid fines of more than a few thousand pounds, which would have had a negligible impact on the crown's debts. Hence the significance of two other witnesses, who provided evidence relating to the bullion trade in the Low Countries, which could potentially be used against the merchant strangers. The first of these, Robert Harrison, had been apprenticed to a goldbeater in Middelburg in Zeeland in about 1601, then traded on his own account in The Hague and Delft, returning to London shortly before testifying on 10 April 1619. He confirmed that English gold was sought after by goldbeaters, because its high bullion content meant it could be alloyed with copper and beaten particularly thin. He insisted the trade had increased substantially during his time in the Netherlands, estimating that Dutch goldbeaters now consumed a weekly quota of more than 100 oz. troy weight of English gold, and he provided evidence of a Dutch skipper smuggling English gold, hidden in a barrel of tar. He also accused Martin Drussett, a stranger living in London, of smuggling bullion both ways between the English goldsmiths and the Dutch goldbeaters. Finally, in May 1619, Harrison briefly returned to the United Provinces to secure affidavits from an Amsterdam merchant and a Middelburg notary confirming that bullion smuggling from London was commonplace. The crown's other deponent, Thomas Morley, having been recruited to the English regiment in the army of Flanders in 1605, presently resigned and took employment with Abraham Lasawe, engraver of the Antwerp mint. Morley testified that the merchant strangers in London (including five of those now being prosecuted) sent £40,000 a year in coin to the United Provinces, as their contribution to the stock of the Dutch East India Company; his source for this information was Lasawe, one of the middlemen in these transactions.[30]

By June 1619, Yelverton believed the evidence he had gathered was sufficient to bring the case against the merchant strangers to trial, and Star Chamber spent a week hearing evidence. But on 18 June the king (having come to London on Lord Chancellor Verulam's forecast of a cash windfall

[29] *Stuart Royal Proclamations*, i. 262–3, 279–81; TNA, STAC 8/25/19, part 1, fos. 17, 19v, 20v, 22, 24v–25, 36r–v.

[30] TNA, STAC 8/25/19, part 1, fos. 13, 15, 38.

to fund his summer progress) ordered the judgement to be deferred until the start of Michaelmas term. As one newsletter writer observed, the crown's evidence was 'rather matter of presumption than proof', while some of the defendants had pleaded the benefit of the pardons of 1603 and 1610.[31] Over the summer, the crown once again attempted to undercut the smugglers' profits with a fresh proclamation reducing the fees the Mint charged for recasting foreign coin, allowing its subjects to refuse clipped coin and reviving the 1587 project for the Mint to issue balances for troy weights to allow local officials to identify 'light' coin.[32] It was presumably this adjustment, and the ongoing Star Chamber case, which depressed the value of sterling on the Dutch exchanges, where a Jacobus fell to 23*s*, (4.5% above par) in 1619.[33]

While the prosecution team worked hard to gather evidence, the defendants had not stood idly by. In May 1619, Richard Carmarden, surveyor of London customs, deposed that in the early stages of the trial, Philip Burlamachi had visited him discreetly at his own house. The latter, protesting that he only exported bullion under licence – he was the crown's chief agent on the foreign exchanges – suggested that 'if it pleased his Majesty to pardon that [which] was past, there might be course taken for the prevention of the like hereafter'. This fits in with news circulating in December 1618 that the merchant strangers had offered the crown a composition of £100,000. If this offer was indeed made, Burlamachi would have been the ideal intermediary, being the defendant best placed to exonerate himself.[34]

With the crown spurning an early deal with the merchant strangers, several of the defendants were seduced by the promises of Garret Day, a scrivener who had originally acted as a solicitor for Sir Henry Britton in the May 1618 case against the London goldsmiths, but who had subsequently been discharged. Seeking better pickings from the defendants, George Stampeel and Robert de Lewe offered him money to secure their discharge from the Star Chamber proceedings (presumably by testifying for the crown), but Day found a more lucrative employment when he persuaded Burlamachi, Stampeel and William Courteen that he could suborn the key prosecution witness, Henry

[31] Brit. Lib., Add. MS. 12497, fos. 33, 52–58; Add. MS. 72253, fo. 45; *Court and Times of James the First*, ii. 174, 177; *Chamberlain Letters*, ii. 245–6

[32] *Stuart Royal Proclamations*, i. 436–9. Notes on the Privy Council debate on the draft of this proclamation can be found in Brit. Lib., Lansdowne 160, fos. 240–241.

[33] TNA, STAC 8/25/19, part 1, fo. 13v; part 3, fos. 53, 61.

[34] TNA, STAC 8/25/19, part 1, fo. 35; *Court and Times of James the First*, ii. 113–14. For the range of Burlamachi's business ventures, see the deposition of his erstwhile clerk Mark Calandrini, STAC 8/25/19, part 1, fo. 83.

Rowland, who had been detained in London's Poultry Compter prison for bankruptcy in May 1619. Rowland must have been in desperate straits, as he apparently retracted his testimony for the remarkably modest sum of £3 6*s*, but the cause of his change of heart was quickly discovered, and at the start of Michaelmas term 1619 the conspirators, having admitted their guilt, were tried *ore tenus* in Star Chamber.[35] Day was fined £2,000, imprisoned and sentenced to the pillory, while Courteen was fined £2,000, Burlamachi 2,000 marks and Stampeel £500.[36]

On 20 July 1619 Sir Julius Caesar took notes of a discussion, possibly between the judges of Star Chamber before they departed on their summer vacation,[37] about the future course of the suit against the merchant strangers. The meeting may have been called to discuss the consequences of Rowland's recantation, but the debate ranged far wider. The testimony of the former apprentices against their masters had already persuaded the crown to indict a second tranche of merchant strangers, while four of the merchant strangers – Nicholas Jacobson, Michel de Horter, Francis Penetiere and one 'Towne' (perhaps Jasper Tyant?) – had agreed to turn crown's evidence, revealing the scale of their smuggling and the names of those for whom they acted. Furthermore, two of the goldsmiths under investigation, Thomas Some and William Lasher, refused to produce their accounts, but another, William Wood, belatedly complied and provided details of sales of £120,000-worth of coin and bullion to a number of the defendants. The judges agreed that Rowland and the other former apprentices whose evidence had proved so invaluable should be re-examined, both to confirm their earlier testimony, and to reveal what they knew of the activities of the second group of defendants.[38]

***

At the start of Michaelmas term, for all the weight of evidence, Lord Chancellor Verulam worried that the case against the merchant strangers might miscarry. Chief justices Sir Henry Montagu and Sir Henry Hobart assured him of their support, but he feared that unless Attorney General

35 *Ore tenus* proceedings were used when matters of fact were not in dispute; the only issue at question was the gravity of the infraction committed. *Les Reportes del Cases in Camera Stellata*, ed. W. P. Baildon (London, 1894) reports many such cases.

36 TNA, STAC 8/25/19, part 3, fo. 33; STAC 8/25/20, fo. 1; Brit. Lib., Add. MS. 12497, fo. 10v; Add. MS. 72299, fos. 28r–v; Lansdowne 162, fo. 265; *Chamberlain Letters*, ii. 266–7; *Letters and Life of Francis Bacon*, vii. 47, 49.

37 The Privy Council did not meet on this day.

38 Brit. Lib., Lansdowne MS. 162, fo. 219.

Yelverton showed more aggression, the court might fail to produce the definitive verdicts and swingeing fines the crown required.[39] Consequently, proceedings during the autumn worked over much of the same evidence and many of the same witnesses as had been examined earlier in the year. Henry Rowland enlarged upon his earlier testimony, going out of his way to implicate Burlamachi's business partner, Giles Vandeputt; he also gave details of his dealings in bullion in 1606–8, after he had gained his freedom and set up as a shopkeeper. William Wood submitted accounts of his dealings with the merchant strangers, while Francis Samborne and George Pigott, former servants of William Haynes – the one goldsmith under investigation against whom no evidence had yet been produced – offered testimony of Haynes's involvement in the bullion trade. Ominously, senior members of the Goldsmiths' Company were now prepared to take the witness stand against their colleagues: Alderman Alexander Prescott, who had sold some of the late Lord Treasurer Burghley's plate to Harris, testified to the latter's insatiable appetite for bullion; while Hugh Myddelton damned Harris, his neighbour in Goldsmith's Row, with the assertion that 'his house was as it were a Prince's Exchequer, by reason of the continual telling of gold & silver, and venting it to the Dutchmen'. Myddelton also insisted that Henry Rowland did not have the reputation as a liar and drunkard that his enemies claimed.[40]

Hearings on the smuggling case, having been delayed by the trial of the disgraced Lord Treasurer Suffolk, eventually commenced on 19 November, when the defendants' counsel moved to have the recent re-examinations of the prosecution witnesses suppressed; Verulam persuaded the other judges to refuse this request. Yelverton dropped the charges brought against eight of the defendants (see table 10.3), but managed to convince the judges of Henry Rowland's credibility as a witness. However, as one newsletter writer noted, while the prosecution had furnished a wealth of evidence about the vast quantity of coin and bullion supplied to the merchant strangers by the goldsmiths, the proof that these immense sums had been smuggled abroad was decidedly thin. Some of the defendants escaped conviction on the grounds that the profits derived from their imports had been invested in English land and businesses, while Peter Vanlore explained that much of his capital had been loaned out to Scottish courtiers. However, as secretary of state Sir George Calvert noted, Yelverton's focus on depositions concerning the ready availability of English gold in the Low Countries, while no more

[39] *Letters and Life of Francis Bacon*, vii. 47–9. Verulam had clearly become disenchanted with Yelverton's conduct of the case by this stage, and the rocky unfolding of the prosecution case in Michaelmas term cannot have restored his confidence in the attorney general.

[40] TNA, STAC 8/25/19, part 3, fos. 7–10, 52v–3, 57v–60v.

Table 10.3: the merchant stranger defendants

Name	Sums exported[1]	Fine or discharge[2]	Fines received[3]	Pardon granted[4]	Other composition[5]
Robert de la Barr	£75,300	£20,000	£5,300	22 September 1620	
Philip Barnardo	£35,140	£10,000	Nil		
Jacques de Best	£38,040	£7,000	Nil		
Philip Burlamachi	£54,300	£2,000 or £4,000	Nil	22 September 1620	loan to Crown
John de Clark	£9,120	£2,000	£21-10-4		
William Courteen	£107,600	£20,000	£2,029-7-6	21 August 1620	
Martin Drussett	£100	Not guilty			
Alexander van Endy	£17,000	Not guilty			
Joos Godscale	£2,667	Not guilty			
Philip Jacobs[on]	£32,450	£3,000 or £5,000	£2,386-16-3	22 September 1620	
Nicholas Jacobs[on]	£19,783	Not guilty			
Hans Levins	£11,000	£2,000	Nil		
Arnold Lulls	£35,250	£8,000	Nil		
Matthew de Quester	£25,570	£4,000	Nil	22 September 1620	
Anthony Tryon	£17,000	£5,000	Nil		
Giles Tyse	£51,498	Not guilty			
Giles Vandeputt	£41,800	£3,000	Nil	22 September 1620	loan to Crown
John de Wolfe	£23,000	£5,000	Nil		
Peter Wybowe	£47,170	£4,000 or £6,000	£1,347-18-2		

1 Brit. Lib., Add. MS. 12497, fos. 9-10.

2 TNA, SP14/111/66—7; Brit. Lib., Add. MS. 72275, fos. 92v-3; Add. MS. 12497, fos. 31v, 63 (N.B. the sources do not all agree about the amounts of the fines).

3 TNA, E401/2431—3.

4 TNA, C66/2226, 2232, 2234, 2276.

5 Brit. Lib., Add. MS. 72275, fo. 94v.

Table 10.4: defendants added to bill in Trinity 1619

Name	Sums exported	Fine or discharge	Fines received	Pardon granted	Other composition
Abraham Beck	£100	Charges dropped			
Jacob Bole	£200	Charges dropped			
Joos Croppenbergh	£18,100	Not guilty			
Segar Corselis	£16,500	Not guilty			
Sir Thomas Coteel	£28,100	Not guilty			
Thomas Coteel	£300	Not guilty			
James Desmaistres	£6,000	Not guilty			
Michel de Horter	£143,855	Not guilty			
Robert de Lewe [L'Eau]	£148,120	£20,000	£9,809-15-0		
John Libart	£7,639	£1,500	£72-3-0	22 September 1620	
John de la Mott	Nil	Charges dropped			
Francis Penetiere	£42,917	Not guilty			
Harman Rickman	£10,000	£2,000	£217-7-0		
George Stampeel	£3,300	£4,000	£425-1-3		
Francis Sopranina	£7,000	Not guilty			
Leonard Sweres [Suarez]	£9,700	Charges dropped			
Moses Tryon	£30,000	£15,000	£2,000	21 August 1620	
Jasper Tyant	£3,300	Charges dropped			
Francis Vanaker	£6,760	Charges dropped		28 June 1622	
Peter Vanlore	£54,750	£4,000 or £8,000	Nil	23 March 1621	loan to Crown
Peter Vanpeene	£1,550	Charges dropped			
Samuel Vissher	£1,700	Charges dropped			

than a circumstantial argument, eventually persuaded the court to accept the credibility of the smuggling charge.[41] Thereafter, it only remained to collate the testimonies of the various goldsmiths to establish the scale of the crime. Master of the rolls Sir Julius Caesar (one of the judges) kept voluminous notes of these debates, concluding that the goldsmiths' accounts revealed sales of £1,183,679 to the merchant strangers. There may have been some element of double counting in these figures, but as they provided only partial information about sixteen years'-worth of smuggling, the vast scale of the fraud could not be denied. Verulam was dismayed to find that Yelverton's careless handling of depositions allowed the brewer, James Desmaistres, at whose tavern much of the smuggling had been arranged, to escape conviction. At an informal meeting with the other judges the day before the verdicts were pronounced, Verulam carefully instructed them not to dwell on the thinness of the evidence, but to focus on ensuring that the fines were proportionate to the scale of the smuggling revealed.[42]

At the sentencing on 8 December 1619, twenty of the defendants were found guilty and fined sums between £1,500 and £20,000, amounting to £134,500 in total. They were imprisoned in the Fleet, pending payment of their fines, although four of them were swiftly released on bail. Lord Chancellor Verulam sketched plans to use this windfall to repair the crown's tottering finances, and pronounced himself determined to 'keep the clock on-going' against those condemned.[43] In February 1620 Robert de Lewe had his stock in the East India Company seized by the crown; while Philip Jacobson, who sold stock at the same time, presumably devoted part of the proceeds to paying his fine. William Courteen, hoping that his role in brokering a match between Buckingham's brother, Christopher Villiers, and a wealthy City heiress would elicit concessions from the favourite, was informed that, while the seizure of his goods and debts might be halted, there would be no reduction of his fine.[44] By August 1620, the Exchequer had received a total of £23,809 18*s* 6*d* (see table 10.3).

[41] Brit. Lib., Add. MS. 12497, fos. 18, 21r–v, 30–32, 34–39; Add. MS. 72253, fo. 75; Add. MS. 72275, fos. 82, 92; Add. MS. 72299, fos. 32–33; *Letters and Life of Francis Bacon*, vii. 60–1, 63–4; *Fortescue Papers*, pp. 96, 99, 102, 106; *Chamberlain Letters*, ii. 276–7.

[42] Brit. Lib., Add. MS. 12497, fos. 9–10, 44, 47–62, 65–68; *Fortescue Papers*, p. 107; STAC 8/25/19, part 3, fo. 60v; *Letters and Life of Francis Bacon*, vii. 67–8.

[43] Brit. Lib., Add. MS. 72253, fos. 79, 81v; Add. MS. 72275, fos. 92–93; *Letters and Life of Francis Bacon*, vii. 69, 74. The first of these sources mentions that £143,000 of fines had been imposed, which presumably includes the £5,833 6*s* 8*d* imposed on Courteen and the others for the subornation of Henry Rowland.

[44] *Fortescue Papers*, pp. 116–18; *Chamberlain Letters*, ii. 284; *Calendar of State Papers Venetian*, ed. R. Brown, et al. (38 vols., London, 1864–1947), 1619–21, at p. 170; *Calendar of State Papers Colonial (East Indies)*, ed. W. N. Sainsbury (5 vols., London, 1862–92), 1617–21,

On 4 February 1620, the crown sought to capitalize further on its success by filing a fresh bill against eighty-seven merchant strangers, twelve of whom had been defendants in the earlier case. This rehearsed similar charges against the merchant strangers as the earlier bill of June 1618, but on this occasion, it explicitly reproduced the arguments of the proclamation of 23 November 1611 in basing its case upon breaches of Edward I's statutes of money, 9 Edward III and 2 Henry IV, cap. 5. The bill also suggested the crown might only seek to enforce these statutes against breaches committed since the proclamations of 1611 – which would bar the defendants from pleading the pardons of either 1603 or 1610 in mitigation of their offences.[45] Commentators who predicted this fresh lawsuit would have a serious impact upon London's trade were proven wrong: the Star Chamber fines of December 1619 caused much discontent among those convicted, several of whom considered emigrating; but the trade slump which affected northern Europe in 1620–1 was primarily caused by the debasement of coinage within much of the Empire and Poland. The prospects of huge profits to be made further east stripped much of northwestern Europe of its finest coin.[46]

The trade crisis, perhaps in conjunction with Attorney General Yelverton's suspension from office in June 1620, persuaded the crown to allow the Star Chamber proceedings to run out of steam. Defendants to the bill of February 1620 continued to file their answers until June 1622, but the acute domestic shortage of coin prompted the crown to avoid pressing the merchants too hard. In August and September 1620, ten of the merchant strangers had their outstanding Star Chamber fines pardoned, while Burlamachi, Vandeputt and Vanlore had their fines waived in return for an interest-free loan of £10,000 to the crown.[47] Moses Tryon, having sued his pardon in August 1620, was still facing proceedings over the crown's seizure of one of his outstanding debts in February 1623, but neither he nor any of the eleven defendants who had not sued pardons paid any further sums into the Exchequer.[48]

---

at p. 408. The latter source misreads de Lewe as 'Delean'.

[45] TNA, STAC 8/25/23, fo. 43. The defendants previously charged in STAC 8/25/19 were: Abraham Beck, Segar Corselis, Joos Croppenbergh, James Desmaistres, Alexander van Endy, Joos Godscale, Francis Sopranina, John de la Mott, Leonard Suarez, Francis Vanaker, Peter Vanpeene and Samuel de Vissher.

[46] *Chamberlain Letters*, ii. 279–80; *Calendar of State Papers, Venetian*, p. 170; Supple, *Commercial Crisis*, 72–96.

[47] Brit. Lib., Add. MS. 72275, fo. 94v; Add. MS. 72253, fo. 81v; TNA, E401/2434; C66/2226/4–5, C66/2232/1–6, C66/2234/2; STAC 8/25/23, fos. 6–42. Burlamachi's share of the loan was apparently paid by Sir Baptist Hickes, who presumably either owed or loaned the money to Burlamachi.

[48] TNA, E126/2, fo. 268v.

***

What does this case tell us about the wider context of Star Chamber proceedings? The surviving papers of the court tell us a great deal about its workings, but by no means the whole story. Unlike most of the court's caseload, bullion smuggling was a high-profile case of international significance: much of the information about this case comes from newsletters to English diplomats in Brussels and The Hague, where interest among politicians and merchants was clearly high. The political nature of the case prefigures the use of the court under Charles I, as does the scale of the fines imposed on the merchant strangers, which far exceeded most Jacobean fines, except for the £30,000 awarded against Lord Treasurer Suffolk and his wife, also in Michaelmas 1619. However, the return on the crown's effort ultimately proved disappointing: Verulam feared in January 1620 King James 'made bondmen (I mean, which have given bonds for their fines) … freemen' by pardoning the offenders. The crown ultimately collected only £7,000 from the Suffolks, £23,800 from the merchant strangers, plus the £10,000 loan from Burlamachi, Vandeputt and Vanlore.[49] Here, as so often in Jacobean England, political considerations trumped the crown's pressing need for extra revenue.

Most Star Chamber cases were founded on charges of riot or conspiracy, which were not difficult for the prosecution counsel to frame, being routine, but the proceedings against the goldsmiths and merchant strangers created significant problems. The goldsmiths around whom much of the main case of 1618–19 revolved were doubtless in breach of 9 Edward III, st. 2, § 3, for having melted English coin, but they were not wealthy enough to bear the huge fines the crown sought. The merchant strangers, by contrast, were proven to have purchased enormous quantities of coin and bullion, and the crown also made a satisfactory case that English gold was freely available in the Low Countries, but evidence of the defendants smuggling coin and bullion on board ships for export was notably lacking, despite the pressure put on the Dutch shipmaster Giles Tyse.[50] There is no evidence that the defending counsel pointed out this flaw in the crown's case, and thus huge fines were awarded, but the fragile grounds on which this verdict rested cannot have escaped notice abroad, and this may help to explain why most of the money was never collected.

Happily for economic historians, the crown's difficulty in finding conclusive evidence of the merchant strangers' breach of any statute with

[49] *Letters and Life of Francis Bacon*, vii. 74.

[50] *Statutes of the Realm*, i. 273–4; TNA, STAC 8/25/19, part 3, fo. 62v.

a financial penalty clause led to the collection of a wealth of circumstantial evidence, which reveals a great deal about the international bullion trade. First, the goldsmiths and merchant strangers shared the profits of their smuggling ventures evenly. Second, the customs officials were clearly not regarded as a serious threat by the smugglers, as any reasonable prospect of interception would have led the strangers to drop the price they were prepared to offer the goldsmiths for their coin.[51] Why were English merchants little involved in bullion smuggling? Because their costs in exporting domestic products were considerably less than those borne by the strangers, who were hobbled by discriminatory customs rates imposed on their exports (particularly English cloth). This led the strangers to resort to many kinds of fraud: shipping goods under the names of English factors, using hot presses to pack more cloth into a bundle than was declared for customs purposes, and the smuggling of bullion.[52] Finally, it should be noted that (according to Caesar's figures) the evidence accepted by Star Chamber amounted to £1.3 million. This clearly represented only a proportion of the actual value of the trade – speculation about the total ranged between three and seven million pounds over the years 1603–19; a staggering sum, which bears comparison with present-day foreign exchange frauds.

[51] For an example of the customs searchers' failure to intercept bullion smuggled by Giles Tyse, see TNA, STAC 8/25/19, part 3, fo. 62v.

[52] This point was made in 1619 by the diplomat William Trumbull in a discussion of the merchant strangers' case with Richard Carmarden, surveyor of London customs: TNA, STAC 8/25/19, part 1, fo. 35.

11. Contemporary knowledge of the Star Chamber and the abolition of the court

*Ian Williams**

The Star Chamber was an important court within the early modern legal system, but one that came to an abrupt end. This chapter is concerned with what contemporaries could learn about the court, and it relates the material and ideas visible in the sources which disseminated knowledge about the Star Chamber to the parliamentary debates that led to its sudden abolition. Claims that parliament abolished the Star Chamber because of 'its acts, its cruelties [and] its extortions' filled early writing on the court.[1] Other scholarship has emphasized dissatisfaction with particular aspects of the court's work, such as the Star Chamber's role in enforcing royal proclamations and fiscal policies.[2]

This chapter confirms historians' understanding that the court was a subject of increasing concern during the personal rule of Charles I. As in the work of H. Phillips and Kevin Sharpe, it shows that the Star Chamber was particularly denigrated for its role in a handful of cases concerning religious matters in the later 1630s.[3] These cases were the subject of significant contemporary interest. The chapter demonstrates that the cases were deliberately well-publicized as part of larger debates about the English

* Associate Professor, Faculty of Laws, University College London. Funding for the consultation of Star Chamber Manuscripts was supported by a British Academy/Leverhulme Trust Small Research Grant (SG151808). My thanks to Jason Peacey, the participants in the Cambridge Legal History Seminar and the UCL Faculty of Laws Staff Research Seminar for their comments on earlier drafts.

[1] J. S. Burn, *The Star Chamber: Notices of the Court and its Proceedings with a Few Additional Notes of the High Commission* (London, 1870), p. 1, expanding on the claim of unlawful jurisdiction and heavy punishment in the abolition statute (stat. 16. Car. I, c. 10).

[2] J. P. Kenyon, *The Stuart Constitution: Documents and Commentary* (Cambridge, 1986, 2nd ed.), p. 106.

[3] H. E. I. Phillips, 'The last years of the court of Star Chamber, 1630–41', *Transactions of the Royal Historical Society,* fourth series, xxi (1939), 103–32, especially at pp. 123–30; K. Sharpe, *The Personal Rule of Charles I* (New Haven, 1992), pp. 680–2.

I. Williams, 'Contemporary knowledge of the Star Chamber and the abolition of the court' in *Star Chamber Matters: An Early Modern Court and Its Records*, ed. K. Kesselring and N. Mears (London, 2021), pp. 195–215.

Church and came to dominate the parliamentary discussions. A particular concern was the role of the bishops as judges in the court.

Most of the criticisms of the Star Chamber appeared in material which can be categorized as 'news', rather than the more 'professional' literature of legal treatises and law reports. The professional literature instead justified the Star Chamber's existence, presented it as a regular part of the legal system and was used, unsuccessfully, in defence of the court. The chapter therefore shows the primacy of popular knowledge of the court over professional learning about it. However, there are hints that some lawyers' views were changing, at least regarding the focal issue of bishops as judges, suggesting a convergence of criticisms from different perspectives.

'Professional' knowledge

A significant body of 'professional' literature about Star Chamber appeared; texts which would have been of particular utility for individuals seeking to work in the court.[4] A handful of law reports of Star Chamber cases appeared in the printed collections of Dyer and Coke, as well as a collection printed in 1594.[5] The printed reports of Coke were cited in later cases in both the Star Chamber and Exchequer.[6] The 1594 collection was predominantly based on material found in print from the medieval yearbooks and other printed texts, although it includes a few sixteenth-century cases which are not printed elsewhere.[7] These printed cases represent only a small proportion of the circulating material on the work of the court. Three manuscript collections of law reports appear to have had significant contemporary circulation.

[4] A fuller discussion of the professional material will be found in I. Williams, '"Out of which books students of the law learn their knowledge": legal publishing in early-Stuart England' (forthcoming).

[5] For Dyer: *Anon* (1558) Dyer 160b–1a; *Onslowe's Case* (1565) Dyer 242b–3a; *Sir John Marvin's Case* (1570) Dyer 288; and *Taverner's Case* (1573) Dyer 322b–3a. For Coke, two particularly important cases were *Twyne's Case* (1601) 3 Co. Rep. 80b and *De Libellis Famosis* (1605) 5 Co. Rep. 125–6. Coke reported eleven more Star Chamber cases (T. G. Barnes, 'Star Chamber Mythology', *American Journal of Legal History*, v (1961), 1–11, at p. 5 n. 12). R. Crompton, *L'Authoritie et Jurisdiction des Courts de la Maiestie de la Roygne* (London, 1594), fos. 29–41, reprinted in English translation as Anon., *Star-Chamber Cases. Shewing What Causes Properly Belong to the Cognizance of That Court* (London, 1630), pp. 13–57 (pp. 1–11 are an introduction which was not previously published). The 1630 text updates references to Elizabeth I to Charles I, but is otherwise simply a translation of the Elizabethan text.

[6] For *De Libellis Famosis* being cited in the Star Chamber, see British Library, Lansdowne MS. 620, fo. 51. *Twyne's Case* was cited in the Exchequer in *R* v *Earl of Nottingham* (undated), Lane 42, at p. 44.

[7] Crompton, *L'Authoritie et Jurisdiction*, fos. 30v–31r, 31v, 32r, 32v, 33r, 35r, 36v and 37r.

The first is an anonymous collection in law-French which begins in 1598 and continues until the second decade of James I's reign. It generally contains fifty cases and survives in at least eight copies.[8] Of these surviving copies, one belonged to the law reporter Francis Moore, and it is through Moore that many of these cases were disseminated in another way.[9] The thirty-five earliest cases in this collection were incorporated into Moore's own collection of cases. This collection was printed in the Restoration, but also circulated in a commercially produced manuscript, although not all copies are of the complete set.[10] These manuscripts include the thirty-five early Star Chamber cases, as well as other Star Chamber cases which feature in Moore's printed reports, such as *Twyne's Case*.[11] The second set of circulating reports is another Jacobean collection, which begins in 1604.[12] It includes 130 reports, up to the end of 1624, albeit with no reports for Trinity term 1618 to Trinity term 1621. Six copies of these reports survive.

The final significant collection of circulating reports survives in three law-French copies[13] and thirteen English copies in varying states of completeness.[14] The full version contains reports of over eighty cases and

[8] All Souls College, MS. 276; Brit. Libr., Add. MS. 25223, fos. 180–203; Brit. Libr., Harley MS. 1330; Folger Shakespeare Library MS. X.d.336; Kansas University MS. 155:4 (a very disordered manuscript); UCL Add. MS. 433A; Folg. Shakes. Libr., MS. V.a.133, fos. 1–89v runs later than the other collections; Cambridge University Library, MS. Gg.2.5, fos. 280r–283v covers 1607–12 with some of the reports for the period omitted.

[9] Folg. Shakes. Libr., MS V.a.133.

[10] Complete texts which include the Star Chamber cases are: Brit. Libr., Add. MS. 25191; Add. MS. 35937; Harl. MS. 4585; Lansdowne MS. 1059. Some manuscripts of Moore's reports do not cover the full temporal range of the complete collection (Harvard Law School, MS. 1206 (formerly MS 2097) only reaches to 1595; Camb. Uni. Libr., MS. Ee.6.12, fos. 1–83v includes the Star Chamber cases to Michaelmas term 1597 (on fo. 80v); Harv. Law Sch., MSs. 107 and 1253 (formerly MS. 5065) reach to the end of Elizabeth's reign, and include the Elizabethan Star Chamber cases). Yale Law School, MS. G.R.29.1 and Lincoln's Inn, Maynard MS. 8 cover the full temporal range but the reports are out of order in places. Not all of the reports in the circulating collection which typically appear in Moore manuscripts have been located in these manuscripts, but the earliest and latest have been, so it seems likely that the other reports are present.

[11] (1602) Moo. KB 638–639.

[12] All Souls Col., MS. 163; Brit. Libr., Stowe MS. 397; Bodleian Library, Brasenose MS 61 (my thanks to David Smith for bringing this manuscript to my attention); Camb. Uni. Libr., MS. Ll.3.2, fos. 1–66; Camb. Uni. Libr., MS. Add. 3105, fos. 133–184v; Harv. Law Sch., MS. 149, Part 3 (digitized: <https://iiif.lib.harvard.edu/manifests/view/drs:425601024$152i> [accessed 23 March 2020]). With the exception of Brit. Libr., Stowe MS. 397 (which is missing some pages at the beginning), the collection begins with a single Elizabethan case, *Radney* v *Raynon* from 1565.

[13] Brit. Libr., Add. MS. 48057, London Metropolitan Archive, MS. CLC/309/MS00532 and Trinity College Dublin, MS. 649.

[14] Full copies are found in: All Souls Col., MS. 177; Bodl. Libr., Brasenose MS. 62; Brit.

runs to a little under 50,000 words in the English version. The English texts are all translations from the law-French.[15] The reports cover the first three years of the reign of Charles I and were copied commercially.[16] The barrister John Lightfoot acquired his own copy in 1636, from the servant of another barrister.[17] The translation of the texts into English may have made them more accessible to non-lawyers, showing the permeability of the 'professional'/lay boundary for at least some legal texts. An English copy was owned and annotated by Francis Russell, the fourth earl of Bedford, and it seems plausible that it was these reports which William Drake was to receive from Gilbert Barrell, an 'exact journall of 3tio Caroli exact Star Chamber Reports'.[18]

Beyond law reports, official material from the Star Chamber also circulated, including orders made about the court's proceedings.[19] A collection of extracts from records referring to the Star Chamber from the reign of Henry VII also circulated in the *Liber Intrationum*.[20] By the seventeenth century, the material was very out of date, and it may be that the text was more useful for legal-antiquarian work, as is visible in some of the treatises written about the Star Chamber.

The earliest of these is William Lambarde's *Archeion*. The Star Chamber material in that book was written from early 1586 onwards.[21] The work combines material on both the Star Chamber and Chancery, as well as some material on other courts. Over forty copies survive in manuscript, and the Star Chamber part also circulated independently,[22] before the book was

Libr., Lansd. MS. 620; Durham University Library, Add. MS. 329; Durham University Library, Mickleton and Spearman MS. 65; Lambeth Palace Library, MS. 1253; and Woburn Abbey, MS. 238. Partial copies include: Bodl. Libr., Rawlinson MS. A 127; Camb. Uni. Libr., MS. Ll.3.2, fos. 73–211; Folg. Shakes. Libr., MS. V.b.70; Harv. University Houghton Library, MS. Eng. 1084; Philadelphia Free Library, MS. LC 14.44(2); and MS. LC 14.44(3).

15 The details of the translations will be discussed in an edition of these reports being prepared for the Selden Society.

16 Copies including text written by the 'feathery scribe' are: Harv. Uni. Hough. Libr., MS. Eng. 1084; Phil. Free Libr., MS. LC 14.44(2); and MS LC 14.44(3) (see P. Beal, *In Praise of Scribes: Manuscripts and Their Makers in 17th-Century England* (Oxford, 1998), pp. 218 and 260).

17 Brit. Libr., Lansd. MS. 620, fo. 39.

18 UCL, Ogden MS. 7/7, fo. 112v.

19 For copies of orders made in the late 1590s, see J. H. Baker and J. S. Ringrose, *Catalogue of English Legal Manuscripts in Cambridge University Library* (Woodbridge, 1996), p. 120.

20 See Baker and Ringrose, *Catalogue of English Legal Manuscripts*, p. 304 and *Select Cases in the Council of Henry VII*, ed. C. G. Bayne (London, 1958), p. xiii.

21 Brit. Libr., Add. MS. 24926, fo. 1 is dated 20 March 1585. It seems most likely that the year here is old-style, which would mean the date is actually 20 March 1586.

22 Baker and Ringrose, *Catalogue of English Legal Manuscripts*, pp. 265–6. Not all of the

printed twice in 1635.[23] The manuscripts include the material printed in Hearne's *Curious Discourses* as a discussion of the Star Chamber by Francis Tate, for the College of Antiquaries,[24] which is in fact an early stage of Lambarde's work on the Star Chamber.[25] Lambarde's work circulated in commercially produced manuscripts.[26] It was sufficiently widespread that Hudson seems to have assumed its availability to a reader of his own treatise from 1621.[27] A seventeenth-century manuscript dealer's catalogue lists a treatise on the Star Chamber as one of the works currently available, together with a treatise on the Chancery, suggesting that this may be a reference to Lambarde's *Archeion*.[28]

William Hudson's treatise survives in over fifty early modern manuscript copies, albeit with quite significant variations in quality and completeness.[29] Finally, there is the text on Star Chamber procedure usually attributed to Isaac Cotton, often with a dedication dated 1622.[30] Both of these texts are from the early 1620s and it seems likely that Cotton's work was inspired by the appointment of the non-lawyer bishop John Williams as the lord keeper who would preside over the court and its proceedings, just as Hudson's work was.[31] One copy of the Cotton text is dated to 1634, showing circulation in Caroline England.[32] Hudson's text also circulated at that time, with John Lightfoot writing in 1636 that manuscripts of Hudson's text were 'now in many hands'.[33]

Lawyers seeking to understand the Star Chamber and its work in the two decades before its abolition would, therefore, have had access to a range

copies of *Archeion* incorporate the Star Chamber material.

23 W. Lambarde, *Archion, or A comentary upon the high courts of justice in England* (London, 1635) and W. Lambarde, *Archeion* (London, 1635).

24 *A Collection of Curious Discourses written by Eminent Antiquaries*, ed. T. Hearne (2 vols., London, 1771), ii. 277–307.

25 See Brit. Libr., Add. MS. 4521, fos. 35–64, which is identical to 'Tate', but attributed to Lambarde at fo. 35.

26 See Beal, *In Praise of Scribes*, pp. 218 and 267, identifying the 'feathery scribe' as one of the copyists of Harv. Law Sch., MS. 1026 vol. 1 (formerly MS. 1034) and Library of Congress, MS. Law M 14.

27 W. Hudson, 'A treatise of the court of Star Chamber', in *Collectanea Juridica*, ed. F. Hargrave (2 vols., London, 1791), ii. 1–239, at p. 2.

28 Brit. Libr., Harg. MS., fo. 207v.

29 Baker and Ringrose, *Catalogue of English Legal Manuscripts*, p. 439.

30 Baker and Ringrose, *Catalogue of English Legal Manuscripts*, pp. 116–17.

31 T. G. Barnes, 'Mr. Hudson's Star Chamber', in *Tudor Rule and Revolution: Essays for G. R. Elton from his American friends*, ed. D. J. Guth, J. W. McKenna (Cambridge, 1982), pp. 285–308, at pp. 296–306.

32 All Souls Col., MS. 256, fo. 413r.

33 Brit. Libr., Lansd. MS. 639, fo. 99v. The date is provided on fo. 23.

of relatively up-to-date material: a procedural treatise and a more wide-ranging one, both from the early 1620s; a set of law reports from the late sixteenth century for almost two decades, overlapping with another Jacobean collection; and a very current set from early in the reign of Charles I. Other reports and texts exist, but with little or no evidence of their circulation.[34]

Lay knowledge of the Star Chamber

Lawyers and actors within early modern government clearly thought some dissemination of criminal law material was desirable.[35] Subjects needed to be informed about the criminal law to avoid breaking it, preventing undesirable behaviour. Such a concern with dissemination is evident in reports of Star Chamber proceedings. There are frequent references to proceedings in the Star Chamber being exemplary, intended to affect behaviour beyond that of the parties to the case.[36] Sometimes the Star Chamber itself ordered that its activities were to be publicized. In the case of *Bertram* v *Sir John Windham* in 1625, the court ordered that '[t]he sentence is to be read in that country church for example', making a public statement of the sentence as an example to the local community.[37]

But knowledge of the Star Chamber and its activities was of interest for more than the exemplary role of its activities in ensuring obedience to the criminal law. Sir William Drake observed in his guide for self-improvement that he should '[f]requent Star Chamber It is an excellent scole for the qualifyinge of a man for action and emploiment'.[38] He linked Star Chamber material with parliament journals and letters of state as 'the most usefull histories of all'.[39] John Holles advised his son to attend the Star Chamber because 'more instruction is to be had at the starr-chamber, then at the globe … yow shall uppon this stage see what yow are to avoyd, what to follow, and by others errors, learn to play your owne part better'.[40] Similar advice appeared in Henry Peacham's *Compleat Gentleman*, which advised

[34] For law reports from Charles I's reign, John Lightfoot's personal collection of reports covering 1624–40 is valuable (Harv. Law Sch. MS. 1101 (formerly MS 1128)).

[35] R. Ross, 'The commoning of the common law: the renaissance debate over printing English law, 1520–1640', *University of Pennsylvania Law Review*, cxlvi (1998), 323–462, at pp. 336–7, 377 and 451 n. 375, contains some good examples.

[36] E.g. Brit. Libr., Lansd. MS. 620, fos. 11r, 11v, 21r, 27v, 32v, 48v, 50r and 65v. Proclamations which refer to the Star Chamber also make reference to exemplary proceedings and punishments there (see below, text at n. 62).

[37] *Bertram* v *Sir John Windham* (1625), Brit. Libr. Lansd. MS. 620, fo. 4 at fo. 5v.

[38] Huntington Library, MS. 55603, fo. *1.

[39] UCL, Ogden MS. 7/7, fo. 112v.

[40] *Letters of John Holles 1587–1637*, ed. P. R. Seddon (2 vols., Nottingham, 1983), ii. 222.

attending Star Chamber to 'enrich your understanding' and recommended observation of the Star Chamber to 'better your speech'.[41]

Knowledge about the court could be acquired in various ways. Drake, Holles and Peacham all advised personal attendance at the court. Star Chamber cases, at least high-profile ones, were popular and seats were paid for.[42] This popularity was sometimes accommodated by the court. In the litigation between the Lake family and the family of the earl of Exeter, the case was to be moved to the Banqueting House to accommodate the expected crowd.[43] This case was identified as a particularly exemplary one, so moving the proceedings disseminated the example more widely.[44]

Attendees might then pass on what they had observed. Early modern diaries include references to diarists hearing information about the Star Chamber.[45] Such oral dissemination was potentially unreliable. In relation to Prynne's conviction for the publication of *Histriomastix*, Ralph Verney noted that '[w]ee country clowns heare various reports', with significant disagreement about the sentence imposed, asking for clarification in a letter.[46] Receipt of news about the Star Chamber by letter was not unusual. John Chamberlain reported cases he considered 'worth remembrance', especially 'any remarkeable matter', in his letters.[47] Cases might be

[41] H. Peacham, *The Compleat Gentleman Fashioning him absolute in the most necessary & Commenable Qualities concerning Minde or Bodie that may be required in a Noble Gentleman* (London, 1622), p. 53. The role of the Star Chamber in education and self-fashioning probably explains the commercial circulation of Walter Mildmay's Elizabethan speeches from the Star Chamber. These survive in Brit. Libr., Harl. MS. 6265, Brit. Libr., Stowe MS. 326; Bodl. Libr., Rawl. MS C 838 and Shakespeare Birthplace Trust, MS. DR 37/3/54. The Star Chamber speeches are grouped together, but each volume includes a wider range of Mildmay's speeches on matters of state. The manuscript dealer Ralph Starkey listed Mildmay's parliamentary speeches as one of the items he had for sale (Brit. Libr., Harl. MS. 537, fo. 83) and it is possible that item would also have included the Star Chamber speeches.

[42] See N. Millstone, *Manuscript Circulation and the Invention of Politics in Early Stuart England* (Cambridge, 2016), p. 262.

[43] *Reports on the Manuscripts of the Most Honourable the Marquess of Downshire Formerly Preserved at Easthampstead Park, Berkshire, Vol. VI: Papers of William Trumbull the Elder September 1616 – December 1618*, ed. G. D. Owen, S. P. Anderson (6 vols., London, 1995), vi. 574.

[44] *Reports on the Manuscripts*, vi. 626.

[45] *The Diary of John Manningham of the Middle Temple, and of Bradbourne, Kent, Barrister-at-law, 1602–1603*, ed. J. Bruce (London, 1868), p. 169; *The Autobiography and Correspondence of Sir Simonds D'Ewes, Bart.: During the Reigns of James I and Charles I*, ed. J. O. Halliwell (2 vols., London, 1845), ii. 104.

[46] *Letters and Papers of the Verney Family Down to the End of the Year 1639*, ed. J. Bruce (London, 1853), pp. 157–8.

[47] *The Letters of John Chamberlain*, ed. N. E. McClure (2 vols., Philadelphia, 1939), ii. 310 and 506.

important for a number of reasons. High-profile cases will be considered later, but observers were not solely interested in such episodes.

Sometimes observers paid attention to the Star Chamber because cases showed that the court might affect the observer or his audience. Simonds D'Ewes noted a 'terrible censure' for staying in London contrary to the king's proclamation that gentlemen should return to their counties.[48] D'Ewes was particularly interested in this case because he had believed that the proclamation did not relate to his circumstances, but after the censure he was less sure and so decided to remove himself to the country.[49] John Chamberlain noted proclamations for keeping of Lent, with the threat of Star Chamber prosecution, which 'being a court not to be dallied withall: makes us all get licences'.[50] The exemplary objective of Star Chamber prosecutions was achieved in these instances.

Other cases were significant because they related to communities of which the diarist or letter writer was a part. John Chamberlain reported one case because it concerned '[o]ur frend little John Moore'.[51] Other cases concerned defendants with whom observers had geographical links. Henry Machyn, a citizen of London, noted when another citizen had been condemned in the Star Chamber;[52] Thomas Crosfield of Queen's College, Oxford recorded prosecutions of people from Oxford in the court.[53] William Wentworth, the future earl of Strafford, sent his father a long report of a case involving a fellow Yorkshireman, Stephen Procter.[54] Such membership of a community might also explain the particular interest in cases connected with the religious policy of the 1630s. Margo Todd suggests that 'puritan self-fashioning … was fundamentally communal rather than individualistic in nature',[55] so godly individuals in the 1630s may have seen the prosecutions of Sherfield, Prynne, Bastwick and Burton, perhaps even John Williams,[56] as prosecutions of members of their own community, a community formed by religious views.[57]

48 *Autobiography and Correspondence of Sir Simonds D'Ewes*, ii. 78.

49 *Autobiography and Correspondence of Sir Simonds D'Ewes*, ii. 79.

50 *Letters of John Chamberlain*, ii. 217.

51 *Letters of John Chamberlain*, ii. 160.

52 *The Diary of Henry Machyn, Citizen and Merchant-Taylor of London, from AD 1550 to AD 1563*, ed. J. G. Nichols (London, 1848), p. 227.

53 *The Diary of Thomas Crosfield*, ed. F. S. Boas (London, 1935), p. 86.

54 *Wentworth Papers 1597–1628*, ed. J. P. Cooper (London, 1973), pp. 57–62.

55 M. Todd, 'Puritan self-fashioning: the diary of Samuel Ward', *Journal of British Studies*, xxxi (1992), 236–64, at p. 252.

56 See below, text at nn. 76–80.

57 This may explain the noting of some of these cases in the diary of Robert Woodford, someone otherwise unconnected with the cases (*The Diary of Robert Woodford, 1637–1641*,

The text of letters might then circulate further. One of Joseph Mead's letters included an account of a Star Chamber prosecution for saying 'That our King [Charles I] was fitter to stand in a cheapside shop, with an apron before him & say What lack yee? Then to governe a kingdome'. In the margin is added a request, 'I pray strike out these words afore you lett any body read the lettre', showing a clear understanding that letters were used to disseminate news beyond the immediate recipient.[58]

Beyond such personal observations and letters, knowledge of the Star Chamber spread through other texts. Royal proclamations were probably one of the most widely circulated sources of information about the court. Proclamations were intended to have a wide circulation, and their initially printed text was further mentioned by letter-writers and disseminated orally.[59] Just under 14% of proclamations during the reign of James I made reference to the Star Chamber, with a lower proportion for the reign of Charles I.[60] Proclamations mainly referred to the Star Chamber as a possible forum for prosecutions of those breaching the proclamation.[61] However, proclamations also informed people about happenings in the court, with some proclamations referring to earlier censures, typically as exemplary punishments with the proclamation disseminating the example more widely.[62] Star Chamber decrees might themselves become proclamations,[63] or be printed as official publications.[64]

Other official dissemination of material about the Star Chamber was rare, only occurring once. In 1637, Archbishop Laud's speech delivered in the trial of William Prynne, John Bastwick and Henry Burton was printed, apparently at the command of Charles himself, probably as a reaction to unofficial circulation of material about the trial.[65] A presentation of the

ed. J. Fielding (Cambridge, 2012), pp. 99 and 176).

58 Brit. Libr., Harl. MS. 390, fo. 454v.

59 For evidence of such dissemination, see C. R. Kyle, 'Monarch and marketplace: proclamations as news in early modern England', *Huntington Library Quarterly*, lxxviii (2015), 771–87, at pp. 776, 779–81 and 784.

60 37 of the 267 proclamations in *Stuart Royal Proclamations, Vol. I: Royal Proclamations of King James I, 1603–1625*, ed. J. F. Larkin and P. L. Hughes (Oxford, 1973). For Charles I, 17 of the 320 issued before the abolition of the court in July 1641 refer to the Star Chamber (*Stuart Royal Proclamations, Vol. II: Royal Proclamations of King Charles I, 1625–1646*, ed. J. F. Larkin (Oxford, 1983)).

61 E.g. *Stuart Royal Proclamations, Vol. I*, p. 296; *Stuart Royal Proclamations, Vol. II*, p. 24.

62 E.g. *Stuart Royal Proclamations, Vol. I*, pp. 137, 193 and 359.

63 *Stuart Royal Proclamations, Vol. I*, pp. 620–1.

64 *A Decree Lately made in the High Court of Starre-Chamber* (London, 1633). The decree concerned engrossing and the supply of victuals.

65 W. Laud, *A Speech Delivered in the Starr-Chamber, on Wednesday, the XIVth of June, MDCXXXVII. At the Censure of John Bastwick, Henry Burton, & William Prinn* (London,

remarks of the defendants was printed several times in the Netherlands, beginning soon after the trial, something about which Laud was concerned, and John Bastwick's *Answer* to the information of the attorney general was also printed, all as part of wider English 'puritan' publishing in the Netherlands.[66] According to an English agent in the Netherlands, 10,000 copies of the defendants' remarks in the Star Chamber had been printed in just one of several printings,[67] compared to an estimated 800–1000 copies of a national proclamation.[68] Bastwick's *Answer* had its title page 'pasted up upon Walls and Posts' in London before being publicly burned.[69] Laud's speech was also read, but its readers included those opposed to its claims. Sir Thomas Barrington, someone 'closely associated with those who were to be leaders in the parliamentary opposition of 1640', bought three copies.[70] Laud's printed speech led to a printed reaction by the pseudonymous Theophilus in 1638.[71]

This particular propaganda battle was unusual for being waged in print, but considerable interest in high-profile cases existed. Material about these cases circulated widely in manuscript, forming part of what Noah Millstone has described as 'a list of forbidden bestsellers of pre-revolutionary England', with interest in such cases also evidenced in letters.[72] The distinction between print and manuscript may nonetheless have been important for dissemination of this material. Peacey has highlighted the high costs of scribally produced copies of state trials.[73] Nonetheless, people who could access and afford such material clearly generated sufficient demand for significant quantities of the manuscript texts to be made.

The earliest of these circulating materials are from the reign of James I: the prosecution of the attorney general, Henry Yelverton[74] and a case against

1637), sig. A3r.

[66] K. L. Sprunger, *Trumpets From the Tower: English Puritan Printing in the Netherlands 1600–1640* (Leiden, 1994), pp. 112, 153 and 175. Versions of the remarks of Prynne, Bastwick and Burton, and of Laud's speech, also appeared in Dutch (pp. 153 and 175).

[67] Sprunger, *Trumpets from the Tower*, p. 153.

[68] Kyle, 'Monarch and marketplace', p. 776.

[69] *The Earl of Straffordes Letters and Dispatches*, ed. W. Knowler (2 vols., London, 1739), ii. 140.

[70] M. E. Bohannon, 'A London bookseller's bill: 1635–1639', *The Library* (4th series), xviii (1938), 417–46, at pp. 419 and 429.

[71] ['Theophilus'], *Divine and Politike Observations Newly translated out of the Dutch language, wherein they were lately divulged. Upon Some Lines in the speech of the Arch. B. of Canterbury, pronounced in the Starre-Chamber upon 14. June 1637* (Amsterdam, 1638).

[72] Millstone, *Manuscript Circulation*, p. 3, see also p. 263.

[73] J. Peacey, *Print and Public Politics in the English Revolution* (Cambridge, 2013), pp. 31–3.

[74] Brit. Libr., Harl. MS. 6055, fos. 1–20v; Stowe MS. 159, fos. 28–37; Folg. Shakes. Libr., MS. V.a.622, fos. 10–44; Kent Library and History Centre, U951/O10/4; Yale Beinecke

Dutch merchants for the export of bullion.[75] But far more Caroline cases appear to have been of interest. In addition to the trial of Prynne, Bastwick and Burton,[76] the proceedings against the earls of Bedford, Clare and Somerset, together with Sir Robert Cotton, John Selden and Gilbert Barrell, survive in many copies.[77] So do the trials of Henry Sherfield,[78] William Prynne for *Histriomastix*[79] and John Williams, bishop of Lincoln.[80] The material circulating varied, ranging from copies of official court records such as informations and decrees to the text of individual speeches by judges.[81] For all types of material, there is evidence of commercial circulation. One of the copies of Prynne's *Histriomastix* trial is in the hand of a known

---

Library, Osborn MS.fb.155, fos. 247–252. The case is noted in John Chamberlain's letters (*The Letters of John Chamberlain*, ii. 311, 323 and 328) and the diaries of Simonds D'Ewes (*Autobiography and Correspondence of Sir Simonds D'Ewes*, i. 155–6) and William Whiteway (*William Whiteway of Dorchester: His Diary 1618 to 1635* (Dorchester, 1991), p. 31).

[75] E.g. Woburn Abbey, MS. 236. The case features in contemporary letters by John Chamberlain (*The Letters of John Chamberlain*, ii. 192, 238, 245–6, 266–7 and 275–6) and the diary of John Holles (*The Letters of John Holles*, ii. 231). See also the chapter by Healy, above.

[76] Manuscript texts of the case include: Bodl. Libr., Tanner MS. 299, fos. 136–161v; Camb. Uni. Libr., MS. Ee.2.1, fos. 4–8; Folg. Shakes. Libr., MS. V.a.248, fos. 31–43; Kansas University, MS D.152(2); Kent History and Library Centre, U951/Z11 and Northamptonshire Archives, FH89.

[77] Bodl. Libr., Rawl. MS. A.127, fos. 55–68; Bodl. Libr., Tanner MS. 299, fos. 207–221; Brit. Libr., Harg. MS. 489, fos. 16–25, 26–47v and 48–57v; Brit. Libr., Stowe MS. 153, fos. 41–47; Brit. Libr., Stowe MS. 159, fos. 15–27v; Folg. Shakes. Libr., MS. V.a.116; Folg. Shakes. Libr., MS. V.b.20; Folg. Shakes. Libr., MS. V.b.277; Folg. Shakes. Libr., MS. X.d.337, fos. 5–10; Harv. Uni. Hough. Libr., MS. Eng 977; Phil. Free Libr., MS. LC.14.87; Trin. Col. Dubl., MS. 721, fos. 102–119v; Woburn Abbey, MS. 33; Yale Bein. Libr., Osborn MS.fb.155, fos. 463–470.

[78] Bodl. Libr., Tanner MS 299, fos. 91–123; Camb. Uni. Libr., MS. Dd.6.23, fos. 42–93; Kansas University, MS C.250; Wiltshire and Swindon History Centre, MS. 1780/8. The case was also noted in various letters: *The Court and Times of Charles I*, ed. Thomas Birch (2 vols., London, 1849), ii. 167–8 and 227; *Newsletters from the Caroline Court, 1631–1638: Catholicism and the Politics of the Personal Rule*, ed. M. C. Questier (London, 2005), pp. 149 and 153.

[79] Bodl. Libr., Tanner MS. 299, fos. 123–134v; Brit. Libr., Add. MS. 11764, fos. 8–29v; Brit. Libr., Stowe MS. 159, fos. 45–78; Camb. Uni. Libr., MS. Dd.6.23, pp. 21–41; Harv. Uni. Hough. Libr., MS. Eng 835; MS Eng 1359; Hunt. Libr., MS. HM 80; Trin. Col. Dubl., MS. 542; MS. 721, fos. 60–95v; Woburn Abbey, MS 9/35/11. Prynne's imprisonment and punishment was noted in the diary of William Whiteway (*William Whiteway*, pp. 127 and 139) and in a letter (*The Court and Times of Charles I*, ii. 224).

[80] Brit. Libr., Add. MS. 45147; Brit. Libr., Stowe MS. 159, fos. 38–44; Camb. Uni. Libr., MS. Ee.2.1, fos. 9–37; Folg. Shakes. Libr., MS. V.a.248, fos. 44–47v; Harv. Uni. Hough. Libr., MS. Eng 1084, fos. 83–116 and Trin. Col. Dubl., MS. 721, fos. 1–38v.

[81] Bodl. Libr., Tanner MS. 299 is a good example. It includes accounts of the trial of Prynne, Bastwick and Burton, its aftermath (fos. 136–146), and the official information initiating the prosecution (fos. 146v–161v).

commercial copyist;[82] the cases against Bishop Williams and Prynne, Bastwick and Burton survive as 'commercially produced' pamphlets all in the same hand.[83] Whether an awareness of the possibility of dissemination influenced the words and actions of participants in these cases is unclear, as is whether such an awareness might have affected the drafting of official records to communicate to an audience beyond the court.

News, opinion and the abolition of the Star Chamber

These texts can all be seen as part of the wider history of early modern 'news'.[84] Such news could be partisan, as in an account of Burton's behaviour at the execution of his sentence which likened him to Jesus.[85] Even if the news itself appeared neutral, it was not consumed uncritically. In his letters John Chamberlain sometimes inserted his own views on the wisdom of using the Star Chamber, or on the sentences imposed there.[86]

Available professional texts on the Star Chamber are different. Most cases were not high profile and did not relate to the kind of matters typically reported as news. Compared to news on the Star Chamber, professional texts also did not focus on issues which might provoke criticism. A good example is the case of *Haines* v *Jordan* from 1627, for the crime of holding an unauthorized consistory. The case was reported as news to Joseph Mead, noting Bishop Laud's 'bitter invective' against the defendant.[87] The same case was also included in the circulating Caroline reports. In those reports Laud's remarks were not mentioned. Instead, the focus was on the existence of an alleged custom which would have authorized the defendant's actions. The only members of the court identified by name, and to whom particular points were attributed, were the legally trained members: Coventry LK, Hyde CJKB and Walter CB.[88] The law report focused on technical points, giving a greater appearance of neutrality and technicality, presenting the

[82] Beal, *In Praise of Scribes*, p. 228, referring to Brit. Libr., Add. MS. 11764, fos. 10v–30v.

[83] Baker and Ringrose, *Catalogue of English Legal Manuscripts*, p. 173, referring to Camb. Uni. Libr., MS. Ee.2.1.

[84] 'News' in the early modern period may not always have been very recent, provided it was currently relevant (J. Raymond and N. Moxham, 'News Networks in Early Modern Europe', in pp. 1–16 in *News Networks in Early Modern Europe*, ed. J. Raymond and N. Moxham (Leiden, 2016), pp. 1–2).

[85] Folg. Shakes. Libr., MS. V.a.248, fos. 42v–43.

[86] *Letters of John Chamberlain*, i. 491 (approving the use of the Star Chamber to prevent duelling) and ii. 246 (the prosecution of Dutch merchants for exporting bullion creating more inconvenience than benefit).

[87] *The Court and Times of Charles I*, i. 276.

[88] Brit. Libr., Lansd. MS. 620, fos. 47v–49.

Star Chamber as like the other central courts, while the letter omitted the crucial legal aspects of the case.

By 1620, fear of the court was being raised by letter writers. Holles worried that it had become too easy to be drawn into the Star Chamber because 'it is neer hand as impossible to keep the common statute, proclamation, and prerogative laws'.[89] According to Chamberlain, this view was widely shared: 'the world is now much terrified with the Star-chamber' because an abundance of proclamations made it too easy to break one.[90] The concern was not directly about the court, but about its activity in enforcing the growing numbers of royal proclamations.[91] Such concern about the court's role, and implicit criticism, became more common during the personal rule of Charles I.

Perhaps more significantly, news writers and readers could interpret the actions of the Star Chamber as explained by concerns other than justice. John Chamberlain noted a Star Chamber prosecution as driven by personalities at court. Chamberlain observed of the prosecution of Sebastian Harvey for errors committed during his tenure as sheriff that '[i]f his daughter could be induced to affect Christopher Villers it is generally thought it had not bin called in question'.[92] As Millstone notes in relation to Walter Yonge, he 'picked out patterns', for example examining the judgements in the case of Henry Sherfield as linked to factions.[93] This 'abuse' of the court was recognized by the earl of Manchester in his defence of it, where he acknowledged the use of the Star Chamber 'for matter of Revenge'.[94] Such analysis of the court could undermine its legitimacy, presenting it as an instrument used by individuals for their own ends, rather than a source of justice.[95]

[89] *Letters of John Holles*, ii. 232.

[90] *Letters of John Chamberlain*, ii. 310.

[91] For similar concerns about statutes, see the remarks of Francis Bacon in *Proceedings in the Parliaments of Elizabeth I*, ed. T. E. Hartley (3 vols., Leicester, 1995), iii. 75.

[92] *Letters of John Chamberlain*, ii. 306. Christopher Villiers was brother to George Villiers, then Marquess of Buckingham and James I's favourite.

[93] Millstone, *Manuscript Circulation*, pp. 190 and 192.

[94] Brit. Libr., Harl. MS. 6424, fo. 73v.

[95] The petition of the soap makers of London to the Long Parliament also raised this issue, complaining that the rival soap makers of Westminster had personally solicited the Star Chamber cases against them and disbursed money in those cases (Anon., *A Short and True Relation of the Soap-busines* (London, 1641), p. 10 and sig. D1v). Although the petition seems not to have been part of parliamentary business until after the abolition of the Star Chamber (*Proceedings in the Opening Session of the Long Parliament: House of Commons. Vol. 6: 19 July – 9 September 1641*, ed. M. Jansson (Rochester, NY, 2005), pp. 450–1), a petition by a soap boiler was submitted to parliament in late May 1641, before the abolition of the Star Chamber (Peacey, *Print and Public Politics*, p. 270). Moreover, the soap makers'

Two particularly significant strands of complaint emerged in parliamentary criticisms of the court in 1640 and 1641. There is considerable congruity between views expressed in relation to news about the Star Chamber and parliamentary criticisms of the Star Chamber before its abolition, although Richard Cust's warning of the difficulties in determining the effects of news on political action must be borne in mind.[96] It is not possible to demonstrate that the circulation of news caused the court's abolition, but it is possible to show a correlation between the views found in circulating material about the court and discussions in parliament before that abolition.

First was the view that the Star Chamber was a source of revenue. John Holles noted as much during the reign of James I. Commenting on the fines levied on the lord treasurer and on Dutch merchants, Holles wrote that 'the starrchamber is lyk a good cow, yeeld good store of milk'.[97] Holles's remark was not overtly critical, but suggests an awareness that the court might be acting for reasons other than mere justice.

During the personal rule of Charles I, newsletters disseminated this view. Early in the 1630s, John Soutcot raised this belief in relation to Star Chamber prosecutions for breaches of proclamations concerning residence in London and the keeping of Lent and fast days.[98] Similarly, it was alleged, and reported in a letter, that the attorney general brought Star Chamber proceedings for breach of a proclamation prohibiting the transportation of gold, but 'he had only been prosecuting such men as were not able to pay the king the one-half of the fine imposed upon them', using the Star Chamber only when revenue could not be raised, and thereby supporting the crown financially.[99] It was observed that the 'complaint reflected much upon the attorney', indicating that this use of the court was seen as unacceptable by some.[100]

The idea that the Star Chamber was to be used to support royal revenue may even have been encouraged (perhaps inadvertently) by the government. In 1627, a royal proclamation explained the need for a further proclamation about the import of tobacco as due to the customs revenue which was then

---

complaints were 'proposed to be remedied' in the Short Parliament (*The Diary and Papers of Henry Townshend, 1640–1663*, ed. S. Porter, S. K. Roberts, I. Roy (Bristol, 2014), p. 46). It is therefore possible that some parliamentarians were aware of the substance of the complaints when considering the abolition of the Star Chamber.

96 R. Cust, 'News and politics in early 17th-century England', *Past & Present*, cxii (1986), 60–90, at p. 87. On the sudden shift in the surviving parliamentary material on the Star Chamber, see below, text at nn. 118–24.

97 *Letters of John Holles*, ii. 231.

98 *Newsletters from the Caroline Court*, pp. 104 and 150.

99 *The Court and Times of Charles I*, ii. 277.

100 *The Court and Times of Charles I*, ii. 277.

being lost. Having explained that the proclamation was about bolstering royal revenue, the text then specified that enforcement was to occur in the Star Chamber, presenting the court as one which was to punish those undermining royal finances.[101] The Star Chamber was, therefore, being associated with the royal revenue more than a decade before the Long Parliament, with hints of criticism in the news on this point.

The earliest parliamentary criticism of the Star Chamber in 1640 was in the Short Parliament, where it was said that the Star Chamber had 'become a very Courte of Exchequer and revenewe to the king by imposition of heavy and deepe Fines which were soe unsupportable that they tend to the utter ruine and subversion of mens estates and Fortunes'.[102] A similar point was made early in the Long Parliament, that the Star Chamber had become 'an arbitrary court of justice to receive gentlemen['s] estates',[103] and in a (draft?) motion about John Williams, bishop of Lincoln, which observed '[t]hat whereas this honorable Court is of late growne most heavye and grevious in the Sentencing of Causes, and to take away the Freeholds of the subject'.[104] Although this does not reappear in reports of later House of Commons proceedings about the Star Chamber, it was mentioned in the House of Lords. According to a diary of House of Lords proceedings, the proposal to abolish the Star Chamber was 'because they meddled with the Liberty & propriety of persons'.[105] The earl of Manchester's defence of the Star Chamber similarly acknowledged two 'abuses' in the court related to income: '[t]o bring the King in a great deal of money by way of Fine' and '[t]o Protect unlawfull Grants'.[106]

The other criticism of the Star Chamber, which appears dominant in the House of Commons material, was that it had become a tool for the enforcement of controversial religious policy at the behest of the bishops. In part this was because the Star Chamber was deciding cases which related to questions of religion and orthodoxy. Laud's speech in the Star Chamber prosecution of Prynne, Bastwick and Burton was a response to the detail of the defences made in the case. It presented the Star Chamber as a

[101] *Stuart Royal Proclamations, Vol. II*, pp. 132 and 134.

[102] Hertfordshire Archives and Local Studies, Gorhambury MS. XII.A.2.a, unpaginated, entry for 15 Apr. 1640.

[103] *Proceedings in the Opening Session of the Long Parliament: House of Commons. Vol. 1: 3 November – 19 December 1640*, ed. M. Jansson (Rochester, NY, 2000), p. 219.

[104] Hertfordshire Archives and Local Studies, Gorhambury MS XII.A.19, unpaginated, first complaint.

[105] Brit. Libr., Harl. MS. 6424, fo. 73.

[106] Brit. Libr., Harl. MS. 6424, fos. 73–v. This also formed part of the petition of the soap makers of London to the Long Parliament (Anon., *A Short and True Relation*, sig. C4r–v and D2r–v).

forum for argument about (disputed) matters of religion, and where the judgement of the court impliedly found one side's views to be correct, to the dissatisfaction of others. This exposed the Star Chamber to criticism. As Bulstrode Whitelocke observed of the bishops' views in that case, 'many of the hearers were offended att it'.[107] Star Chamber judgements touching on controversial matters of religion themselves predictably became matters of controversy and dissatisfaction.

Laud's speech in the case was apparently printed by royal command.[108] The Caroline regime thereby presented the Star Chamber as a court appropriate for, and concerned with, enforcing controversial religious orthodoxy. The official dissemination of Laud's speech could have been seen as a warning that those who did not agree with contemporary ecclesiastical policy risked more than ecclesiastical sanction; they faced prosecution in the Star Chamber with the backing of the crown. Such a view may have undermined the Star Chamber's legitimacy. It was after this case, for example, that Nehemiah Wallington referred to the Star Chamber as an 'unlawfull corte'.[109]

Beyond the challenge to the legitimacy and acceptability of the Star Chamber imposed by involvement in a controversial area, a related concern was that the Star Chamber had simply become a tool for the bishops, who abused it to pursue their own agenda. Once again, the Star Chamber was presented as a source of injustice. This was a key component of the printed texts disseminating news and views about the prosecutions of Prynne, Bastwick and Burton. John Bastwick's *Answer* to the attorney general's information presented the Star Chamber prosecution as one undertaken by prelates who were displeased with him,[110] while Prynne described the case as arising because the 'prelates find themselves exceedingly agrieved and vexed against what wee have written concerning the usurpation of their calling'.[111] This complaint may have been exacerbated by a visible change in the court in the second half of the 1630s. From 1636 the number of bishops sitting regularly as judges increased to three: the two archbishops were joined by William Juxon, bishop of London, as lord treasurer.[112] This

[107] *The Diary of Bulstrode Whitelocke, 1605–1675*, ed. R. Spalding (Oxford, 1990), p. 87.

[108] See above, text at n. 65.

[109] *The Notebooks of Nehemiah Wallington, 1618–1654: a Selection*, ed. D. Booy (Aldershot, 2007), p. 122.

[110] J. Bastwick, *The Answer of John Bastwick, Doctor of Phisicke, To the Information of Sir John Bancks Knight, Attorney universall* (n.p., 1637), p. 7.

[111] *A briefe relation of certain speciall and most materiall passages, and speeches in the Starre-Chamber* (Amsterdam, 1637), p. 19.

[112] Phillips, 'The Last Years', p. 114. Earlier in the reign of Charles I there were usually only two ecclesiastics sitting as judges in the court (see, e.g., text at n. 134 below).

enhanced ecclesiastical presence perhaps gave an impression of a greater role for the bishops as decision-makers in the court, particularly as this change occurred only the year before the case of Prynne, Bastwick and Burton; a case concerning religious matters. That all three bishops were vigorous in implementing changes in the Church in the 1630s could only have exacerbated the sense of the court being used for the bishops' ends.[113]

The view of the court as a tool of the bishops was repeated by Nehemiah Wallington in his notebooks, identifying the prosecutions as the work of 'our lordly Bishopes and prelates'.[114] Wallington, however, synthesized the Star Chamber's actions in this case with another criticism of the court. In Burton's 1636 criticism of the *Book of Sports*,[115] the *Divine Tragedie*, the trial and conviction of Prynne for the publication of *Histriomastix* was presented as unjust. This injustice was attributed to the attorney general, William Noy, to whom Burton attached considerable responsibility for the *Book of Sports*. Burton therefore presented the case as one in which Noy prosecuted, and persecuted, Prynne for a licensed book 'compiled onely out of the words and sentences of other approved Authors', and which appeared before the queen engaged in activity (acting on stage) of which Prynne expressed strong disapproval. Noy's conduct of the trial was also presented as unjust.[116] Wallington copied the relevant passages from the *Divine Tragedie* into his notebooks, just after his report of the prosecutions of Prynne, Bastwick and Burton in 1637, thereby linking the two distinct prosecutions of Prynne. In doing so, Wallington formed a more general view of the unjust uses to which the Star Chamber was put by both bishops and the king's own attorney.[117]

The criticisms of the Star Chamber's role in matters of religion and unjust proceedings by the bishops appear in early December 1640 in the Long Parliament. The Star Chamber and High Commission were joined together in the committee to consider the petitions of Prynne, Burton and others.[118] A subsequent focus in the House of Commons from March 1641 was a bill to remove the bishops from secular matters, especially the Privy

[113] For Neile and Juxon as two of the 'good "Laudians"', see A. Foster, 'Church policies of the 1630s', in *Conflict in Early Stuart England: Studies in Religion and Politics 1603–1642*, ed. R. Cust and A. Hughes (Harlow, 1989), pp. 193–223, at p. 211.

[114] *Notebooks of Nehemiah Wallington*, p. 121.

[115] *The Kings Maiesties declaration to his subiects, concerning lawfull sports to bee vsed* (London, 1633).

[116] H. Burton, *A Divine Tragedie Lately Acted, or a Collection of sundry examples of Gods judgements upon Sabbath-Breakers* (n.p., 1636), pp. 43–4.

[117] *Notebooks of Nehemiah Wallington*, pp. 122–3.

[118] *Proceedings in the Opening Session of Parliament, Vol. 1*, pp. 438 and 441.

Council and the Star Chamber.[119] In the surviving diaries and reports about proceedings in the House of Commons, these concerns entirely replace other complaints about the Star Chamber.[120] Even complaints about the Star Chamber in enforcing ship money, raised in the earl of Strafford's impeachment proceedings in the first half of 1641, do not seem to have featured in parliamentary debates about the court itself.[121]

The idea that Star Chamber cases were the work of the bishops was repeated in Prynne's petition to the Long Parliament, where he stressed the 'malicious practices and persecutions of some Prelates and Churchmen'. Prynne linked this to matters of controversy in religion, explaining that his persecutors were in fact responsible for 'errors and innovations' in the Church of England.[122] Given innovation in religion was a concern of both the Short and Long Parliaments, Prynne's petition presented him as a victim of religiously motivated persecution; persecution for defending that which parliament was also concerned to protect (or restore), with the Star Chamber as a means to impose false religion.[123] In doing so, he seems to have set the agenda for discussion of the Star Chamber in the House of Commons in the Long Parliament. Prynne was able to link his case to views already expressed in printed material circulating about the court; material which may have been more accessible than manuscript texts.[124]

Strong parallels thus existed between criticisms of the court in news material, especially recent material (some of which was printed), and

[119] *Proceedings in the Opening Session of the Long Parliament: House of Commons. Vol. 2: 21 December 1640 – 20 March 1641*, ed. M. Jansson (Rochester, NY, 2000), p. 710 and *Proceedings in the Opening Session of the Long Parliament: House of Commons and the Strafford Trial. Vol. 3: 22 March – 17 April 1641*, ed. M. Jansson (Rochester, NY, 2001), pp. 234–5, 237 and 311. On these proceedings generally, and their background, see W. M. Abbott, 'Anticlericalism and episcopacy in parliamentary debates, 1640–1641: secular versus spiritual functions', in *Law and Authority in Early Modern England: Essays Presented to Thomas Garden Barnes*, ed. B. Sharp, M. C. Fissel (Newark, 2007), pp. 157–85.

[120] The issue of religion does not appear in accounts of House of Lords proceedings that I have identified. However, the earl of Manchester alluded to it when he observed about the proposed abolition of the Star Chamber that 'to tak away the use for the abuse is like that Bill against Bishops called Root & Branch' (Brit. Libr., Harl. MS. 6424, fo. 73).

[121] J. Rushworth, *Historical Collections of Private Passages of State* (8 vols., London, 1721–2), viii. 582–9.

[122] *The severall Humble petitions of D. Bastwicke M. Burton M. Prynne And of Nath. Wickins, Servant to the said Mr Prynne, To the Honourable house of Parliament* (London, 1641), pp. 1–2.

[123] For concern about innovation about religion in the Short Parliament, see Hertfordshire Archives and Local Studies, Gorhambury MS XII.A.2.a, entry for 15 Apr. 1640. For the Long Parliament, see *Proceedings in the Opening Session of Parliament Vol. 1*, pp. 35, 38, 39, 43, 44, 101, 102, 106 and 111.

[124] See above, text at n. 73.

political discussions about the court before its abolition. However, ideas found in professional literature were not irrelevant in the parliamentary proceedings about the court. The act which abolished the Star Chamber stated that the jurisdiction of the court was based upon a statute of 1487, for the punishment only of offences specified in that statute, '[b]ut the said Judges have not kept themselves to the points limited by the said Statute'.[125]

The professional literature of the late sixteenth and seventeenth century generally did not take this position. Professional texts often described contemporary practice, and the Star Chamber did not confine itself to matters mentioned in the 1487 statute. For example, in the preface to the 1630 printing of *Star-Chamber Cases* the jurisdiction of the court covered 'misdemeanors not especially provided for by the Statutes'.[126] Material circulating in print and manuscript presented the court as older than 1487 and therefore not dependent upon any statutory warrant for its authority.[127]

The presentation of the Star Chamber in the abolition statute as a court whose authority derived from statute, and with a statutorily defined jurisdiction, was therefore contrary to the dominant position in the circulating professional literature devoted to the Star Chamber. This literature was presumably important in shaping the views of the legal profession. It certainly seems to have informed the views expressed in the Long Parliament by the earl of Manchester, former chief justice of the King's Bench Henry Montagu. Montagu declared that 'the Star Chamber was not erected nor limitted 3.H.7. but that it had been in practise many 100 years before'.[128] Montagu also identified the Star Chamber as the King's Council sitting judicially, a point made in Lambarde, and cited the same passage from *Bracton* as was used in Hudson's *Treatise*, suggesting influence from that work too.[129]

The formal justification for the abolition of the Star Chamber therefore suggests that the view of the court's authority presented in the abolition statute was different to the understanding of the court among

[125] Stat.16.Car.I, c.10 (*Statutes of the Realm*, v, pp. 110–11), referring to stat.3.Hen.VII, c.1 (*Statutes of the Realm*, ii, pp. 509–10).

[126] [Anon.], *Star-Chamber Cases*, p. 1.

[127] E.g., *Archeion or, a Discourse upon the High Courts of Justice in England by William Lambarde*, ed. C. H. McIlwain and P. L. Ward (Cambridge, Mass., 1957) pp. 80–3 and Hudson, 'A Treatise of the Court', pp. 9–16. The exceptions are *Onslowe's Case* in Dyer (see above, n. 5) and F. Pulton, *A Collection of Sundrie Statutes* (London, 1618), p. 3 of the Henry VII statutes, where the statute is described as about the 'authoritie of the Court of star-chamber'. Pulton's work was reprinted in 1632, 1636 and 1640.

[128] Brit. Libr., Harl. MS. 6424, fo. 73v.

[129] Brit. Libr., Harl. MS. 6424, fo. 74r; *Archeion*, ed. Ward and McIlwain, pp. 81–3; Hudson, 'A treatise of the court', p. 9.

the legal profession. In surviving parliamentary material, the professional understanding of the court is only visible in the House of Lords debate, following which the House of Lords was hesitant to abolish the court.[130]

However, while ideas found in the professional literature on the Star Chamber were deployed in the defence of the court, that literature may not have reflected developments in the thinking of at least some members of the legal profession. In his reading in the Middle Temple in 1640, Edward Bagshawe concluded that bishops could not act as secular judges.[131] It is unclear how widely Bagshawe's views were shared, although when he left London after his reading was ended, forty members of the Temple rode with him, suggesting some support.[132]

Dissatisfaction with the bishops is present in the professional material on the Star Chamber. The 1625–9 reports included the prosecution of a servant of the earl of Lincoln, for dispersing letters which encouraged people to refuse to pay the Forced Loan.[133] The text, unusually, reports the remarks of the two bishops sitting in the court: 'Laud Bishopp of Bath & Neale Bishopp of Durham sayd that the sowing of division & setting of dissention between the king & his people was treason in him that contrived that letter'.[134] Even more unusually, the author of the report added some commentary: '[n]ote that the two Bishopps can spye treason in a case which concernes the kings prerogative when the judges which spake before could not see it nor any of the lords which spake after'.[135] There is implied criticism here, that the

[130] *The Diurnall Occurrences, or Dayly Proceedings of Both Houses, in this Great and Happy Parliament, from the third of November, 1640, to the third of November 1641* (London, 1641), pp. 165 (28 June 1641) and 176–7 (1 July 1641); Bedfordshire Archives and Record Services, MS. St John J1386, unfoliated (report of proceedings on 21 June 1641). The House of Lords approved the bill to abolish the Star Chamber on 2 July 1641 (*Journal of the House of Lords: Volume 4, 1629–1642* (London, 1767–1830), p. 298).

[131] Brit. Libr., Stowe MS. 424, fos. 3–36v at fos. 15v–16. This text appears to be of the reading which Bagshawe intended to deliver before his reading was suppressed; it includes material which according to other accounts was to be delivered, but was in fact not. Stowe MS. 424 discusses episcopal judges generally, whereas an account of the reading as delivered refers only to bishops as justices of the peace (Brit. Libr., Harl. MS 1222, fos. 105v–106v), although the reasoning would apply to other secular jurisdictions.

[132] Brit. Libr., Harl. MS. 1222, fo. 109v. The claim by MPs that bishops could not be involved in the capital proceedings against the earl of Strafford was anticipated in Bagshawe's reading (on the issue in relation to Strafford, see Abbott, 'Anticlericalism and episcopacy', pp. 157 and 165), suggesting either knowledge of the text by others or that Bagshawe was setting out more widely held views.

[133] Brit. Libr., Lansd. MS. 620, fos. 38r–v. The case and commentary is found in both the law-French and English versions of the reports.

[134] Brit. Libr., Lansd. MS. 620, fo. 38v. cf. *The Court and Times of Charles I*, i. 222–3.

[135] Brit. Libr., Lansd. MS. 620, fo. 38v.

bishops in the court supported the king's prerogative with a view of treason which went beyond the boundaries of that offence as understood by the lawyers, and therefore perhaps that the bishops went beyond the law.

At this point, the circulating law reports move closer to some of the criticisms of the court which emerged in the later 1630s, about inappropriate actions of the bishops as judges. The point is not identical, but is related; the bishops in the Star Chamber had their own agenda and views, different to that of English law, and perhaps were using the Star Chamber to enforce it. This concern may have been exacerbated by lawyers familiar with Prynne's *Histriomastix* trial, one of those about which material circulated. According to some accounts, Prynne's offence of seditious libel was identified by both the archbishops as 'treasonable', like the view of the bishops criticized in the circulating reports.[136] However, in the *Histriomastix* trial, both of the chief justices also referred to treason in relation to Prynne's offence, seemingly adopting the idea of treason used by the bishops in the prosecution of the earl of Lincoln's servant, unlike the earlier judges.[137] Concerns raised by the circulating reports may therefore have been confirmed by the later case.

If readers of the reports accepted this concern about the views and influence of the bishops, there was overlap between views of the Star Chamber formed by professional literature and opinions shaped by news about high-profile cases.[138] This shared dissatisfaction, directed to the role of the bishops in the court, dominated the attacks on the Star Chamber preceding its abolition.

[136] *Documents Relating to the Proceedings Against William Prynne, in 1634 and 1637*, ed. S. R. Gardiner (London, 1877), pp. 26 and 27.

[137] *Documents Relating to the Proceedings against William Prynne*, pp. 18–20.

[138] Not all readers of the 1625–9 reports did accept the expressed views uncritically. In Brit. Libr., Lansd. MS. 620 much of the text has been struck through, and on fo. 39r John Lightfoot wrote that despite possessing the text, 'it is not of my owne Colleccion' and that he had received it only in June 1636.

Index

www.ingramcontent.com/pod-product-compliance
Ingram Content Group UK Ltd.
Pitfield, Milton Keynes, MK11 3LW, UK
UKHW021840100926
8556IPUK00004B/452

9 781912 702893